55.00

THE STATE
AND THE
ACADEMIC LIBRARY

**Recent Titles in
Contributions in Librarianship and Information Science**

The Librarian, the Scholar, and the Future of the Research Library
Eldred Smith

Social Science Reference Sources: A Practical Guide
Revised and Enlarged Second Edition
Tze-chung Li

Books and Blueprints: Building America's Public Libraries
Donald E. Oehlerts

Dilemmas in the Study of Information: Exploring the Boundaries of Information Science
S. D. Neill

The Library and Its Users: The Communication Process
John M. Budd

Books Behind Bars: The Role of Books, Reading, and Libraries in British Prison Reform 1701–1911
Janet Fyfe

Technological Innovations in Libraries, 1860–1960: An Anecdotal History
Klaus Musmann

Democracy and the Public Library: Essays on Fundamental Issues
Arthur W. Hafner, editor

Research Libraries—Yesterday, Today, and Tomorrow
William J. Welsh, editor

Critical Approaches to Information Technology in Librarianship: Foundations and Applications
John Buschman, editor

THE STATE AND THE ACADEMIC LIBRARY

Edited by VICKI L. GREGORY

Contributions in Librarianship and Information Science, Number 76
Gerard B. McCabe, Series Adviser

GREENWOOD PRESS
Westport, Connecticut • London

Library of Congress Cataloging-in-Publication Data

The State and the academic library / edited by Vicki L. Gregory.
    p.   cm.—(Contributions in librarianship and information science, ISSN 0084–9243 ; no. 76)
  Includes bibliographical references and index.
  ISBN 0-313-28108-4 (alk. paper)
  1. Academic libraries—Government policy—United States—States. I. Gregory, Vicki L., 1950–   . II. Series.
Z675.U5S735   1993
027.7′0973—dc20   93-13013

British Library Cataloguing in Publication Data is available.

Copyright © 1993 by Vicki L. Gregory

All rights reserved. No portion of this book may be reproduced, by any process or technique, without the express written consent of the publisher.

Library of Congress Catalog Card Number: 93–13013
ISBN: 0-313-28108-4
ISSN: 0084-9243

First published in 1993

Greenwood Press, 88 Post Road West, Westport, CT 06881
An imprint of Greenwood Publishing Group, Inc.

Printed in the United States of America

The paper used in this book complies with the Permanent Paper Standard issued by the National Information Standards Organization (Z39.48-1984).

10 9 8 7 6 5 4 3 2 1

This work is dedicated to my husband, William Stanley Gregory, who has, during such free time as his law practice would allow, read, re-read, and commented upon the various drafts even when he would have much rather been doing something else, such as watching the game (which he still managed to do, often simultaneously), and graciously tolerated the grumpiness during the preparation of this book that is the "privilege" of any author.

Contents

List of Charts   ix

Preface   xi

1   Introduction   1

PART I   **The Nature and Function of State Government as It Relates to Academic Libraries**   7

2   The State Governmental Environment—Governors and State Legislatures   9

3   State Coordinating Agencies of Higher Education   23

4   State Libraries   33

PART II   **The Interaction between State Government and Academic Libraries**   39

5   State Funding—The Key to Control   41

6 Academic Library Networking and Automation—An Academic Approach to the Funding Conundrum	59
7 Multitype Library Cooperative Networks—The Use of Overarching Agencies	73
8 Program Review—Macromanagement or Micromanagement?	89
PART III Case Studies of the Interaction between State Government and Academic Libraries	**99**
9 The Florida Center for Library Automation—A Relationship That Ultimately Succeeds *Margaret A. Hogue and Michele I. Dalehite*	101
10 Public Academic Libraries in Massachusetts— Reorganization Redux *Janet Freedman*	123
11 Networking in the University System of Georgia— A Case Study in Successful Interaction *Ralph E. Russell*	143
12 Colorado Alliance of Research Libraries: The Role of the State *George R. Jaramillo and Helen I. Reed*	153
Appendix A Acronyms Used in this Work	163
Appendix B State Coordinating Agencies of Higher Education	167
Appendix C State Library Agencies	173
Selected Bibliography	179
Index	187
About the Editor and Contributors	195

List of Charts

Chart 3-1	Coordinating Agency Structures in the United States	24
Chart 5-1	Formula Variables and Weights: Clapp-Jordan, ACRL, and Washington State Formulas	52
Chart 9-1	Florida Department of Education Organizational Structure	105
Chart 9-2	Florida Board of Regents Organizational Structure	107
Chart 10-1	Library Expenditures Per FTE Student	125
Chart 10-2	ERM Purchasing Power	126
Chart 10-3	Number of Titles Per FTE Student	126
Chart 10-4	Current Serials Subscriptions	127
Chart 10-5	Library Staff Per FTE Student	127
Chart 10-6	Library Budget UMass Amherst vs Ten Northeast Peers	128

Preface

This book grew out of my earlier research in the area of state coordinating agencies of higher education and academic libraries. That previous research has been updated and expanded to include all major aspects of state government that have some effect on academic libraries. The chapters dealing with state libraries and multitype library cooperative networks are based on survey research completed during 1991–1992.

The book is divided into three main sections. Part I deals with those state officials, entities and agencies that affect, to greater or lesser degrees, the operations and/or budgets of academic libraries, including governors, legislatures, coordinating agencies of higher education, and state libraries. Part II deals with the effect of state governmental control on specific library programs and concerns, including library automation, cooperative programs, library funding, and program review.

Case studies involving specific library programs in four selected states constitute Part III, which is the heart and soul of this work. Emphasis is placed on the role of the state in respect to those major areas of concern to academic libraries where state governments have or are currently most directly influencing the programs and services of academic libraries. Among the most significant of these major areas are: networking, especially computer networking, of academic libraries; and library budgets, both in terms of the formulation process, structures and outcomes.

Michele Dalehite and Margaret Hogue discuss the development of the

Florida Center for Library Automation (FCLA), which handles automation for the nine state universities in Florida, and the relationship between FCLA and the newly established College Center for Library Automation, which is involved with the automation of the libraries of all of Florida's state-supported community colleges.

Janet Freedman describes the current status of the public university libraries in Massachusetts and details that state's movement toward formula funding while describing, as well, a major shift in governance structure in Massachusetts from a statewide governing board to a state coordinating council. She also details how major governance change in Massachusetts has come about for some universities by means of consolidation on the institutional level.

Ralph Russell discusses networking in the State University System of Georgia in terms of the automation programs of that system's libraries and the efforts to accomplish resource sharing among them. Dr. Russell describes the development of Peachnet, a statewide telecommunications network for the University System of Georgia, to which all thirty-four of Georgia's institutions of higher education are anticipated to be connected in 1993. He points out that several of the Georgia institutions with on-line systems in place have offered the use of their systems as "hosts" for the benefit of other Georgia institutions. He also discusses the development of the Georgia joint borrowing card, which can be used by students and faculty members of any state institution to check out books at their own or any other state institution.

George Jaramillo and Helen Reed discuss the development of the Colorado Alliance of Research Libraries (CARL) from a partially state-supported library operation to a much more independent nonprofit corporation and, in 1988, to the addition of a for-profit corporation, CARL Systems, Inc., to enhance the ability of CARL to market its products more aggressively. They point out that CARL is unique in its early mix of private and public support, both at the city and state level, due to the different kinds of research libraries initially involved in the project—public universities, private universities, and the Denver Public Library.

While in a work such as this it is impossible to describe each and every way that current forms of state-level governance of higher education have had significant impact on academic libraries, the theoretical background and specific examples discussed should prove useful both to practitioners and to students in library programs who seek an appreciation and understanding of the basics of the process of interaction between the state and its institutions' academic libraries. The success of this interaction determines to a large degree the quality of academic library services available at public institutions of higher education in the United States today. Likewise, it is hoped that the experiences in the several states described in Part III may be of use to librarians in other states around the country who may be attempting to break new ground.

Chapter 1

Introduction

THE POWER SHIFT FROM THE INDIVIDUAL INSTITUTION TO THE STATE

The traditional patterns of public, post-secondary educational governance in the United States that arose with the development of state-supported institutions of higher education in the nineteenth century have been broken. A palpable shift of power has occurred from the once mostly autonomous individual public universities in the United States toward entities at the state government level. Many critical decisions, ranging from operational questions to broad policy matters, are being made for public colleges and universities outside those institutions either by relatively new or newly empowered branches or agencies of state government. This process of increased centralization may have involved in some states only an increased accountability to a state coordinating council or to a statewide governing board, but just as often it has entailed a direct shift of control, occasionally on a micromanagement level, to the state legislatures and/or the state governors and administrative agencies. This shift of power has had and will most likely continue to have a significant impact on all sections of the state universities, including their libraries.[1]

A number of factors have influenced this change. In relation to the post-World War II role of state responsibility for public higher education, a major impetus to the assertion of control was obviously the rapid growth of higher education in the 1950s and 1960s, owing to first the GI Bill and later to rising levels of American affluence and the baby boom. Rising enrollments naturally led to greater expenditures and increased demands on state revenue sources. The growing magnitude of state support of higher education and the increased complexity of the higher education institutions themselves thereby naturally gave rise to state-level concerns for increased accountability.

When the great postwar economic boom finally ended for good in the 1970s and tax revenues began to fall in relation to the costs of ever-expanding governmental functions, the attention and concern of the states over how their money was being spent again increased. In the 1980s, a period of basically steady or declining college-level enrollments, many legislators and state executives began to question seriously for the first time the need for continually escalating higher education budget requests. By creating coordinating councils or boards, legislators and/or governors often hoped to distance themselves from the situation while at the same time gaining more control over higher education in their state.[2]

A second factor in the power shift from institutions to the state, which is also directly related to the expansion of higher education in the 1950s and 1960s, is the increased number (and relative percentages) of people from all of society's levels and backgrounds who began to have a stake in higher education. As more and more people of all economic and social classes came to attend a college or university, those same people began taking a more active interest in the programs and policies of their state institutions and thus the proportion of the population who came to care about state higher education rose dramatically. By the last third of this century, the state university had become, much more than ever before imagined, an institution for all the people of the state; with the effective broadening of the franchise accomplished through a better educated populace, civil rights laws, etc., increased concerns about equal access, program offerings, and institutional control by the traditional upper classes attracted legislative and gubernatorial as well as federal interest.[3]

A third factor, today somewhat forgotten but hard to ignore, is the highly publicized, and probably over-publicized, student and faculty turmoil of the latter half of the 1960s and early 1970s. The apparent conflict in values between the campus and the general public, whether with respect to the Vietnam War, social policy, or popular music, as perceived by the general public, led many state legislatures, finding themselves stymied in the politically popular (among the voting populace) but no longer constitutionally permissible tendency to push state universities into the traditionally perceived role of *in loco parentis*, to combat the perceived "sex, drugs, and rock and roll" culture of the campus in other ways, for example, by increasing the level of financial and governance controls and current accountability demanded of its public universities.[4]

Introduction

In 1970, President Charles Johnson of the University of California emphasized to the academic senate of his university:

Make no mistake, the university is a public institution, supported by the people through the actions of their elected representatives and executives. They will not allow it to be operated in ways which are excessively at variance with the general public's will. By various pressures and devices the university will be forced to yield and to conform if it gets too far away from what the public expects and wants. In the process the university will be severely damaged, through drastic inadequacy of support, through loss of valuable personnel, and through loss of autonomy.[5]

Dr. Johnson obviously recognized a speeding train when he saw one and thought it wise to suggest that his faculty get off the tracks.

A final factor in the power shift is the ever-growing influence, even through the Reagan years, of the federal government.[6] Congress, in the Higher Education Facilities Act of 1963, effectively encouraged, indeed mandated, for all intents and purposes, statewide coordination by requiring that those states wishing to participate in the various federal programs provided for in that act:[7]

... shall designate for that purpose an existing State agency which is broadly representative of the public and of institutions of higher education (including junior colleges and technical institutes) in the State, or, if no such State agency exists, shall establish such a State agency, and submit to the Commissioner through the agency so designated or established..., a State plan for such participation.[8]

In Title II of the Higher Education Act of 1965, Congress dealt specifically with academic libraries, requiring that:

Each institution of higher education which receives a grant under this part shall periodically inform the State agency (if any) concerned with the educational activities of all institutions of higher education in the State in which such institution is located, of its activities under this part.[9]

In the Educational Amendments of 1972, the scope of the activities of the state agency so designated or established was broadened by Congress to include vocational schools and private institutions. Section 1203 of the same act authorized grants to the designated State Commissions to pursue comprehensive statewide higher education planning.[10] According to a study done by the Carnegie Foundation for the Advancement of Teaching, the Educational Amendments of 1972 constituted the primary impetus for the creation of no less than fifteen new statewide agencies for the coordination of higher education.[11]

The basic tension between the state and the public institutions of higher education is the balance between the state's concerns and demands for utility and accountability versus the institutions' needs for academic freedom and autonomy. According to Robert Berdahl:

> A major source of friction is that many in academe are trying to protect too much, and many in state government are trying to claim too much. Both sides fail to recognize that academic freedom and university autonomy, though related, are not synonymous, and that university-state relations in the one area may quite properly differ from those in the other.[12]

Berdahl believes that coordinating boards of higher education play a crucial role in helping both sides of the partnership determine substantive policies, as well as whether the "various tensions stay benign or become pathological."[13]

Higher education operates in many contexts, especially important among which for public colleges and universities is the political context. From the late 1940s and increasingly so from the 1960s, the various state agencies for the governance of higher education have become a critical determinant of the development and nurturing of public institutions of higher education and their constituent parts, including their academic libraries.

NOTES

1. See, for example, Aims C. McGuinness, Jr., *The Search for More Effective State Policy Leadership in Higher Education: Recent State Higher Education Studies and Trends in Coordination and Governance* (Denver: Education Commission of the States, 1986); and Michael L. Skolnik and Glen A. Jones, "A Comparative Analysis of Arrangements for State Coordination of Higher Education in Canada and in the United States" *Journal of Higher Education* 63 (March/April 1992), pp. 130–32.

2. Leonard E. Goodall, "Emerging Political Issues for State Coordinating Boards" *Journal of Higher Education* 45 (March 1974), p. 220.

3. Thomas E. Johnson, *Role of the State in Planning and Coordination of Autonomous Institutions of Higher Education* (Lansing: Michigan State Department of Education, 1977), p. 6.

4. J. Victor Baldridge et al., *Policy Making and Effective Leadership* (San Francisco: Jossey-Bass, 1978), pp. 62–63.

5. Quoted in Kenneth P. Mortimer and T. R. McConnell, *Sharing Authority Effectively* (San Francisco: Jossey-Bass, 1978), p. 196.

6. Skolnik and Jones, "A Comparative Analysis," p. 136.

7. In 1980, Congress eliminated the requirement that states establish planning commissions and replaced it with a simplified "state agreement." However, by 1980, most states had gone beyond simple planning commissions to creating coordinating boards or consolidated governing boards. The withdrawal of the federal

Introduction 5

mandate and funds, however, did cause the demise of the planning commission in Wyoming, leaving that state without any overall state agency for higher education.

8. Section 105, Public Law No. 88-204, 77 Stat. 367 (1963).

9. Section 208, Public Law No. 89-329, 79 Stat. 1227 (1965).

10. Sections 1202, 1203, Public Law No. 92-318, 86 Stat. 324–325 (1972).

11. *The Control of the Campus* (Washington, D.C.: Carnegie Foundation for the Advancement of Teaching, 1982), p. 38.

12. Robert Berdahl, "Public Universities and State Governments: Is the Tension Benign?" *Educational Record* 71 (Winter 1990), p. 38.

13. *Ibid.*, p. 38.

Part I

THE NATURE AND FUNCTION OF STATE GOVERNMENT AS IT RELATES TO ACADEMIC LIBRARIES

The vitality of libraries as educational agencies depends upon the wise actions by public decision makers and others who provide resources to educational institutions. The American Library Association identifies four realities for educational reform within a learning society. The four realities are:
1. Learning begins before schooling.
2. Good schools require good school libraries.
3. People in a learning society need libraries throughout their lives.
4. Public support of libraries is an investment in people and communities.
—American Library Association
Task Force on Excellence in Education
1984

Chapter 2

The State Governmental Environment—Governors and State Legislatures

While all of the states in the United States recognize that free elementary and secondary education is an important, and sometimes constitutionally mandated aspect of state governmental responsibilities, free or heavily subsidized higher education, while accepted as a permissible function of state government, is not necessarily perceived as an absolute duty of the state.[1] Therefore, higher education often finds itself in the thick of the legislative process—protecting its turf and competing with many other agencies for the always hard-to-come-by appropriation dollars. Any state university or college is, by definition, subject to some control by the state in which it exists, and will necessarily always be dependent to a greater or lesser degree upon the appropriations made to it periodically by the government of the state in and by which it is established. These appropriations are usually the result of recommendations by the state's chief executive officer, its governor, which recommendations are transmuted through the appropriations process into an act of the state legislature, an act which in turn may be subject to gubernatorial approval, veto or amendment as determined by the state constitution.[2] In addition to the obviously critical appropriations process, the oversight function performed by governors and state legislatures over institutions of higher education dictates a review of their respective roles and motivations.

Each state's interest in higher education in general ideally involves a multi-faceted concern with state needs for higher education services, with programs geared to meet state and local needs, while making appropriate geographical and other differentiations of mission among the public institutions set up to meet these needs, and with efficiency and cost-effectiveness in performing essential services. Individual institutional interests are, of course, not always necessarily identical with those of the state government as a whole. An individual institution inevitably wishes to enhance its status, to grow in size, and to ensure itself of constantly expanding or at least stable financial support, regardless of the needs of other universities and colleges, regardless of desirable patterns of collaboration and cooperation, and regardless of costs and the economic circumstance of the state government.[3] It is the balancing of the overall state interest against the individual institutional interest that must be seen as the heart of both the governance and the appropriations processes.

Remarkably, political questions external to higher education per se have not had great impact on these processes. Commenting on the tumultuous era in higher education from 1960 to 1980, Clark Kerr, former President of the University of California, has written:

[Concerning the period 1960–1980] State support [of higher education], by contrast [to the federal government], has been much more constant and committed across the board. Legislatures also by and large and even surprisingly and remarkably, held steady during the period of student protests, passing few antagonistic laws and maintaining fiscal support even as public opinion became largely critical. State legislatures proved to be the most constant source of support and the greatest centers of stability with much rhetoric but little adverse action. Governors varied greatly— some protecting higher education, some attacking. Overall, governors, in the area of public higher education, have become the one most dominant force, but with differing and changing agenda. They have become the new persons of power in public higher education.[4]

There appears to exist today a renewed recognition by governors and legislators of the central role that each state's higher education system must play in the state's economic future, both with respect to the ability to attract new industry (especially high-technology companies) and with respect to the state's overall social, economic, and cultural well-being.[5] From the library perspective, the latter is an area in which the academic libraries can play a major role. Arising from this concern can be seen the fueling of a new sense of urgency regarding the effectiveness and responsiveness to the state's system for governing and financing higher education.

THE CONSTITUTIONAL FRAMEWORK

From a technical perspective, the powers of a state government over its constituent parts, agencies and subdivisions, such as its institutions of

The State Governmental Environment 11

higher education, are much more comprehensive than that of the federal government over the states themselves. The U.S. constitution was traditionally viewed as involving essentially the division of pre-existing governmental powers through the delegation by the constituent states of portions of their sovereignty to another entity, the federal government. In theory then, at least, the federal government is not a national government in the truest sense, but rather a grantee of delegated state powers. All undelegated powers are reserved to the states, and indeed unless specifically prohibited by the Constitution, the powers delegated by the states may still be exercised by them concurrently with their exercise by the federal government.

But at the state level, the situation is reversed; generally speaking, unless the state constitution otherwise provides, the constituent parts of the state, its agencies, its political subdivisions and its institutions owe their very existence and all of their powers to the decision makers at the central state authority. State constitutions are thus best viewed not as grants of power, as is the case with the United States Constitution, but rather as limitations on the exercise of power. As a result, state executive branches and legislatures necessarily possess extremely broad powers respecting their state's creations and institutions and exercise controls over them as plenary as those of any European parliament, except as such controls may be limited by either the state or federal constitution.

In some cases, this fact of life may not be so clear or self-evident. A state university may, for instance, enjoy a constitutionally established governing board or board of trustees the membership of which virtually cannot be touched by an envious governor or legislature, but in no state does such a board possess the constitutional authority to levy taxes or otherwise provide by itself through appropriation from the state treasury for the support of the university. By contrast, public school districts for elementary/secondary education in most states have considerable authority to levy property taxes for the support of their schools, though this power is usually subject to the approval of the voters. Community college districts in various states, perhaps because they are seen as extensions of the public schools, also have the authority to levy a general property tax subject to voter approval.

The distrust of government historically expressed by delegates to state constitutional conventions have rendered many state constitutions rather restrictive documents, a jealous body politic requiring that it be consulted through referenda on constitutional amendments on many questions (Alabama's highly restrictive constitution, for instance, now amended by the state's voters over 550 times since 1901, probably takes the prize in this category today, but it is by no means alone in terms of excessive length and arguable over-specificity, especially if the numerous voter initiatives attached to various western-state constitutions such as California's are considered.) As a result, state-funded higher education, which is a matter a state could obviously control under its conventional plenary powers, is sometimes raised to constitutional status through the enshrining therein of governance provisions removing, to some degree, certain higher education institutions from some aspects of the sphere of legislative authority. Thus, historically, some self-perpetuating state university boards of trustees for a time found themselves able to thumb their collective nose at attempts by governors or legislatures to "control" their universities until, that is, higher education became too expensive to operate primarily on the tuitions paid by the well-heeled parents of the college-bound. Constitutional status becomes of little avail when the university president arrives hat in hand at the Ways and Means Committee of his state's legislature.

In view of the reality that state universities and colleges must depend for a significant portion of their income requirements on moneys appropriated by their state legislatures (to which, of course, they may add such charges as they are authorized to make respecting tuition and fees applicable to students, as well as moneys earned with respect to such contracts, grants, gifts and sales as they may be able to generate), the interaction of state issues versus institutional priorities becomes critical, regardless of the state constitutional environment. And this interaction ultimately occurs most noticeably and often most noisily in the legislative forum.

STATE LEGISLATORS

Who, if anyone, represents the state as a whole within a legislature is sometimes difficult to determine. Legislators in most states, in their self-perceived (and voter-expected) roles as ombudsmen for their districts, inevitably take pride in how well they can provide for the colleges and universities in their districts, and many a legislator will think nothing of obtaining an appropriation of money for a new university building in his district or blocking a statewide policy in order simply to satisfy his institutional constituents—all without regard for statewide interests as a whole. Even discounting the "old school ties" that may be involved, the rationality of such actions from a political point of view is often confirmed through the campaign contributions, good seats at the big game, honorary degrees and general red carpet treatment afforded when the legislator visits the campus. Sometimes the political rewards are even more overt. In Alabama, for instance, some college presidents have appeared in televised campaign commercials for their favorite state legislators during election contests.

An utterly cynical view is not, however, always justified. Legislators in many states are known for taking a much more than casual interest in basic higher education issues, and this is highly laudable since courageously backing "reform" is usually not the surest ticket to re-election. Inevitably, however, there are varying degrees of focus. For instance, in Florida, the legislature typically uses its budget-making authority to address such generalized concerns as the quality and content of undergraduate education programs generally, with special appropriations made each year intended to address special needs. This is certainly a praiseworthy approach. But also in Florida, lawmakers have never been above using budget bills to continue a seeming tradition of providing what some may argue to be sinecures at universities for departing legislative colleagues.

Whatever the interests and the motivations, in many states it is the legislature that plays the dominant role in higher education matters, sometimes to the exclusion of the executive and/or the coordinating agency (which itself may be under gubernatorial control), and effective relations with the law-making branch of government are essential to the success of the statutory coordinating or governing mechanisms, and the individual institutions of higher education as well.

In some states, state legislatures have traditionally treated state-owned institutions as subject to the same procedural and budgetary controls as those applicable to other state agencies. But for the most part the institutions have enjoyed a degree of independence from day-to-day control that only the establishment of the coordinating agencies has abridged. Legislatures have tended historically to take the trustees' word for things and to respect the "corporate" independence of the institutions. Increasing costs and the complexity of higher education have significantly altered this relationship.[6]

In other states, most notably in Pennsylvania, public institutions of higher education are treated as if they were simply state-assisted, but privately controlled entities and thereby exempt from most state procedural controls concerning budget matters. In still other states, the pattern is mixed.

Legislative oversight of institutions of higher education typically tends to fall within the established pattern applicable generally to legislative review of executive branch activity. The effectiveness of these patterns of oversight is necessarily dependent upon local and legal form and practice, party politics, and the political strength of the executive branch or the coordinating agency. Legislative oversight of higher education institutions can be seen to fall into four basic areas: (1) policy matters, both as to formulation and as to the reform thereof, (2) personnel matters, including trustee appointments or confirmation, (3) revisions to institutional structure or coordinating agencies and (4) controls on expenditure.[7]

Policy Matters. While the complexities that often result in the highly generalized type of legislation so characteristic of the efforts in the United States Congress are not so endemic at the state level, it is nevertheless true that imprecise standards often riddle most legislation concerned with matters of higher education policy. "Higher Education Improvement" acts full of high-blown phrases more warm and fuzzy than substantive abound, and such acts will typically shift the burden of precise definition and implementation to the institutions themselves or to the state coordinating agency, a situation which many a legislator, feeling himself blameless in the matter, then proceeds to characterize as the fox guarding the hens. When legislators become surprised by the institutional exercise of the effective autonomy that generalized legislation provides, the result can be a 180-degree turn toward "sharp-shooting" type legislation that suffers from over-specificity and all of the ambiguities that inevitably winnow into legislative language whenever bills are passed in the heat of a moment of legislative ire. Because the committee structure in many state legislatures is not very highly developed and rarely adequately staffed, the opportunity for careful review of the details needed to properly formulate matters of policy simply may not be present. And where legislative turnover is heavy from term to term the absence of experience undoubtedly plays a major role.

In states where governors are relatively weak, legislative committees often have eagerly attempted to take over matters of policy and general state interest. This has become especially true as legislators in most states have in recent decades become "more professional" in that they meet more often during the year, they typically receive rates of legislative pay (not to mention lobbyist-provided emoluments) commensurate with a living wage and their legislative jobs are no longer viewed as strictly part time avocations and tools for building business back home in the district. For the most part in the higher education area, however, legislatures have fortunately not formed themselves as roving commissions to look into all sorts of matters of institutional detail; indeed, the rise of the coordinating agencies to undertake such tasks seems to indicate that they probably will not do so in the foreseeable future.

Personnel. Most legislatures possess some constitutional or legislative powers of either confirmation or appointment with respect to Boards of Trustees of institutions of higher education in their state and over the membership of the state's higher education coordinating agency. Typically, this control arises from "advise and consent" type provisions in state constitutions. Only rarely, and usually then only in cases of governors in deep political trouble, is "advise and consent" successfully converted by legislators into "control," but there can be no doubt that the legislative influence over trustees whose appointments are contingent upon legislative confirmation is not insignificant. This is an arena where partisan or ideological conflict (and occasionally the performance of the football team) can easily come into play, and some legislators may even try to enhance their own positions either through attempting to obtain, where allowable under state constitutions, appointments to an institution's board as trustees or employment positions for themselves or their spouses, relatives and supporters at state institutions. While most states have extensive merit systems that are intended to prevent the legislature from reaching too far down the organizational chart of an institution, it cannot be denied that the legislative process involves not only matters of policy but of political self-promotion and survival.

A typical state constitution will include significant provisions concerning the impeachment or removal of public officials, but in the higher education field the exercise of such power by legislatures is extremely rare. The impeachment process is typically both arcane and time-consuming and while the possession of the impeachment power obviously gives a legislature such legal justification as it might need to hunt down those it considered to be wrongdoers, the restrictions on legislative staff and the overwhelming nature of other policy interests and matters undoubtedly contribute to the paucity of action by legislators in this area.

Structural revision. In matters of structural policy and revision, legislatures can and often do look for ways to intrude into the decision-making process of institutions and into those of coordinating agencies as well. While this power is most often seen in legislative efforts to establish specific programs (or to terminate them), the position of the state coordinating agency notwithstanding, some legislatures have taken to requiring extensive reports respecting structural revision or reform from "blue-ribbon" committees or from individual institutions or the coordinating agency. But such reports, which are usually lengthy and liberally salted with jargon, are all too often ignored by legislators who lack the time to read legislative bills, much less turgid reports, and this approach has not borne significant fruit. Thus, the requirement for written reports is likely not to be particularly meaningful as a method of legislative oversight. Undigested and unread, most such reports making suggestions for change or reform simply gather dust.

One technique for policy control that has begun to come into some favor in recent years is the concept of the legislative veto. To implement such an approach, substantive legislation is written in a way that requires, as a procedural matter, any administrative action taken pursuant thereto, such as the establishment of a new program at a particular state college, either to be later approved by the legislature before it can become effective or remain suspended for some stated period of time in order to allow the legislature an opportunity to determine whether to repeal it. While examples of this sort of legislation are relatively rife in the public school area in connection with such matters as teacher testing or textbook selection, it is a method of control rarely practiced in higher education.

Finally, it is noteworthy that many lawmakers have begun to insert into legislation the requirement that particular members of the legislature, either ex-officially, e.g., Speaker of the House, President Pro Tempore of the Senate, etc., or as named by presiding officers of the houses of the Legislature, are to be members of agencies or boards that ordinarily or traditionally have had an executive flavor. While this approach appears not to be extensive yet in the field of membership on coordinating agencies, with the executive branch usually in firm control of appointments, it certainly is a power that the legislatures could, in the absence of a strong governor, exercise in the future should they choose to do so.

Appropriations. The traditional and most effective way in which a legislative body may exercise power over the state's institutions is, of course, in the exercise of the power of the purse. The control of expenditures and the provision of moneys through taxation is the basis on which legislative bodies first asserted their rights against the sovereign power of the executive. State constitutional provisions typically mandate, as does Article 1, Section 9 of the United States Constitution, that "No money shall be drawn from the treasury, but in consequence of the appropriations made by law."

As state legislatures have grown in sophistication and as their staffs have grown it has been at least partially possible for them to exercise significant oversight through control of the appropriation process itself, but it is probably no exaggeration to say that most agency and institution heads, if they are worth anything at all, can usually win over enough legislators to justify their budget. After all, it is what university presidents are in the final analysis hired for. But if budget review is the chief instrument for oversight of state institutions of higher education, it is also true that for the most part the involvement of legislatures in the budget process ends with the approval of the bills providing for appropriations. Viewed from this angle, even budgetary control is relatively ephemeral.

Another problem with the exercise of control through the budget process is that legislators typically fail to undertake any thorough consideration not only of the budget document placed before them by the executive branch but also of any possible alternatives thereto. In order to meet this deficiency, the establishment of the coordinating agency as the "sifter-out" of various alternatives has resulted. This approach works effectively, however, only in situations where the coordinating agencies are vested with real power and are able to prevent the eruption of bilateral relationships between individual institutions and the legislature itself. In state budgets there is probably nothing more complex than the education components thereof, and in the case of higher education the likelihood of effective legislative oversight must decrease directly in proportion to the level of complexity. Legislators simply cannot know all that is going on: in the slightly paraphrased but nevertheless immortal words of the late Senator Everett Dirksen "A billion here, a billion there, and pretty soon it adds up to real money."

Political scientists William Keefe and Morris Ogul wrote, almost thirty years ago, "To have a great legislature a nation or state must have greatly interested citizens, the most talented of whom are willing to run for office. Critics, whatever their preferences as to legislative design or function, seem to agree that the central element in the strength of any legislature is the quality of its members."[8] Achieving this ideal in the United States in the 1990s remains difficult. No other nation on earth suffers from a more complex system of electing its legislators, and it is important to keep in mind that, in the decisions that they make in any area, they will inevitably tend to be remarkably parochial. "All politics is local" is the old saying, and it is certainly true at the state legislative level. Legislators simply do not take direction well from those sources that will have no bearing on their legislative careers; with America's weak political party system, the average state legislator is typically independent of anything except his local support. And when, as is the case today, most legislatures are remarkably stable in terms of their membership, with few legislators being defeated at election time, radical departure from the political compromises of previous years is unlikely. If old policies will usually look new to those who made them, it is likewise true that, without the infusion of new blood, new policies and directions are necessarily unlikely. Large questions are therefore almost always viewed by legislatures in the light of local interest, because that local interest is from whence they derive their political self-preservation.

Thus, it should come as no surprise that legislators consider colleges and universities within their districts to be their "pet" institutions, and when a particular legislator rises to eminence within the body of which he is a member, the institution that he "represents" can be expected to prosper as well. Coordinating agencies necessarily find themselves in tension with the basic goals of the typical legislator, therefore doubling the agency's problem.

The legislative process itself is beyond the scope of this work, but suffice it to say that the generalizations made above certainly apply to the actions taken within the framework of the typical committee system that forms the backbone of legislative action as well as to actions on the floors of the legislature and those of the individual legislators when interacting with the various public and private interest groups that haunt the halls of every statehouse in the nation.

GOVERNORS

In many states, though perhaps now in fewer instances than was once the case owing to today's more frequent and longer legislative sessions, the governor is the key figure in state government, sometimes as a result of constitutional grants of power, but more often through force of personality and the institutionalized ability to exercise considerable political leverage through the appointment and budgeting processes. To the extent that a governor has authority to make coordinating/governing board appointments, this power is usually among his strongest tools for influencing, over the long-term, the direction and quality of his state's higher education system. While in some states the governor may initiate the budget process without restriction, the force of history and precedent prevents the speedy implementation of major or basic changes even where the legislature is generally receptive to the governor's initiatives. Long-established institutions and programs are never easily abandoned or even cut back. When cutbacks come, they are usually statewide in scope, resulting in the spreading of limited state resources among too many institutions, thereby potentially rendering those not possessed of substantial independent means of support vulnerable to charges of mediocrity. While a governor may wish to avoid the intense bickering among various institutional interests, because such can often be seen as a deterrent to successful competition for new high-technology industry and jobs in the state, there may be little he can do about it directly. The governor is, after all, a politician and must make concessions and facilitate compromise. The state initiatives for economic development, high technology workplaces and improvements in the quality of educational programs do not necessarily have to take a back seat, however, and they can reflect the desirability of a tendency toward centrally directed higher education policies; here is where the governor, through coordinating agency appointments, can have a lasting impact.

A governor typically functions as the catalyst for legislation of all types at the state level. Many state constitutions provide that the governor may propose specific items of legislation for consideration by the legislature at each session, and his proposals are typically the ones that go to the top of the legislative agenda. Some states have even considered the adoption of constitutional provisions that would make certain gubernatorial proposals, such as the budget, the paramount order of legislative business. This has been tried in Alabama with respect to the budgetary process, essentially without success in that the provision in question allowed for its regimen to be suspended by supermajority vote of each house, which is currently done as a simple matter of rote custom before the consideration of each bill prior to the passage of budgets during each regular legislative session.

Also, the governor typically has the power to call special sessions and, in most states, the power to veto, either on a line item or a generalized basis, actions of the legislature with which he is unsatisfied.

In relation to the institutions of higher education, however, the governor has a bigger role than simply that of agent for the initiation and development of legislation. As a state's chief executive officer, he has an opportunity to serve as the focal point for state aspirations and desires, to place the emphasis in his state on matters that he considers important. In most states, gubernatorial budget-making powers are immense. The sheer volume of work necessary to prepare a budget virtually guarantees that legislators will not have the opportunity to do more than skim the surface of any budget document, chipping away at the edges for special items of constitutional interest, polishing the veneer but otherwise not much affecting the general drift and direction of the budget.

The broad constituency of the state at large gives a governor an opportunity to attract public attention to his or her ideas and to link them with the obvious advantage of the governor's typically being the most easily focused-upon element of state government. It would be a mistake, however, to characterize governors simply as the true agents of the aspirations of the state at large vis-à-vis the narrow parochialism of individual legislators. Their political pressures are different, but are not likely to be any less narrow and focused than those of individual legislators. For instance, the governor will likely be a graduate of only one, or at most two, state schools and can have friends and acquaintances at only so many of the institutions. Concomitantly, only so many of an institution's leading lights are likely to have supported any particular governor politically. But a governor does enjoy one overweening power, and that is the ability, as a result of the powers inherent in a governorship, to persuade. The best policies in the world are worthless if political support cannot be rallied in their favor. As much as one might not like it, the undeniable fact is that such support is rarely accomplished through logic and reason. Personal contact, persuasion, cajolery, the return of support for support given, the bestowing of rewards and the meting out of political retribution are the things that accomplish the job in our systems of state government.

EDUCATION COMMISSION OF THE STATES

The state governmental environment cannot be fully appreciated without consideration of the role of the states' most successful cooperative venture in the educational arena, the Education Commission of the States, which was established in 1965 by interstate compact. The Commission was formed with a dual propose: to bring state governments together as a counterweight to the increasing role of the federal government in educational matters, and to give governors and state legislators a common meeting ground on which to exchange information about their educational interests. The Commission is made up of seven commissioners from each participating state: the governor, two legislators, and four other individuals, usually appointed by the governor.

The Commission in 1973 published a report of a Task Force chaired by Robert W. Scott from North Carolina concerning the coordination, governance, and structure of postsecondary education. The members of the task force included one state senator, one state representative, one state budget officer, two state coordinating officers, one head of a statewide multi-campus system, one officer of a state board for community colleges, one state university president, one private university president, two professors of higher education, and three representatives of higher education associations. The report was entitled "Coordination or Chaos?"[9] and contained the task force's conclusion that there simply was no one "best way" for planning, program review, and budget review at the state level. The task force, not surprisingly, declared that the public responsibility for postsecondary education resided in the legislative and executive branches of state government and implied that this responsibility should be neither shirked nor delegated.

A later study,[10] published in 1980 by the Education Commission of the States, identified five major issues confronting state governments: (1) educational quality; (2) accountability; (3) social justice; (4) inflation and limited resources; and (5) the need for institutional cooperation. Few would argue with these, but how to address them successfully is the inevitable problem.

THE EFFECT OF COORDINATING AGENCIES ON THE ROLES OF GOVERNORS AND LEGISLATORS

In essence, until the rise of statewide governance agencies for higher education, the relationship between a particular institution of higher education and its state government remained almost purely bilateral—institution versus legislature or governor—and since most legislatures typically sat for only limited periods of time and most governors tended to respect the independence of the institutions (Huey P. Long's fabled relationship with Louisiana State University being the arguable exception to prove the rule), once the university president brought home the proverbial bacon, great freedom of action in its use and consumption was usually assured. With the rise of the coordinating agencies, the individual institutions' level of independence necessarily declined.[11]

The rise of such agencies does not necessarily, however, mean that true political power has come to reside in them. As noted in a 1971 report prepared by the Carnegie Commission on Higher Education,

> Apart from its budget appropriation functions, perhaps the single most significant power of the state legislature over the state's colleges and universities is in coordination. While the planning functions may be carried on in another agency, in many states the ultimate authority for plan approval rests with the legislature, and in all states significant elements of the plans cannot be implemented without legislative appropriations. It is the legislature that creates the structure for co-

ordination in the state and it is the legislature that, in most instances, provides the impetus and mechanisms for planning. The nature of the mechanisms established and the delineation of authority and responsibilities delegated by the legislature to coordinating and planning agencies, play key roles in the development of the state system.[12]

By removing the bilateralism that could exploit the "old-school" tie, and substituting therefor (to a greater or lesser degree from state to state) a multilateral presentation to the legislative body, the power of the governor and the legislature itself may arguably have become significantly enhanced by the coordinating agencies.

The coordinating agency at the very least provides the governor and often the individual legislators as well with the *sine qua non* of political power with respect to matters involving higher education—some degree of knowledge as to what is really going on statewide with all the money vanishing from the state coffers that has been earmarked and appropriated for the state's colleges and universities. This enhanced role of governors and legislatures ensures that careful examination of their motivations and methods must always be kept in mind when considering questions involving higher education funding and governance.

NOTES

1. Clyde F. Snider in collaboration with Samuel K. Gove, *American State and Local Government*, 2nd ed. (New York: Appleton-Century-Crofts, 1965), p. 542.

2. The appropriations process for public education has in recent years come under increased scrutiny by state courts on the basis of state constitutional provisions purporting to require "equitable" distributions of state moneys for the benefit of public school students. The U.S. Supreme Court has ruled that there is no right to an "equal" education per se under the Federal Constitution (outside of matters involving racial discrimination and the like), but activist judicial reinterpretation of broad state constitutional provisions has resulted in some states in significant changes in the allocations and amount of state resources devoted to public school education. These court decisions have not yet, however, altered the fundamental nature of the higher education governance and appropriations processes and thus are not within the scope of this work. It should not be presumed, however, that the judicial branch will not come to play a more important role in the future or that "equity" for public school children might not be accomplished at the expense of state-supported higher education.

3. John D. Millett, *Conflict in Higher Education: State Government Coordination versus Institutional Independence* (San Francisco: Jossey-Bass, 1984), p. 26.

4. Clark Kerr, *The Great Transformation in Higher Education 1960–1980* (Albany: State University of New York Press, 1991), p. 154.

5. Education continues to enjoy its traditional high priority. For an overview

and rankings of the issues considered to be of highest priority by the members of 44 legislatures and the legislative bodies of the District of Columbia and Commonwealth of Puerto Rico, see National Conference of State Legislatures, *State Issues 1991: A Survey of Priority Issues for State Legislatures* (Denver: National Conference of State Legislatures, 1991).

6. Edith K. Mosher and Jennings L. Wagoner, Jr., *The Changing Politics of Education* (Berkeley: McCutchan Publishing Corporation, 1978), p. 238.

7. William J. Keefe and Morris S. Ogul, *The American Legislative Process, Congress and the States*, 2nd ed. (Englewood Cliffs, New Jersey: Prentice Hall, Inc., 1968), p. 429.

8. Keefe and Ogul, *The American Legislative Process*, p. 121.

9. Education Commission of the States, *Coordination or Chaos?* (Denver: Education Commission of the States, 1973)

10. Education Commission of the States, *Challenge: Coordination and Governance in the 1980's* (Denver: Education Commission of the States, 1980).

11. Robert J. Barak and Robert O. Berdahl, *State Level Program Review in Higher Education* (Denver: Education Commission of the States, 1978), p. 242.

12. Carnegie Commission on Higher Education, *The Capitol and the Campus, State Responsibility for Postsecondary Education* (New York: McGraw-Hill, 1971), p. 22.

Chapter 3

State Coordinating Agencies of Higher Education[1]

Some form of agency-based statewide coordination of higher education is today extant virtually throughout the United States.[2] Such statewide coordination may be said to take the form of either (a) a coordinating board in most cases with a mix of regulatory[3] and advisory powers[4] or (b) a consolidated governing board.[5] The exceptions are Delaware and Vermont, which have appointed planning agencies only, and Wyoming, which has only one state-supported university, therefore arguably obviating the need for interinstitutional coordination in that state. Some of the states with a consolidated governing board also have an overarching statutory coordinating or planning agency for higher education. No research studies (as opposed to personal opinion essays) have found one form of statewide coordination structure to be intrinsically superior to another. The reasons for the establishment of coordinating agencies by states are, of course, those discussed in chapter 1 respecting the reaction to rising levels of concern by the state in its higher education institutions.

Information on and an attempt at classification of existing coordinating structures in the forty-nine states that have some kind of coordinating agency or agencies for higher education is set forth below.

The consensus view is that coordinating agencies are established to accomplish multiple objectives. When the majority of the coordinating agencies were established in the 1950s and 1960s, the typically stated major purpose of their organization was to ensure the orderly growth and

Chart 3–1
Coordinating Agency Structures in the United States

Coordinating Board, advisory or regulatory	Governing Board	Governing Board plus an advisory coordinating board
Alabama	Georgia	Arizona (1)
Alaska	Hawaii	California (2)
Arkansas	Idaho	Florida (3)
Colorado	Iowa (4)	New Hampshire
Connecticut	Kansas	New York (5)
Delaware (6)	Maine	Oregon
District of Columbia	Mississippi (8)	Pennsylvania (7)
Illinois	Montana	
Indiana	Nevada	
Kentucky	North Carolina (9)	
Louisiana	North Dakota	
Maryland	Rhode Island	
Massachusetts (10)	South Dakota	
Michigan	Utah	
Minnesota	West Virginia (11)	
Missouri	Wisconsin	
Nebraska		
New Jersey		
New Mexico		
Ohio		
Oklahoma		
South Carolina		
Tennessee (12)		
Texas		
Vermont (6, 13)		
Virginia		
Washington		

(1) Arizona has two boards with governing and coordinating authority, the Board of Regents for the three universities and the State Board of Directors for the community colleges. In addition, there is an advisory body, the Arizona Commission for Postsecondary Education.
(2) California has a three-tier system of higher education, the university system, the state college system, and the community college system. On top of all three systems in an advisory capacity only is the California Postsecondary Education Commission.
(3) Florida has a consolidated governing board for the State University System. The community colleges have their own individual governing boards plus a coordinating committee in the State Department of Education. There is also an overall advisory coordinating agency, the Postsecondary Education Planning Commission.
(4) The Board of Regents governs the three public universities, and the State Board of Education is over the community colleges.

Chart 3–1 (continued)

(5) New York has two large public-university systems, the State University of New York and the City University of New York, both with their own system administration. The New York Board of Regents provides coordination of all segments of public education including elementary and secondary schools.
(6) Planning agency
(7) There are 14 regional "state-owned" colleges and universities that make up the State System of Higher Education under the consolidated governing board. Pennsylvania also has 4 "state-related" institutions— Lincoln, Pennsylvania State, Temple Universities and the University of Pittsburgh—which receive substantial portions of their finances from the state. A third set of colleges are considered "state-assisted." They are private, but receive state money for certain academic programs. The State Department of Education provides overall coordination for all aspects of higher education in the state.
(8) The Board of Trustees of State Institutions of Higher Learning is the coordinating and governing board for the 8 four-year institutions, and the State Board for Community Colleges is the coordinating and governing board for the two-year institutions.
(9) The University of North Carolina System is governed by a single board, with a less powerful board providing advice for each campus. The community colleges are governed locally, with coordination by the State Department of Community Colleges.
(10) In 1991, Massachusetts eliminated a statewide Board of Regents and replaced it with the Higher Education Coordinating Committee. Two regional universities, the University of Lowell and Southeastern Massachusetts University were incorporated into the University of Massachusetts under a superboard.
(11) Recently West Virginia eliminated a statewide Board of Regents and replaced it with two new boards: one governing the research universities and professional schools that make up the new University of West Virginia System; the other oversees the operation of the state's two-year and four-year colleges.
(12) The regional and community college system is governed by the Tennessee Board of Regents. Both the regional and the university systems are coordinated by the Tenneessee Higher Education Commission.
(13) Four-year institutions, other than the University of Vermont, and the community colleges are governed by the Vermont State Colleges Board of Trustees. The University of Vermont is governed by its own Board of Trustees. The Vermont Higher Education Planning Commission does the statewide planning for all higher education.

development of higher education in their respective states through effective planning. The "planning for orderly growth" function was to be accomplished by means of both coordinating and actually clarifying the role and mission of the various institutions, thereby ensuring the diversity of types of institutions and programs sufficient to meet the growing educational needs of the state (although homogeneity may sometimes have been the actual result). Another typical objective was to ensure access for all qualified citizens of the state to higher education commensurate with their interests and needs. Other common objectives are the avoidance of unnecessary duplication of academic programs, and institutional accountability to the state. A concomitant objective is the development of a clearinghouse for the accumulation and analysis of the information necessary for continuous state and institutional planning to meet changing conditions and needs.[6]

Differences in scope of authority, grant of powers, and variations in formal structures from state to state have naturally resulted in some coordinating agencies emphasizing one or more of these objectives to the exclusion or de-emphasis of others, but most agencies have included substantially all of these objectives in their formal charge.

Having a statewide, rather than an institutional, perspective, state coordinating agencies find themselves in a position to deal capably with matters that go beyond the scope and capabilities of individual institutions. While the promise implied by such capability has unfortunately not always been realized, examples of such activities abound, and some are reviewed in some detail in the chapters constituting parts II and III of this work.

VOLUNTARY COORDINATING AGENCIES

In several states, voluntary associations preceded the formal establishment of state coordinating agencies. Generally, these groups were formed through institutional initiative, more often than not to forestall the creation of a single, statewide governing board or a coordinating agency imbued with legally-binding comprehensive powers. These voluntary groups were often composed of the presidents of institutions participating in them, sometimes joined by trustees (e.g., the Ohio Inter-University Council) or business officers (e.g., the Indiana Inter-institutional Study Committee). The "power" exercisable by a voluntary group could only be influential in nature, since the group's capabilities were necessarily derivative only of the authority of its individual members in their official capacities. Thus, by their nature, these groups suffered from their lack of synergy and were inevitably forced to function almost exclusively on the basis of consensus and through the personal powers of persuasion of key participants. Although some of these groups were moderately successful for a time, they generally proved too weak to serve as vehicles for effective coordination. Major controversies among competing institutions, such as the establishment of branch campuses, simply could not often be resolved by agreement among the group members; to use a slightly over-wrought analogy, the members never viewed themselves as oligopolists dividing their states into exclusive territories or their respective curricula into exclusive spheres of influence. The members typically viewed higher education as something other than a business, and while the tendency to carve out empires is certainly no less pronounced in the field of higher education than in any other arena of human endeavor, the problem was more that reasonable people can and do differ on what is the "best" thing to do, and if there is no arbiter or method to determine what is the "final," if not necessarily the "best" word, then failure is inevitable. According to Robert Berdahl, comparative experience generally suggests that voluntary coordination "is unable to make tough decisions because it usually operates on a principle of near unanimity; thus, vigorous objection from one member is enough to freeze its progress."[7]

The inability of voluntary agencies to resolve effectively the major issues in higher education led state legislatures to look for methods to resolve those issues—and therefore to the eventual replacement of voluntary coordinating agencies. The number of voluntary coordinating associations peaked around 1960, when there were six such agencies, but by 1976, each of these groups had been replaced either by a statutory coordinating council or by a statewide governing board.

COMPOSITION OF COORDINATING AGENCIES

The history of statewide higher education coordination reveals a close relationship between an agency's composition, that is, its membership, and the power it exercises. Voluntary associations proved to be ineffective largely because they were made up entirely of institutional representatives who had their respective institutional interests at heart and who were not disposed toward actions that would necessitate the surrender of institutional prerogatives. These groups and their members could and did provide leadership in planning for all areas of higher education, but without noninstitutional, that is, public members, to serve as the "balance tippers" between institutions, these groups were ultimately incapable of performing any effective role as mediators or arbitrators among the various competing institutions. Even in the case of statutory coordinating councils, it is the existence of public members (usually a majority of public members) on the council that serves as a guide or litmus test to the separation of those councils having only advisory power (of which there are only five currently), from those exercising at least some regulatory functions. State political authorities, it may generally be said, are suspicious of the institutions and tend to be unwilling to grant substantial powers to agencies composed exclusively or even mostly of college presidents or trustees.[8] Whether lawmakers, who typically lack the level of educational attainment of college presidents, are afraid of being outwitted or simply detect a superior attitude in the demeanor of the classic university hierarchy, it is an undisputable fact that today coordinating councils have evolved legislatively to the point where the majority of the members are public, rather than institutional members, and it is only in conjunction with this feature that a general increase in the power and influence of these agencies is noticed.

COORDINATING BOARD AUTHORITY

A coordinating board with regulatory powers characteristically possesses authority in three principal areas: 1) program approval for new and/or existing academic programs and approval for new campuses; 2) planning authority for higher education generally; and 3) budget review and recommendation power to the state executive and/or legislative branch. The level of coordinating board authority varies greatly along a continuum from boards with very limited advisory functions to strong boards with regulatory power over all three areas mentioned above. Examples also exist of agencies that do not fully exercise such legal powers as they may appear to possess as well as agencies that exercise unauthorized powers in indirect, and sometimes rather circuitous ways. The variation in authority among coordinating boards more often than not relates to intangible personal and political factors as opposed to the existence of formal legislative grants of power. These factors may include the prestige and influence of board members, and the confidence and respect of the state legislature for the board's staff work and recommendations.

In some states the coordinating board must struggle mightily to restrain the colleges and universities, most of which hope to expand their academic programs and missions, sometimes at the institutional expense of the programs and missions of others. In some states it is a losing battle. All too often the institutions carry considerably more weight with the legislature, through alumni ties and direct lobbying efforts, than the coordinating agency.

The Center for Research and Development in Higher Education at the University of California at Berkeley issued in 1971 a report entitled, "Coordinating Higher Education for the '70s,"[9] essentially a handbook on those activities ideally to be undertaken by a state coordinating agency. This report advocated the utilization of coordinating boards or councils and pronounced them superior to consolidated governing boards since the coordinating board would have the power to act as an "umbrella" for a variety of public institutions and agencies of higher education. The report also recommended a minimum of five spheres of influence or authority for coordinating boards: 1) to perform continuous planning; 2) to serve as a clearinghouse for and gatherer of information from all postsecondary institutions statewide; 3) to review and approve all new and existing degree programs and campuses; 4) to review and recommend operating and capital budgets for higher education; and 5) to administer student financial aid programs and federal grant programs to the state institutions.

In the late 1970s, states significantly increased their efforts to develop comprehensive master plans for all their various institutions of higher education. These efforts reflected a significant broadening of state concern from the field of public higher education alone to all of postsecondary education. This new broader scope for planning lent itself to coordinating boards more readily than to governing boards, which generally do not perform state governmental functions with respect to independent institutions or to public institutions that they do not govern (often community colleges or technical institutes). To perform true statewide planning, states with consolidated governing boards began to create separate coordinating boards with overarching planning authority for all of higher education in the state. Because coordinating boards do not have powers over personnel decisions or internal fiscal operations and control, dissimilar to the powers of governing boards discussed below, it is the typical major function of such boards to develop a systematic and complementary approach to utilization of the available resources, including the available library resources, of the state and its various state institutions in order to meet the wider educational needs and interests of the state as a whole.

CONSOLIDATED GOVERNING BOARDS

Consolidated governing boards generally have the responsibility not only for coordinating but also for directly governing the institutions of higher education in a state. Of the twenty-one states currently having statewide governing boards, the boards in eight of those states have governing authority over senior institutions only, but in the other thirteen states the governing authority extends to two-year institutions as well as senior institutions, thus making those boards truly comprehensive in purview. The states with governing boards for only senior institutions (or a separate board for the community colleges as in Arizona) are: Arizona, Florida, Iowa, Kansas, Mississippi, North Carolina, Oregon, and South Dakota.

In an extensive, landmark study conducted by Lyman Glenny in the 1950s, Glenny, who accurately forecasted the increasing concern on the part of the state governments with the organization of higher education, found that governing boards were measurably more successful than coordinating boards in obtaining funds from state legislatures, and that the institutional autonomy existing under coordinating boards was more marked than that existing under governing boards.[10]

It is commonly thought that there has been a trend toward single, statewide, consolidated governing boards. Indeed relatively new ones were established in Wisconsin and North Carolina in the 1970s, but out of the fifteen or more states that have considered this option since that time, either legislatively or in formal ways by the executive branches, only one state, Massachusetts, adopted this solution; and that state has since reverted to a coordinating board, revising in 1991 its governance structure for public higher education[11] (see also chapter 10). Other states that recently looked seriously at creating a single governing board have so far chosen to retain and strengthen an existing coordinating mechanism while maintaining a separate system or systems of institutional governance.[12]

A 1980 report by the Education Commission of the States noted that no "best" model had emerged for the governance of state higher education; however, the report did state that the logically expectable has resulted: smaller states have tended to favor the use of statewide governing boards and larger states, i.e., those with more complex (or more extensive) systems of higher education, are more likely to have coordinating boards.[13]

AUTHORITY OF CONSOLIDATED GOVERNING BOARDS

The primary difference between coordinating boards and consolidated governing boards is that a consolidated governing board possesses the authority to govern individual campuses directly, usually appointing and evaluating the chief administrative officer of each campus under its control. A consolidated governing board can intervene whenever necessary in the internal affairs of any campus, often reaching down into areas such as those involving approval of internal personnel policies and actions, and the establishment and revision of admission standards. More basically, the governing board is concerned with developing and actually implementing the total operating and capital budgets of each individual campus, a type of authority not characteristically conferred upon coordinating boards.

Differences among agencies within the categories of "coordinating board" and "governing board" can often be almost as great as those between the two categories themselves. For example, although some older governing boards in smaller states have not moved beyond the ministerial functions required to run the institutions under their control, a very different statewide perspective is characteristic of consolidated governing boards established more recently because the governor and the legislature in those states saw the need for tough policy choices in an era of declining enrollments and shrinking financial resources.

COORDINATING AGENCIES AND ACADEMIC LIBRARIES

A mid-1980s survey and interview-based study of state coordination of higher education and academic libraries[14] resulted in findings indicative of the proposition that successful interactions between the academic libraries of public institutions and those institutions' state coordinating agencies are, and have historically been, achieved mainly in those states possessing either regulatory coordinating boards or consolidated governing boards. It was also found that a change in the type of state coordinating agency, whatever the change, for example, converting an advisory agency into a regulatory board or going from a regulatory board to a consolidated governing board, resulted in an increased level of activity and contact between the academic libraries and the coordinating agency. This seeming "Hawthorne effect" could typically be traced to the effort of those involved to bring about changes in the coordinating agency, an effort no doubt bred from dissatisfaction with the older agency—a dissatisfaction that may have itself been engendered because of an unwillingness on the part of persons at the various institutions to work together.

In that same 1980s study, survey data indicated that most library directors felt state coordinating agencies were evidencing an increasing level of concern for and attention to the needs of academic libraries. Responses from ARL library directors indicated that they most affirmatively noted this trend. In addition, it was found that the presence of a permanent advisory committee of librarians (usually library directors) attached to or reporting to the coordinating agency was a key component of successful relations between the coordinating agency and academic libraries. In states without such a committee, it is apparently difficult to keep (or even place) library concerns before the membership and staff of the coordinating agency. Without such an organizational springboard it is apparently particularly difficult for strong library-oriented leadership, whose presentation of library concerns to the coordinating agency would have the weight and authority that is so necessary to carry the day against multifarious competing concerns, to emerge.

Another important factor in successful academic library/coordinating agency relations was found to be the existence of a person, preferably one with a library background, on the permanent staff of the coordinating agency whose continuing responsibilities included the academic libraries as a major component thereof. The record bears out the assertion implicit here: in states where library cooperative programs are successfully implemented, a position responsible for academic libraries almost always exists at the coordinating board level, although it is not always filled with a librarian.

Coordinating boards and consolidated governing boards can and do play a major role in academic library funding and programs. In part II of this work, the way these agencies influence academic library activities and programs will be examined in detail.

NOTES

1. The phrase "coordinating agency" will be used to indicate generically any type of higher education coordinating structure—consolidated governing boards, regulatory coordinating boards, or advisory coordinating boards.

2. Only Wyoming at present has no coordinating agency, the coordinating function being vested in the only state university, the University of Wyoming, and the Wyoming College Commission for the state's seven community colleges.

3. The term "regulatory coordinating board" is used here to denote a state-mandated agency that does not supersede institutional or segmental governing boards but does have final approval power in at least some key policy areas.

4. An advisory coordinating board provides advice and recommendations on higher education to the institutions and state agencies, but it has no powers of final approval with respect to any key policy areas.

5. The term "consolidated governing board" is intended to describe a board which functions as a unitary governance and coordination instrumentality for all aspects of higher education within a state, except, in some cases, public community colleges.

6. Richard M. Millard, *Today's Myths and Tomorrow's Realities* (San Francisco: Jossey-Bass, 1991), p. 3.

7. Robert O. Berdahl, "Public Universities and State Governments: Is the Tension Benign?" *Educational Record* 71 (Winter 1990), p. 39.

8. Robert O. Berdahl, *Statewide Coordination of Higher Education* (Washington, D.C.: American Council on Education, 1971), pp. 47– 48, 52.

9. Lyman A. Glenny et al., *Coordinating Higher Education for the '70s* (Berkeley: Center for Research and Development in Higher Education, University of California, 1971).

10. Lyman A. Glenny, *Autonomy of Public Colleges: The Challenge of Coordination* (New York: McGraw-Hill, 1959).

11. Goldie Blumenstyk, "Massachusetts' Reorganization of Public Education Gives Wide Powers to Secretary, 11-member Council," *Chronicle of Higher Education* 37 (July 24, 1991), pp. 17A-18A.

12. *State Postsecondary Education Structures Handbook 1986* (Denver: Education Commission of the States, 1986), p. 5.

13. Education Commission of the States, *Challenge: Coordination and Governance in the 1980s* (Denver: Education Commission of the States, 1980).

14. Vicki L. Gregory, "State Coordination of Higher Education and Academic Libraries," *College & Research Libraries* 49 (July 1988): pp. 315–24; Vicki L. Gregory, "Library Cooperative Programs and Coordinating Agencies of Higher Education," *Library and Information Science Research* 10 (Summer 1988): pp. 305–29.

Chapter 4

State Libraries

A state library may be described as that particular state governmental agency that has responsibility for the extension and development of public library services in its state; additionally, the state library is usually its state's entity responsible for the administration of the federal government's Library Service and Construction Act (LSCA) funds for that state.

Historically, state libraries were concerned primarily with service to state government, to public libraries and, in some states, to school libraries. With the advent of LSCA moneys, the state libraries have begun to broaden their purview. For instance, since not all state-financed library programs and LSCA-funded library programs are solely for public libraries, state libraries are in a position to influence and aid in the development of all types of library services. In addition, when Title III of LSCA, dealing with interlibrary cooperation, became law in 1966, it "gave leadership responsibility [to the state library] for statewide multitype library networks, thus causing state library development agencies to widen their scope from public libraries alone to all types of libraries within a state."[1]

Today, academic and state library agencies are becoming increasingly interdependent. Academic libraries are often dependent upon their state libraries to coordinate library programs that cross traditional type-of-library boundaries, and in such cases must necessarily look to their state library. Likewise, state libraries look to academic libraries in their states as both important participants in the state library's function and as major resource centers for information access and delivery within and throughout the state. In a number of states, new legislation has been passed, or old laws amended or re-interpreted, to allow state library agencies to work directly with academic libraries in just this way. Academic libraries and state libraries obviously share many of the same concerns and can benefit from mutual cooperation, as opposed to the competition for state funding that is an unfortunate historical norm in some states.[2]

LEGAL BASIS FOR MULTITYPE LIBRARY PROGRAMS

Legislative approaches to multitype library programs involving state libraries and academic libraries range from a single sentence in a statute providing broad authority for multitype library cooperation to comprehensive legislation supported by extensive regulations actually creating multitype organizations. Somewhere in the middle are specific legislative initiatives involving funding of multitype library programs such as reciprocal borrowing or a common borrower's card, interlibrary loan, collection development, union catalogs, and shared automated systems. According to a survey published in 1991, 34 states then had specific legislation authorizing cooperation among different types of libraries, with eleven additional states reporting the existence of such cooperation but without actual multitype library legislation or regulations. Probably a key factor in such a high level of achievement in this area is that all fifty states support cooperative projects with funding under LSCA Title III.[3]

Several examples will serve to illustrate the wide variety of legislation in this area. In June 1988, Colorado enacted the "Colorado Library Law," which specifically states that it is the policy of the State of Colorado:

[T]o promote the establishment and development of all types of publicly-supported free library service throughout the state to ensure equal access to information without regard to age, physical or mental health, place of residence, or economic status, to aid in the establishment and improvement of library programs, to improve and update the skills of persons employed in libraries through continuing education activities, and to promote and coordinate the sharing of resources among libraries in Colorado and the dissemination of information regarding the availability of library services.[4]

In section 103 of the Colorado Library Law the phrase "publicly-supported library" is further defined to include specifically the academic libraries of the state's publicly supported colleges, universities, community colleges and junior colleges as well as the state's public libraries, school libraries maintained by a school district and special libraries operated by publicly-supported associations, agencies, or other groups.

In section 105, which describes the powers and duties of the Colorado State Librarian, five specific powers and duties are listed for the State Librarian in regard to publicly-supported libraries other than public libraries, the first of which is directly related to multitype library cooperation; it is the statutory duty of the Colorado State Librarian "to further library development and encourage contractual and cooperative relations to enhance resource sharing among all types of libraries and agencies throughout the state."[5] Buttressing Colorado's legislatively expressed intent in multitype library cooperation is section 118, which provides for the establishment, by the Colorado State Library, in cooperation with the research libraries in Colorado, of an automated catalog available for use by all publicly or privately supported libraries in Colorado.

In 1991, North Dakota enacted a multitype library authority act,[6] and the state legislature provided $50,000 for startup of a statewide multitype library authority committee. The act mandates that this committee establish one multitype library system during the 1991–1993 biennium and one or more additional multitype library systems in each succeeding biennium. Libraries, with approval from their boards of trustees, may submit a membership application to the Multitype Library Authority Committee to join a regional multitype library authority. Each member must be willing to provide access to its collection, reciprocal borrowing privileges, and interlibrary loan service to any person residing within the "service area" of the multitype library system.

The relatively new Colorado and North Dakota laws are among the most comprehensive and detailed in the nation and are noteworthy in being essentially "freestanding" in that the powers to be exercised under them are not derivative or dependent upon those of any other constituted authority or institutions, but are in both cases derived directly from the state.

A state that has amended its library legislation to include multitype library cooperation is Illinois. "The Illinois Library System Act,"[7] originally passed in 1969, amended in 1983,[8] presently includes the following:

Because the state has a financial responsibility in promoting public education, and because the public library is a vital agency serving all levels of the educational process, it is hereby declared to be the policy of the state to encourage the improvement of free public libraries and to encourage cooperation among all types of libraries in promoting the sharing of library resources. In keeping with this policy, provision is hereby made for a program of state grants designed to establish, develop and operate a network of library systems covering the entire state.[9]

The act goes on to detail procedures for the conversion of existing public library systems to multitype library systems, including the submission of an application respecting a new system to the state librarian, whose approval is required before the multitype system can begin operations.

Yet another approach is seen in Florida, where no specific law at all authorizes the creation or recognizes the existence of multitype library systems, but the powers granted to the state library have been deemed broad enough to allow that agency both to encourage and to engage in such cooperative ventures. The general language of the law authorizing the Florida State Library Agency is itself quite broad:

The division [Department of State, Division of Library and Information Services] may, upon request, give aid and assistance, financial, advisory, or otherwise to all school, state institutional, academic, free and public libraries, and to all communities in the state which may propose to establish libraries, as to the best means of establishing and administering libraries, selecting and cataloging books, and other facets of library management.[10]

The examples set forth above are by no means fully representative of all the various legislative avenues taken by states in regard to the legal basis of multitype library cooperation. As in most areas, each state is unique in many ways in its approach to the matter of library cooperation in its state with different circumstances and historical developments having dictated different legislative solutions and approaches.

STATE LIBRARIES AND ACADEMIC LIBRARIES

Because of the relative paucity of published materials focusing on the relationship between state libraries and academic libraries, in the course of preparation of this chapter of this work a survey instrument was sent to the state librarians of all fifty states. The data collected from the survey emphasized relationships between state libraries and academic libraries specifically, and the relationship between state libraries and those multitype library systems that address all types of libraries in the state, including academic libraries. The generalizations and observations discussed below are based on 36 responses (a 70 percent return rate) to that survey questionnaire.

First, state librarians appear strongly to believe that both public and academic libraries have much to offer their patrons through collaboration in cooperative ventures. They also agreed that LSCA funds have encouraged an increase in the level of cooperation between public and academic libraries. When asked if LSCA funds were a major source of funding for the technology to facilitate multitype library cooperative programs, the majority agreed that they were, but it should be noted that about a fourth of the respondents indicated that LSCA funds had not been used at all in this manner in their state. One state librarian asserted that collaboration and coordination among libraries is the "only route to follow" with the new technologies, and that it will be the creation and structuring of cooperatives, not the technology itself, that will be critical to the state's future and the country's future as well.

The state librarians were also asked to judge whether multitype cooperative programs had been successful in their state, to which question the overwhelming majority answered that multitype programs had been successful. As an example of their assessment of multitype library programs, Nancy M. Bolt, State Librarian of Colorado stated:

I've worked in many states and I have never seen multitype cooperation like it exists in Colorado. There are seven regional library service systems that were created as multitype in the early 1970s. Almost all statewide projects have representation from all types of libraries. The Systems have regular retreats to which librarians from all types of libraries attend. Almost everything we do is multitype oriented. The larger public and academic libraries have accepted a responsibility to serve smaller, less well-off libraries.[11]

In another assessment of multitype library programs, Jim Scheppke, Acting State Librarian of Oregon, stated that:

The most successful multitype cooperation occurs when it is planned "bottom-up" and not "top-down." The state library agency should not force multitype cooperation, but should encourage it and provide start-up funds when necessary. Ongoing organizational funding should be a local and not a state responsibility.[12]

When the state librarians were asked if academic librarians in their state recognize the role of the state library agency in regard to all types of libraries, the majority agreed that they did, but there were more negative responses than to the questions discussed above. The conclusion most logically to be drawn is that while state librarians strongly feel that there is much to be gained through multitype library programs, they are not as a whole quite so sure that academic librarians recognize the (implicitly important) role of state library agencies in these ventures. Even in resource sharing networks composed mainly of academic libraries, an overwhelming majority of the state librarians (81 percent) felt that the state librarian should have an important advisory role to play on the governing board of the network. However, state librarians also feel that both the state coordinating agency and the state library agency should be involved in the governance of multitype library cooperative systems.

In many states, the existence of LSCA Title III funds have obviously encouraged multitype library cooperative programs. Even without the LSCA funds, the current economic situation and the rapid increase in the number and type of information sources being published create an environment that encourages, even demands, resource sharing. However, as studies of multitype library systems have shown, state and federal funds have been the chief source of funding for multitype programs.[13] The growing existence of automated systems in all types of libraries provides the ability to share information about collections needed for cooperative collection development, improved interlibrary loan access, and other means of sharing information resources. Studies have shown that in multitype library systems not only do academic libraries provide resources for public and school libraries, but public and even school libraries have been shown to provide unique materials, both books and periodicals, for patrons of academic libraries.[14] These kinds of programs do bring more players from different types of libraries into the decision making process for the network and thus have an impact, most likely positive but certainly not negative, on how academic libraries function.

NOTES

1. Genevieve M. Casey, "Administration of State and Federal Funds for Library Development" *Library Trends* 27 (Fall 1978), p. 159.

2. Charles T. Townley, Charles R. Peguese and Kenneth G. Rohm, Jr., "Academic Library-State Library Agency Relationships: The Pennsylvania Needs Assessment," *College & Research Libraries* 49 (May 1988), pp. 239–40.

3. Keith Michael Fiels, Joan Newmann, and Eva R. Brown, comp., *Multitype Library Cooperation, State Laws, Regulations and Pending Legislation* (Chicago: Association of Specialized and Cooperative Library Agencies, 1991), p. xii.

4. Colorado Revised Statutes, Title 24, Article 90, Part 1, Section 102.

5. Colorado Revised Statutes, Title 24, Article 90, Part 1, Section 105(2a).

6. 1991 North Dakota Laws, Chapter 596, codified as N.D. Cent. Code section 54–24.3–01 *et seq.*(1991).

7. Laws of Illinois, Chapter 81, Sections 111–126.

8. Public Act 83–411, section 1.

9. Laws of Illinois, Chapter 81, Section 111.

10. Florida Statutes, 257.04(2).

11. Quoted by permission of Nancy M. Bolt, State Librarian of Colorado.

12. Quoted by permission of Jim Scheppke, Acting State Librarian of Oregon.

13. See, for example, Betty J. Turock, "Organizational Factors in Multitype Library Networking: A National Test of the Model," *Library & Information Science Research* 8 (April/June 1986), p. 130.

14. Betty J. Turock, "Performance Factors in Multitype Library Networking," *Resource Sharing and Information Networks* 3 (Fall 1985), pp. 15–38; Barbara Markuson, "Analysis of Requirements of On-Line Network Cataloging Services for Small Academic, Public, School, and Other Libraries" (Bethesda: ERIC Documentation Reproduction Service, 1977), ED 140 861.

Part II

THE INTERACTION BETWEEN STATE GOVERNMENT AND ACADEMIC LIBRARIES

Our common vision of networking is an environment in which libraries can provide each individual in the United States with equal opportunity of access to resources that will satisfy their and society's information needs and interests. All users should have access on a timely basis to the information that they require without being faced with costs beyond their own or society's means.

To realize this vision, there must be technical and intellectual sharing of resources between the public and private sectors; local, state, and federal governments must fulfill their various responsibilities to individuals and society; and the diverse missions of the several types of libraries must be accomplished. As this vision becomes a reality, there will emerge a diverse but coordinated structure of networks rather than a monolithic one. Active research, rapidly developing technology, collaborative leadership, common standards, and shared communications will provide means by which the system will be further shaped as an interlocking series of local, state, regional, national, and international relationships that are capable of serving the nation's information needs.

—Network Advisory Committee
Library of Congress
1986

Chapter 5

State Funding—The Key to Control

The state's annual (or in a few states biennial) budget typically reflects the heartbeat of the political process at the state level; for that reason its budget should be viewed as the state's most important political policy statement. Every state possesses a finite sum of resources that must be spread among a number of essential and some not so essential state services. Whether any particular object of expenditure, such as higher education, is "essential" is, of course, a debatable point. Ultimately "essentialness" is conclusively influenced more by the point of view of the decision makers than by abstract considerations of the ultimate utility and desirability of any particular object in question, or even by legislative or constitutional determinations of "essentialness," which will always be the subject of differences of opinion.

In any event, the state budget itself undeniably serves several, certainly essential, purposes. One is to establish demonstrably the politically perceived need for and desirability of certain proposed new activities; an appropriation carries with it an *ipso facto* (at least facially) presumption of legitimacy of purpose where (as everywhere) resources and means are limited and wants and desires infinite. Another purpose of the budget is simply to distribute available resources to support previously authorized purposes and activities (which have established their legitimacy in an earlier period) during a given fiscal period. The amount of money allocated to higher education thus must necessarily compete with a large number of other state services for a fair share of the proverbial pie.

Michael J. Ross, in a 1987 study of state and local politics, pointed out that

> A key point to remember about budgets is that they are political documents. Although budgets have the appearance of accounting ledgers with columns of numbers and a bottom line that balances, they are really expressions of deeply held political values and ideological preferences. Programs that pursue goals that governors or legislatures care about, or that benefit politically powerful interest groups, will be generously funded. Those that do not, will not.[1]

In most states, the publicly-supported institutions of higher education present budget requests to their state higher education coordinating agency, which may hold hearings or engage in other fact finding activities before preparing either a consolidated[2] or aggregated[3] budget request for higher education, which is in turn submitted to the state governor and/or an executive or legislative branch budget bureau. While state budgets generally are prepared in the executive branch by a budget agency or department subordinate to the governor, legislatures enjoying well-funded committee structures and staff jealously and zealously guard the "power of the purse," often challenging a governor's budget at every turn and sometimes even abandoning the basic structure of the budget presented to them and substituting their own collective wisdom for that of the executive. Lyman Glenny, a well-known expert in the area of higher education finance, believes that "no phenomenon found in studying state budget practice seems likely to have as much impact on colleges and universities as the growth in number, size, and professional capacity of legislative budget staffs."[4] As legislative staffs add capable (or not so capable) budget analysts, that staff is less likely to rely on the recommendations of the state coordinating board or of the governor and his (or her) budget bureau, tending to undertake its own in-depth reviews.[5] Of course, there are significant restraints to what the legislature can do to the governor's budget; these restraints may include constitutional restrictions on deficit spending for current or operating expenditures, the earmarking of certain tax revenues for specified purposes, and contracted commitments respecting debt principal and interest payments and retirement programs, as well as the practical restraints of limited-length legislative sessions, the imposition of more politically pressing legislative matters, party loyalty, etc.

Due to the necessarily incremental nature of state budgeting (true zero-based budgeting remains a chimerical ideal) most of the battles are necessarily fought only on the margins. Legislatures are generally concerned mostly over new expenditures or those proposed expenditures that are to be greatly increased over the previous state allocation. Preexisting fund allocations reflect the results of earlier wars that the combatants, even the losers, would generally not wish to refight; thus, the obtaining of new or substantially increased funds is where the current political battle lines are almost always drawn and fought over.[6]

These state political battles become of concern to academic libraries simply because the libraries are an integral part of their respective institutions of higher education; thus, examination of the issues involved in the various types of budgets used for higher education in general should be made, a correlative part of which involves the types and examples of the library budgeting process.

GENERAL ISSUES IN HIGHER EDUCATION FUNDING

In an assessment of what may be termed the "societal" factors affecting the current relationship between institutions of higher education and state governments, Jonathan Fife notes four conditions that, in his view, undeniably affect public higher education:

First, the majority of college students attend state supported institutions. Second, there is a general dissatisfaction with the quality of the output from higher education institutions. Third, in the foreseeable future there will be more competition for public funds, especially from areas such as social security, Medicare and Medicaid, day care, and crime prevention. Fourth, the public holds elected officials accountable for how well public monies are spent. Those factors translate into the undeniable fact that public colleges must continue to be concerned with their relationships with state government if they are to meet public expectations and to receive sufficient public funding. This will call for not only strong leadership, but also statesmanship. The days of competition between, and separation from, state governments and public institutions have passed.[7]

The higher education growth experienced following World War II and continuing through most of the 1960s naturally resulted in higher percentages of available state financial resources being consumed by higher education. Of necessity, budget agencies and state legislatures became aware of a need for a more systematic, and preferably more objective, approach to controlling the expenditures of those public funds set aside for higher education. Accountability for the use of public funds became the watchword as higher education came to be more critically viewed from the state level. Conversely, the state institutions, having traditionally enjoyed a high level of independence (sometimes based more on neglect than a healthy respect for academic freedom), were naturally enough concerned with protecting themselves from a new, and arguably more sinister, type of state control, which took the form of budgetary restraint. In many states the use of budgeting formulas was established as a political compromise in an attempt to satisfy both the state government and the individual institutions of higher education. These formulas were generally introduced and touted as methods (a) to ensure to all institutions a more or less "guaranteed" base level of support, (b) to avoid having to deal with each institution on an individual basis, (c) to provide a certain degree of interinstitutional equity in terms of equal funding for similar programs, and (d) to provide greater effectiveness in measuring specific needs.

Not all states have taken the formula budget route; some have retained the types of budgeting traditionally applied to state level agencies such as highway departments or fish and game agencies, that is, line-item or lump sum budgeting. Other states have experimented with new kinds of budgeting, such as so-called performance or program budgeting. Several of these approaches are briefly described below, and each can be seen to have both defects and advantages. Certainly, no single approach to budgeting can be expected mechanically to resolve in all, or even perhaps most, cases the complexity and inherent conflict that exists in the funding of higher education and other state services. The human political element must eventually come to the fore to settle, if not permanently resolve, the conflicts.

Many experts today argue for the "deregulation" of higher education. Thompson and Zumeta maintain that higher education should generally be seen to function in many respects as a sort of regulated industry. From this perspective, the state coordinating agency typically is seen as offering considerable benefits to the students (the consumers) by controlling the programs (the service) and the institutions (the utilities that provide the service to the consumers), by exercising influence over the size and distribution of programs, the kinds and numbers of new programs, and the production of degrees. The agency can also be seen as monitoring, if not controlling, the prices charged to consumers, (student tuition rates) and protecting the students in their role as rate paying consumers.[8] (The analogy falls down a bit when one considers that the taxpayers may be seen as the true ratepayers; perhaps, though, the railroad land grants of the last century and TVA, REA, and other subsidy programs of this century assist in supporting the parallel.) Certainly, a rationale can be constructed against such a regulatory approach. It can be convincingly argued that the concerns about quality and accountability that lead to regulation may be destroying what the state government actually wants to preserve. Regulation always tends to lead to excessive paperwork and restrictions that in turn tend to produce rigidity in administration, which leads to the stifling of creativity and prevents the flexibility needed in higher education to promote the elusive "quality" factor so highly sought after in college and university programs.[9]

But if the regulated industry analogy is accepted as being reflective of the current reality in most states, focusing on specific areas where "deregulation" may be needed could be useful. The major area of concern here would have to be fiscal controls and the need for institutions to be able to exercise more flexibility in management. Government and flexibility are not often found together, and several areas have been identified where, from a budgetary standpoint, more flexibility is likely needed: 1) institutional authority to carry funds over from one fiscal year to the next, including authority either to expend or to invest these funds; 2) authority to procure, contract for, and dispose of property independent of unified state systems for property control; 3) authority to allocate, and reallocate as needs change, funds among categories of appropriations during the fiscal year; and 4) authority to review and to set policy in sensitive areas such as purchasing equipment and funding employee travel.[10]

A certain degree of control by the state over higher education is both inevitable and desirable due to the size of the public institutions and the percentage of each state's tax moneys expended by those institutions. The concern is over the amount and kind of regulation. Too much regulation can lead to rigidity, to excessive numbers of administrators to deal with state-mandated reports and forms, and to less money for the classroom, the laboratory, or for library resources, but too little regulation likely leads to chaos and the survival of only the politically fittest.

BUDGET TYPES

Review of current state budget practices reveals that the budgets typically utilized for higher education may be placed in five general categories: 1) the object of expenditure or line-item budget; 2) the lump-sum budget; 3) the formula budget; 4) the performance budget; and 5) the program budget. Each will be examined below in turn.

Line-item budgeting. Currently the most prevalent form of state budgeting is the object of expenditure or line-item budget. This type of budget is essentially incremental in nature, with emphasis placed upon examining changes in particular data or criteria from one year to the next as opposed to establishing a linkage between the budget amounts and stated objectives or long-range plans. At the time of Isaac Littleton's study in 1977, over half of the states' institutions of higher education had to first justify their respective requests by line item. State budget agencies, legislatures, and governors then made their decisions for each institution separately. Where line-item budgeting is used:

[t]he political clout of the institution is usually an important factor in obtaining adequate library funding in these institutions. The library must compete with the many other needs of the campus. In the final showdown, adequate funding for the library is dependent upon the priorities given to the library needs by campus

administrators and the skill in convincing budgeting authorities of the need of the funds requested.[11]

Lump-sum budgeting. As its name connotes, lump-sum budgeting results in allocation to each recipient organization for a single fiscal period of simply a specified amount of money. Lump-sum budgeting allows administrators maximum flexibility in expenditures but obviously provides for very limited built-in accountability. As in the case of line-item budgeting, lump-sum budgeting contains no inherent mechanism for establishing relationships between expenditures in any one year and the long range plans and goals of either the institution or the state.[12]

Performance budgeting. The performance budget has not been widely used in higher education and library funding. Advocates of this type of budgeting stress its emphasis on efficiency through its focus upon unit costs in terms of service outputs. In its simplest form, moneys are allocated on the basis of performance indicators and outcome measures. As applied to educational settings, it would not, however, be correct to characterize the method as simply a "dollars-per-degree" approach because performance budgeting does attempt to use qualitative as well as quantitative measures of results. Tennessee, for instance, uses a form of performance budgeting which allocates incremental funds, up to two percent of each institution's budget, on the basis of performance ratings with respect to several selected indicators.[13]

Program budgeting. This type of budgeting is probably best known in terms of its most sophisticated version (which comes complete with an acronym), the Planning-Programming-Budgeting System (PPBS). Program budgeting is intended to force a continuous link between planning and budgeting and thus between organizational objectives and expenditures. This type of budget generally makes use of or at least pays homage to the zero-sum or zero-base approach, meaning that financial considerations are returned to the first dollar or zero rather than using the previous year's allocation as a beginning point. A simplified version of PPBS designed specifically for libraries is the ALMS (A Library Management System) developed at California State University, Northridge.[14] While PPBS has been largely discarded at this writing (ALMS proved politically unworkable in California), other versions of program budgeting still exist in some higher education applications.

Formula budgeting. Formula budgeting approaches for higher education institutions vary greatly in their complexity from fairly simple formula allocation of certain set percentages of available moneys per student credit hour to the division of earmarked funds based on complex mathematical formulas; however, even many of the latter may be seen as essentially enrollment driven. In the last few years there have been attempts to develop more "accurate" and sophisticated formulas based on such concepts as marginal cost analysis, as in Indiana, or "fixed-and-variable cost" formulas such as those used in Wisconsin and Florida. One of the great appeals of formula budgeting to state legislatures and state officials generally has always been its seemingly impartial and objective approach to funding. The elimination of favoritism and political maneuvering, however, may be something of a mirage. Obviously the political elements will inevitably come into play whenever a formula is being developed or decided upon or whenever revision of the formula is required or desired. Formulas, even at their very best, are at root no more than a combination of technical judgments and political agreements. However, the political conflicts having to do with formulas are not battles which must necessarily be fought at every session of the legislature. Once a formula is established, no matter how it is based or how illogical it may seem to some, it naturally becomes entrenched and therefore much harder to deviate from in order to play favorites; thus, to many governors and state legislatures formula funding does seem a preferable approach since it can and typically does remove many of the political battles in funding higher education away from their doorsteps. The unwanted child is not thereby orphaned—it simply arrives at the state coordinating agency.

BUDGETING TECHNIQUES AS APPLIED TO LIBRARIES

In 1973, the Association of Research Libraries (ARL) conducted a survey[15] of budgeting techniques used in ARL libraries. The results of that survey indicated that 78 percent of the ARL libraries at that time used the traditional line-item budget approach and 3 percent the lump-sum technique where the library budget was an integral part of the university budget, that is, when the library was reflected as only one of the many cost centers of the parent organization. The survey also revealed that those libraries using formula funding generally had had the technique imposed upon them from the outside, usually by state legislatures. The compilers of the ARL study also discovered that many of the "parent" institutions preferred formula budgeting over any other budget technique. It should be noted, however, that at the time of the ARL study the impact of steady or declining enrollments had yet to become keenly felt. Periods of declining enrollments would not likely make formulas so popular—their strict use can be devastating to the operation of an institution since neither fixed nor variable operating costs typically decline proportionately to decreases in enrollment, and the closing of the institution's doors is not out of the question. The ARL study also identified examples of program and performance budgeting being used in academic and research libraries.

Of course, in practice, budgeting techniques are not always pure examples of any of the five major types described above. For example, formulas may be used in lump-sum budgeting to calculate, based on established criteria, the amount of money which should be appropriated as a lump sum to the institution or governing board as is done in Georgia. Formulas can also be embedded in performance and program budgeting approaches. Even line-item budgets may include some aspects of formula budgeting; for example, a formula based on the number of current periodical titles and size of the collection could easily be used to generate a line-item amount for binding in a library's budget.

A few states, such as North Carolina and at one time Texas, have provided in their higher education budgets for restricted library budgeting. In such cases, coordinating agencies allocate funds appropriated by the legislature directly and specifically to the academic libraries. Theoretically, such an approach can be utilized with any of the types of budgets, except where funds are allocated as a lump-sum to the institution as a whole. As a result of his study, completed in 1977, Littleton concluded that "from the library's point of view, it [restricted library budgeting] is desirable because an institution's administration cannot divert funds needed by the library to other purposes as has been done in some states with lump sum institutional budgeting." Littleton further states that libraries in states with direct funding allocations from the coordinating agencies of higher education have generally fared well.[16]

While there is little conformity among states in the methods of funding their higher education institutions' academic libraries, there does seem to exist a trend toward some increased use of formulas in state funding despite the problems with formula funding in times of economic stress and the declining enrollments of many institutions.

Formula budgeting for libraries. As with funding formulas generally, formula budgeting approaches for libraries vary greatly, ranging from an allocation of an arbitrary percentage of the total university budget to allocations based on complex mathematical formulas, most of which are essentially enrollment driven.[17]

The use of formulas in the library sphere is not at all new. An early study of library formula budgeting published by Arthur McAnally in 1963[18] found that in many states at that time statewide coordinating agencies were using systematic formula budgeting in connection with library funding. The chief characteristic of the budget formulas then in use in connection with libraries was found to be, as it remains today, variety. McAnally found that just about every library standard known to the profession was used in the funding process in one or more states, and often in combination. The standards most often used did fall into four general classes: 1) arbitrary standards; 2) per student or enrollment bases; 3) comparisons; and 4) unit or operations costs. McAnally predicted in 1963 that, as statewide agencies gained more experience, libraries would receive more and more of their attention.

At roughly the same time, James L. Miller conducted a study[19] of the use of formulas and cost analysis in higher education that included a discussion of formulas used in budgeting for library expenditures. Among those states utilizing formulas for estimating library costs, he found a number of different approaches: for instance, 1) Oklahoma and Tennessee utilized a fixed percentage of instructional costs; 2) Kentucky used a fixed dollar amount per full-time equivalent student; 3) Florida used a modified version of the standards devised by the American Library Association; 4) Texas used a ratio of library staff to enrollment with a separate calculation for purchase of books and other expenses; and 5) California utilized a series of ratios of library staff to specific workload measures such as the number of volumes added, with a separate calculation for the purchase of books and payment of other expenses.

During 1971–1972, Kenneth Allen studied budgeting techniques in academic libraries.[21] Utilizing a questionnaire, he conducted field interviews of directors, associate and assistant directors, heads of appropriate divisions of selected libraries, vice-presidents for business and finance, deans, budget officers and budget managers of the institutions visited. Allen identified five major types of budgeting which either were then currently in use, had been previously used, or were planned to be used in the near future in the libraries studied: 1) traditional budget based on object of expenditures (line-item budget), 2) program budget, 3) performance budget, 4) Planning-Programming-Budgeting System (PPBS), and 5) formula budgeting. Allen described the major budgeting formulas utilized by academic libraries, which included: 1) the Clapp-Jordan Formula, 2) the Washington State Formula, 3) the Voigt Formula, and 4) formula variations.[21] (Each of the major named funding formulations are discussed briefly below.) In Allen's opinion, formula budgeting appeared to be the emerging trend in academic libraries. He also stated that, for the most part, formula budgeting was being imposed on libraries from the outside.

To the extent that this imposition is politically motivated, it can be harmful. Under this condition the formula can become a way to allocate scarce resources among competing units and, most unfortunately, might be a tool for punitive but impersonal action on the part of a legislative body. Intelligent formula development demands the recognition of the differences in academic profiles of the institutions within the system. If this is not done, then much time and energy can be spent in the jockeying for position in quantitative terms, developing areas of noncomparability or working up budget presentations outside the formula—a game of upmanship for survival.[22]

By 1977, Littleton found that librarians and faculty were questioning formulas based solely on enrollment and number of programs. He also found that librarians in research libraries were especially concerned about those formulas that were being applied uniformly and mechanically, without distinction or difference, both to colleges lacking graduate or research programs and to major research universities.[23]

Likewise, a 1975 study respecting factors underlying library collection development prepared by the Committee on Library Resources of the Faculty Senate of the State University of New York resulted in the conclusion that it is extremely important to reexamine library allocation priorities "at a time when enrollments are stabilizing, particularly if collection growth is tied to student FTE [full-time equivalent] growth."[24] Some of the additional factors expressed in the Faculty Senate report as needing inclusion in the formula were: differential costs and publication rates among disciplines; the purpose(s) of the collection (teaching, research, or basic use); and the level and variety of academic programs. In addition, certain operational factors were also deemed important and worthy of special consideration: user population; the size and adequacy of existing holdings; the accessibility of other libraries; the degree to which holdings are scattered in branch libraries (to determine the amount of necessary duplication); loss and physical deterioration of materials; and the rapidly increasing costs of books and periodicals.

According to a study conducted by Mary P. McKeown,[25] by 1982 at least twenty-five states were using some formula or guidelines approach for determining library funding in their statewide budget process. Of the twenty-two states for which data detailing the formulas then in use was available, McKeown found that seventeen states utilized a separate formula for library support, while in five cases the library was included within a formula for either all academic support activities or for general administrative support. McKeown found three methods typically being used to calculate formula amounts for library support: 1) rate per base unit (used in sixteen states); 2) percentage of base factor (used in six states); and 3) base factor-position ratio with salary rates (used in one state, Michigan). McKeown also classified the base factors used in library formulas into three categories: 1) credit hours (six states), 2) full-time equivalent students (ten states), and 3) number of volumes (one state, Michigan). In addition, most of the twenty-five states differentiated in the formula the resources needed for library support by level of student enrollment (undergraduate, masters, doctoral), and/or by discipline, and/or by institution type. Nine states also gave recognition to fixed costs as a component of their formula.

LIBRARY STANDARDS AND FORMULAS USED IN BUDGETING

ACRL Standards

One of the most common standards used in determining what constitutes an appropriate level of library funding are the ACRL standards for college libraries. First formulated in 1959, these standards originally called for the library budget to equal at least 5 percent of the total educational and general budget of the institution, with a qualification that the percentage must be higher (1) if the library's holdings are seriously deficient, (2) if rapid expansion is occurring in student population or course offerings, or (3) if the institution supports a wide range of courses at the Master's level or programs of independent study.[26]

In the 1975 revision of the ACRL standards for college libraries, the recommended, but not mandated, standard had risen to 6 percent of the college's total educational and general expenditures.[27] By the time of the approval of the 1986 ACRL Standards for College Libraries, the percentage was firmly established at 6 percent.[28] Also, in both the 1975 and the currently-effective 1986 standards, a standard exists for collections which incorporates a modified version of the Clapp-Jordan formula (see below).

The current ACRL standards for university libraries,[29] which were adopted in 1979, are much more qualitative in nature than the college library standards and call for no fixed percentage of the university's budget to be allocated to libraries; however, the 5 and later 6 percent standard has typically been used in university library budgeting.

Clapp-Jordan Formula

The Clapp-Jordan Formula[30] is based on several variables reflective of typical library needs. The formula takes into account the size and characteristics of the institution's student body, the size and research commitment of its faculty, and the extensiveness of the curriculum. Beginning with a core or "opening day" collection and adding increments by weighting the above factors to arrive at a minimum adequacy of volumes, the formula has enjoyed some popularity. Developed in the 1960s for use by Ohio academic libraries for assessing the adequacy of their collections, the formula has since been used as a basis for budget formulas in several other states, and variations of the Clapp-Jordan formula have been found, as noted above, in the ACRL standards for college libraries beginning with the 1959 standards and carrying forward with the various revisions and modifications up to the present standards.

Washington State Formula

The Washington State Formula[31] uses a library resource formula based upon the Clapp-Jordan Formula and a library operations formula that includes a staffing portion, which is designed to provide adequate staffing levels. The staffing portion of the formula is one that was proposed but not implemented for the University of California System. Such a formula

Chart 5-1
Formula Variables and Weights: Clapp-Jordan, ACRL, and Washington State Formulas (Bound Volumes and Equivalents)

Variable	Clapp-Jordan Weight	ACRL Weight (1975)	Washington State Weight (Unmodified)
Basic or Opening Day Collection	50,750	85,000	85,000
Allowance per FTE Faculty	100	100	100
Allowance per FTE Student	12	15	15
Allowance per Honors Student (25%)	12	—	—
Allowance per Undergraduate major	335	—	—
Allowance per Masters Field:			
when no Doctorate offered	3,050	6,000	6,100
when Doctorate offered	3,050	3,000	3,050
Allowance per Doctoral Field	24,500	25,000	24,500

was later implemented in the California State College System. Certain changes were made in the weights assigned to some of the variables, but the formula for minimum adequacy of holdings is very similar to the Clapp-Jordan formula (see chart 5-1).

The main emphasis of the Washington State formula can be described as one of balance between library resources and staffing. First designed in the 1960s to respond to special problems occurring during a period of growing enrollments, the formula was revised in 1976 to take into account the impact of falling enrollments. The State of Washington considers audiovisual services, institutional archives, and special libraries, such as health sciences and law libraries, to be noncomparable and, therefore, these are not funded utilizing the formula.

The library operations portion of the formula consists of two parts: staffing and binding. The staffing portion considers FTE students weighted at four levels of instruction, total institutional FTEs, costs of maintenance of the current collection, and costs of new acquisitions in addition to a base level of staffing assumption. The binding portion of the formula calculates the binding cost of periodicals based on the number of current subscriptions to be bound plus an additional percentage amount to provide for rebinding of prior bound volumes. There is also an operations cost calculation determined on an incremental basis, with the cost of inflation factored in plus anticipated costs for travel, goods, and services.

Despite its name, this formula has been used successfully outside of the State of Washington. For example, Florida currently utilizes a modified version of the library resources portion of the Washington State formula in its formula budget calculations for the libraries of the State University System of Florida.

Voigt Formula

The Voigt Formula[32] is unique in that it was designed especially for general universities having extensive doctoral programs. The formula features an emphasis on acquisitions of currently-published materials separate from any retrospective material purchases. Since most doctoral-granting institutions could be expected to have large collections, the Voigt formula's emphasis on current materials is meant to judge how well the library is maintaining that collection at the doctoral-study level. Similar in many ways to the Washington State Formula, the Voigt Formula can be considered a modification or refinement of the Clapp-Jordan Formula.

EFFECTS OF FORMULA BUDGETING

First, it should be stressed that funding formulas are, for the most part, used in calculating an "asking" budget to be presented to the state coordinating board and executive branch of state government. In most states, once the money is appropriated by the state legislature, it is distributed to the institutions of higher education and their constituent parts however the legislature has decided, which is not necessarily (and in most states typically not) in the same amount as generated by the formula. Furthermore, if the state funds have not been appropriated in a strict line-item manner, the recipient institution's administrators will probably be able to distribute funds among the various units of the university according to their own priorities, regardless of how the funds were formula generated. In only a few states does the statewide governing board actually use the formulas for allocating lump-sum legislative appropriations among the various state institutions. Hence, the funding formula approach is all too often used simply as a "wish-list" budget that nearly everyone expects will be ignored. If undertaken in that manner and in such a political context, formula budgeting may not be worth the effort and may actually be counterproductive in the library arena either through raising librarians' expectations unrealistically or providing a basis for justifying objectively unjustified reductions in an institution's library expenditures when the institution's overall appropriation falls short of the formula-driven amount.

Although there are problems with formula funding during both periods of declining enrollments and periods of rapid growth, since the funding figures generated thereby are usually based on historical data such as enrollment or credit hour production at a particular point in time, the approach can provide a significant benefit for academic libraries when the library formula used to "drive" a library appropriation results in the actually passing through the institutional or system administration of formula-derived funding directly to the library. Unfortunately, library budget formulas are too often seen by college and university administrators as a "cash cow" for obtaining institution funding that can be diverted to other urgent (or not so urgent) needs.

LIBRARY FUNDING AND THE STATE COORDINATING AGENCY

In a study concerning state coordinating agencies and academic libraries in fifteen states completed in 1987,[33] it was found, not surprisingly, that funding continues to be essentially the major issue confronting the libraries of public institutions. As a part of the study, library directors, chief academic officers of the institutions, and staff members of the state coordinating agencies were surveyed as to their perception of the funding process for academic libraries in their respective states. A majority of all three groups (and, most significantly, two-thirds of the chief academic officers and coordinating agency staff members) responded that they believed that state coordinating agencies were then exercising a key role in obtaining financial support for academic libraries. In an attempt to determine how well the agencies were seen to be performing in that role, all three groups were also asked to respond using a Likert scale to the statement that state coordinating agencies have diverted funds from research libraries. Fears have been expressed in more than a few articles in the library literature that such would be at least a possible (and some have suggested inevitable) outcome of library funding influenced by state coordinating agencies.[34] The responses to the survey, however, did not indicate a general perception on the part of the directors of either research libraries or other academic libraries that any such diversion was in fact taking place in the fifteen states covered by the study. It was found that of those surveyed in states that were then using some type of restricted library funding (where the university could not lawfully simply divert library funds to other types and objects of expenditures), most of the library directors and chief academic officers agreed that the policies and practices of their state coordinating agencies were beneficial in terms of the amount of money their particular institution's library was actually allocated. But interestingly, in states where restricted budgeting of the type described above was not utilized, library directors and chief academic officers tended to be neutral or opposed to the use of that approach. There would appear to be little justification for this level of conservatism and this can be said not based simply on the perceptions, as noted above, of those who have "tried it and liked it." Observations in those states visited in the 1987 study for on-site interviews that had been using a form of restricted library funding indicated that the libraries in those states were apparently both better equipped generally and more adequately staffed than in the states observed that were not using restricted funding. Though these observations are necessarily personal in nature and cannot rise to the status of strictly objective quantifiable data (being only one person's perception), restricted library funding appears to provide "better" results from a librarian's point of view.

One often held and occasionally expressed opinion of administrators with which librarians must often contend is that any academic library may be viewed as a "bottomless pit," capable of ingesting unlimited sums of money. One frequently quoted paragraph from a 1968 article by Robert F. Munn sums up this view:

One important consideration is the fact that many academic administrators view the library as a bottomless pit. They have observed that increased appropriations one year invariably result in still larger requests the next. More importantly, there does not appear to be even any theoretical limits to the library's needs. Certainly the library profession has been unable to define them. This the Administration finds most disquieting.[35]

Obviously, in times of shortfalls in state revenues, to be viewed as a "bottomless pit" is not a particularly healthy position for academic libraries to find themselves in. If "x" amount of dollars will satisfy at least the expressed and clearly articulated demands of an academic department, and the same sum will only scratch the surface of that which the library says it needs (i.e., if the library is seen as aspiring to the collection of the British Museum or the staffing levels of the Library of Congress), the tendency of state officials and college and university administrators will probably be to reach out and touch that which is within their grasp and satisfy the academic department. If it appears to administrators that they cannot possibly completely satisfy the library with the funds available they may be discouraged from even trying. Much, therefore, is to be said for tempering the application of formula parameters, etc., with a self-enforced rule of reason. Politics is the art of the possible and budgets and funding allocations are at the heart of politics—asking for the impossible may thus become self-fulfilling and confirmational in result.

Funding is clearly a fundamental issue respecting the relationship of academic libraries of publicly supported institutions and state government. The next two chapters deal with library automation and networking and multitype cooperative programs, all of which are dependent for success on state funding to varying degrees.

NOTES

1. Michael J. Ross, *State and Local Politics and Policy: Change and Reform* (Englewood Cliffs, N.J.: Prentice-Hall, 1987), p. 206.

2. A "consolidated budget" is one in which all institutional requests are lumped together; for example, all library requests for all the state's public universities might be grouped under a specific budget line for library support/resources.

3. An "aggregated budget" is one which is simply a compilation of all the various institutions' budget requests, with each institution's request broken out separately.

4. Lyman A. Glenny, *State Budgeting for Higher Education: Interagency Conflict and Consensus* (Berkeley: Center for Research and Development in Higher Education, University of California, 1976), p. 98.

5. Richard M. Millard, "Power of State Coordinating Agencies" in *Improving Academic Management* (San Francisco: Jossey-Bass, 1981), p. 77.

6. Jack M. Treadway, *Public Policymaking in the American States* (New York: Praeger, 1985), p. 111.

7. Edward R. Hines, *Higher Education and State Governments: Renewed Partnerships, Cooperation, or Competition?* (College Station, Texas: Association for the Study of Higher Education, 1988), p. xix.

8. Fred Thompson and William Zumeta, "A Regulatory Model of Governmental Coordinating Activities in the Higher Education Sector," *Economics of Education Review* 1, no. 1 (1981), pp. 27–52.

9. Harold H. Enarson, "Quality and Accountability: Are We Destroying What We Want to Preserve?" *Change* 12, no. 7 (1980), pp. 7–10.

10. James R. Mingle, ed., *Management Flexibility and State Regulation in Higher Education* (Atlanta: Southern Regional Education Board, 1983), ED 234 705.

11. Isaac T. Littleton, *State Systems of Higher Education and Libraries: A Report for the Council on Library Resources* (Washington, D.C.: Council on Library Resources, 1977), p. 50.

12. Shari Lohela and F. William Summers, "The Impact of Planning on Budgeting," *Journal of Library Administration* 2 (Summer/Fall/Winter 1981), p. 176.

13. Anthony W. Morgan, "The New Strategies: Roots, Context, and Overview," *New Directions for Institutional Research* 43 (Sept. 1984), p. 10.

14. Betty Jo Mitchell, *ALMS: A Budget Based Library Management System* (Greenwich, Conn.: JAI Press, 1983).

15. Association of Research Libraries, "Review of Budgeting Techniques in Academic and Research Libraries," *ARL Management Supplement* 1 (April 1973), pp. 1–4.

16. Littleton, *State Systems of Higher Education and Libraries*, p. 52.

17. For a more detailed discussion on formula funding in eight selected states, see Vicki L. Gregory, "Development of Academic Library Budgets in Selected States with Emphasis on the Utilization of Formulas," *Journal of Library Administration* 12, no. 1 (1990), pp. 23–45.

18. Arthur M. McAnally, "Budgets by Formula," *Library Quarterly* 33 (April 1963), pp. 159–71.

19. James L. Miller, Jr., *State Budgeting for Higher Education: The Use of Formulas and Cost Analysis* (Ann Arbor: Institute of Public Administration, University of Michigan, 1964).

20. Kenneth S. Allen, *Current and Emerging Budgeting Techniques in Academic Libraries, Including a Critique of the Model Budget Analysis Program of the State of Washington* (Washington, D.C.: Council on Library Resources, 1972).

21. For further information about specific formulas and the application of formulas see Vicki L. Gregory, "Formula Funding in Academic Libraries" in *Encyclopedia of Library and Information Science* v. 49, Supplement 12 (1992), pp. 259–67.

22. Allen, *Current and Emerging Budgeting Techniques*, pp. 27–28.

23. Littleton, *State Systems of Higher Education and Libraries*, pp. 50–52.

24. State University of New York, "Factors Underlying Collection Development," *Faculty Senate Bulletin* 10 (June 1975), p. 5.

25. Mary P. McKeown, "The Use of Formulas for State Funding of Higher Education," *Journal of Education Finance* 7 (Winter 1982), pp. 277–300.

26. Association of College and Research Libraries, "Standards for College Libraries," *College & Research Libraries* 20 (July 1959), p. 275.

27. Association of College and Research Libraries, "Standards for College Libraries," *College & Research Libraries News* 9 (Oct. 1975), p. 298.

28. Association of College and Research Libraries, College Library Standards Committee "Standards for College Libraries, 1986," *College & Research Libraries News* 47 (March 1986), p. 200.

29. American Library Association, Association of College and Research Libraries, and the Association of Research Libraries, "Standards for University Libraries," *College & Research Libraries News* 4 (1979), pp. 101–10.

30. Vernon W. Clapp and Robert T. Jordan, "Quantitative Criteria for Adequacy of Academic Library Collections," *College & Research Libraries* 26 (Sept. 1965), pp. 371–80.

31. For a more in-depth analysis of the Washington State Formula before modification in the mid-1970s, see Kenneth S. Allen, *Current and Emerging Budgeting Techniques in Academic Libraries* (Washington, D.C.: Council on Library Resources, 1972).

32. Melvin J. Voigt, "Acquisition Rates in University Libraries," *College & Research Libraries* 33 (July 1975), pp. 262–82.

33. Vicki L. Gregory, "State Coordination of Higher Education and Academic Libraries," *College & Research Libraries* 49 (July 1988), pp. 315–24.

34. See for example, James F. Govan, "The Better Mousetrap: External Accountability and Staff Participation," *Library Trends* 26 (Fall 1977), pp. 255–67.

35. Robert F. Munn, "The Bottomless Pit, or the Academic Library as Viewed from the Administration Building," *College & Research Libraries* 29 (Jan. 1968), p. 52.

Chapter 6

Academic Library Networking and Automation—An Academic Approach to the Funding Conundrum

The technological innovations of the last two decades that have made available, at relatively low cost, levels of computer data processing capability that were heretofore the province of virtually only the federal government, the military, NASA, and a very few of the nation's elite research centers and universities have had the significant effect of bringing about much more actual interaction between academic libraries and the state. As this technology has become available for library use, state budgeting agencies and institutions of higher education have found a new item on the wish-list of most academic libraries in their state: special funding for library automation and networking. In a number of states these requests for special funding, when made on an institution-by-institution basis, have actually had the effect of leading state legislatures to encourage or even mandate a centralized, as opposed to a piecemeal, approach. A typical example of a more or less pristine application of this philosophy is described in chapter 9 by Dalehite and Hogue, who detail the instigation and implementation of the automation process in both the State University System and Community Colleges in Florida. In other states, where certain individual institutions in those states may have run ahead of others in the arena of application of computer technology to libraries, more concern about linking different library automation systems has been evident. Examples of such states are discussed in chapters 11 and 12, which deal with the libraries in Georgia and Colorado.

The advent of the technology necessary to link library catalogs and other bibliographic data bases within a state has been seen by many decision makers in state government, once they become aware of the implications of such applications of automation technology, as a way to provide for the sharing of the academic and other library resources within a state and thereby keep down, or at least bring under some degree of control, the rising expenses being incurred in the collection development portions of library budgets. Fortunately, librarians have seen the advantages of these state data bases in making cooperative collection development more feasible than it has ever been in the past and are, therefore, not so at odds with budget administrators on this question as might be expected.

Prior to the automation revolution, efforts at cooperative collection development had often failed because of: 1) limited funding, 2) failures of communication among participants, and 3) difficulties in providing physical access to materials. Automation, including the existence of the Internet, has made sharing data and resources much easier and more practical for academic libraries and improved the chances for successful cooperative collection development, hopefully thereby freeing up funds for other library-related uses.

The Missouri Research and Educational Network (MOREnet) is a fiber-optic based computer network that links computers at member institutions throughout Missouri and provides access to the Internet. (The membership of MOREnet at present consists of thirteen four-year colleges and universities, Missouri's Coordinating Board for Higher Education, and SHAREnet, a consortium of school districts in the Kansas City area.) The Internet provides the libraries with access to electronic mail, electronic bulletin board and discussion forums, library catalogs, electronic journals, and bibliographic and other specialized data bases.[1]

A review of library networks generally and an exposition of the development and the special characteristics of the various networks implemented in several states is important to an understanding of the impact of automation and networking in the academic library context.

LIBRARY NETWORKS

The National Commission on Libraries and Information Science (NCLIS) has defined library networks in such a way as to include a broad range of services, organizations, types and modes of communication:

Two or more libraries and/or other organizations engaged in a common pattern of information exchange, through communications, for some functional purpose. A network usually consists of a formal arrangement whereby materials, information, and services provided by a variety of types of libraries and/or other organizations are made available to all potential users. (Libraries may be in different jurisdictions but agree to serve one another on the same basis as each serves its own constituents. Computers and telecommunications may be among the tools used for facilitating communication among them.)[2]

Library networks generally may be said to share three major objectives. The first, of course, is to make resources throughout the network available to the users at each participating library. Second, the network should accomplish, if not a decrease, at least a slow down in the rise of per-unit library costs by increasing the productivity of the library staff. The third objective, and librarians should like it to be seen as the most important, is to furnish information to a user when and where he or she needs it.

Some of today's statewide library networks include only one type of library (e.g., public, academic, etc.). Other networks involve all types of libraries and information centers. (See chapter 7, which is concerned with these multitype library networks.) Administrative structures vary widely, as do services and membership. An important common thread, however, is that strong statewide networks require: 1) adequate and dependable funding, 2) a legal basis, 3) a willingness on the part of the members to yield some local autonomy, and 4) a structure that can encompass growth and change.

Huntington Carlile classifies the structure of state government library networks as follows:

On the state level, governmental library networks usually take one or two forms. The most familiar is the state library, which today is taking on a greater leadership role in many states under new legislative mandates to plan and implement new library services, funnel funding, and provide authority and example leadership. The other type of state library network is that type organized as part of a State Board of Education. This was initiated in 1932 by the Oregon State Board of Higher Education and has been duplicated in such areas as the New England Board of Higher Education and the Minnesota Higher Education Coordinating Board.[3]

Carlile maintained that the latter type of network, while extremely flexible, is also subject to the accidents and vagaries of history and politics. He also stated what should be fairly obvious but may not always be seen: the factor most immediately important to funding authorities for libraries in regard to the sharing of library resources through a network format is the potential for saving tax money. The utilitarian purposes for which a network may be organized in order to provide for the member libraries and their patrons are necessarily secondary to those providing the funding— if the network can do the job "just as well" then that may be all that has to be shown. Improvements in service and availability of materials to researchers are not the key selling points. Some may find the wonders of automation and its promise of better services intriguing, but in all cases, in order to provide initial funds for a network, governing authorities generally must perceive a return on their investment in terms of future savings.[4]

Fortunately, the case should be an easy one to prove. Due to technological advances in library automation systems, networking, and telecommunications, libraries today can enjoy geometrically increased speeds of access and increased confidence in the availability of needed resources held elsewhere in the network, thereby gaining flexibility in the expenditure of book and periodical funds. Through allowing one library to depend upon many others in the network for infrequently used materials, networks permit each participating library to spend its own money on books and periodicals that are the most used and needed by its own patrons.

All of this is well and good, but as Richard DeGennaro pointed out, there exists an ever-present danger in overselling the potential benefits of network membership: academic administrators and state coordinating agency members and their staffs may, as a result of such an oversell, acquire unrealistically high expectations about the cost savings that will result, thereby providing them with an excuse for reducing future budgetary support for libraries.[5] As anyone who has dealt with an automation project can attest, Murphy's law and its corollaries are applicable: nothing is as easy as it seems, few things work right the first time, and if anything can go wrong it will—and it will cost more money!

Five groups of stimuli may play a leading role in cooperative planning for intrastate library networking. The first of these is the professional associations which may bring together librarians and other information specialists for the purpose of the development of networks. The second group consists of state agencies such as coordinating agencies of higher education. The third group consists of what are sometimes termed "ad hocracies," that is, groups of interested people with no official base but with a specific idea in mind. Such groups are usually action-oriented but are often ineffective due to the lack of a base from which to influence decisions. The fourth group consists of the planning bodies, such as state library commissions, that can create official participatory planning and development groups. The last group of stimuli are external planning requirements, such as those that dictate the strictures surrounding LSCA moneys, which require a statewide advisory council to develop a long-range library program in order for a project to qualify for LSCA funds.[6]

Gerald Brong points out that, when undertaking any cooperative program, the decision makers must be fully committed to the idea of the program from the outset. Having to return to an administration or a state agency to "re-sell" the idea frequently leads to the decision makers then either pocket vetoing the plan by simply doing nothing or identifying new and always compelling grounds why the plan cannot work. These new reasons, of course, did not occur to them the first time around.[7]

An example of the good results that can be obtained when the prudence to involve the decision makers from the start is heeded is the development of Alabama's Network of Alabama Academic Libraries (NAAL). NAAL's creation grew out of a concern expressed by the Council of Graduate Deans, an advisory committee to the Alabama Commission on Higher Education (ACHE) (which committee is composed of the deans of graduate programs in the state's universities), respecting the ability of the academic libraries in Alabama to support graduate education adequately. In 1982, the Council of Graduate Deans requested the Council of Librarians (another advisory council to ACHE consisting of the library directors) to conduct an in-depth survey of the current ability of the academic libraries to support graduate education and, more importantly, to go beyond that and to devise a cooperative plan that would allow problems to be addressed jointly in a fashion that none of the libraries could do alone. The study[8] and the plan so devised by the Council of Librarians was reviewed and later endorsed by the Council of Graduate Deans, the Council of Chief Academic Officers, and the Council of Presidents. It is perhaps not insignificant that two members of the Council of Presidents served on the original committee which set up NAAL, and that Dr. James Vickrey, then President of the University of Montevallo, served as its chairman.

Many state systems of higher education encourage statewide cooperative projects and library networking for the purpose of more effectively sharing library resources. A brief examination of a few of these efforts will illustrate the variety of activities and programs undertaken by state networks of academic libraries. (Part III of this work gives the reader an in-depth look at academic library networks in Florida and Georgia.)

ALABAMA—NETWORK OF ALABAMA ACADEMIC LIBRARIES (NAAL)

The membership of NAAL consists of (1) general members, that is, libraries in both public and privately supported institutions which provide graduate education, and (2) non-voting, cooperative members, which include research libraries in non-educational institutions. An additional requirement for NAAL membership is that the library must also be a member of OCLC/SOLINET.

NAAL was established for the stated and specific purpose of facilitating resource-sharing among the libraries of institutions providing graduate education in Alabama. A logical first step was to create a statewide data base of available resources; therefore, the first major effort on the part of NAAL was a retrospective conversion project of all member libraries' bibliographic records for books and the loading of these records and/or holdings into the OCLC data base, thereby creating a statewide data base. As member libraries began to finish their retrospective conversion projects, emphasis shifted to collection development.

This second major NAAL project of statewide collection development had the purpose of enabling institutions to maintain the collection levels required to support their graduate programs while reducing the need to duplicate lesser used and more expensive materials. Two distinct programs were, and continue to be, covered under the collection development project: instructional support for graduate study and research support. The instructional support program is intended to help raise the local acquisition rate in particular disciplines to the level required by the particular graduate programs that such disciplines support. The research support program helps to add new materials to the aggregate of materials held in the state by NAAL members. The type or kind of these added materials tend to be those expensive and highly specialized materials that any individual institution might have been less likely to acquire with its own local resources, but can now be acquired with NAAL funds because they can be made available for sharing among the other NAAL members. The awards under both collection development programs are competitive, with all NAAL members having to submit a proposal that describes the academic program(s) that will use the collection, and a collection assessment report that includes the following:

A. strength of each collection in relation to available materials;
B. strength of each collection in relation to other collections on the same subject;
C. deficiencies and gaps in coverage within each subject collection;
D. deficiencies and gaps in coverage within the statewide resources;
E. current and anticipated demands of the graduate program supported by the collection;
F. unique collections and resources; and
G. institutional resources available to maintain and strengthen the collection.[9]

To participate in the research support program, the library must be currently collecting materials in the subject area at RLG Conspectus level 4 or 5. NAAL has prepared a manual[10] for use in assessment of library collections for use in this project and for the purpose of new program review (see also chapter 8).

NAAL is also intimately involved and concerned with document delivery. A quick and relatively easy way of acquiring needed material from another NAAL member was seen as an obvious necessity if libraries were to be able to depend upon other members of the network for needed materials. During the fiscal year 1988–1989, NAAL received a grant under the Higher Education Act Title II-D, Library Cooperation and Technology Program, to test the feasibility of using telefacsimile equipment to reduce the time necessary to deliver documents to the users. With the assistance of the federal grant, NAAL established a statewide network to fax photocopies of needed material from one NAAL member to another, thereby significantly decreasing the turnaround for interlibrary loan requests, with NAAL funds paying for the basic monthly charges for each institution's dedicated telefacsimile telephone line. More conventionally, NAAL also funds package delivery by United Parcel Service for items not feasible for fax transmission.[11]

Among NAAL members no fees, including photocopy charges, are charged to the users of interlibrary loan. Thus, the scholar is assured of access to research materials in all NAAL libraries without geographical or financial barriers, and the resources of all NAAL libraries can be viewed as one large statewide collection.

MINNESOTA—MINNESOTA INTERLIBRARY TELECOMMUNICATIONS EXCHANGE (MINITEX)

Although MINITEX would today certainly qualify as a multitype and multi-state library cooperative with academic, public, special (particularly governmental), and school library members, at the time it was founded in 1969 (initially as a two-year pilot project), it was simply a teletype custom library program for academic institutions in Minnesota. The stated purpose of MINITEX was to make library resources as accessible as possible by promoting and making easier the use of existing resources. The program was designed around the assumption that no library can be self-sufficient or responsive to all individual user demands. MINITEX supplements local resources and enables libraries to provide services which would be difficult, or even impossible, to offer independently. MINITEX has made a primary contribution to quality education in Minnesota through service to faculty in both research and classroom preparation in addition to service to students.

The Minnesota Union List of Serials (MULS), which consists of a continuously updated list of periodicals, titles and holdings of the major Minnesota academic, state agency, and public libraries, is one of the key programmatic offerings of MINITEX. MULS was established in the 1970s when it became clear that a data base identifying where serials were held was necessary for an efficient resource sharing program. The union list has reportedly aided significantly in collection development decisions and in service to library patrons. MULS also supports cataloging, resource sharing and collection development in relation to serials.

By 1976, the Bush Foundation had provided grant money to Minnesota's Higher Education Coordinating Board (HECB) that allowed MIN-

ITEX to offer the services of OCLC to its member libraries. The significance of the Bush grant and other private grants to participating libraries is that the grant money provided the opportunity for all the libraries to enter the system at the same time on a cooperative basis and thereby to more quickly fully share the benefits and efficiencies of the OCLC online system. By 1986, MINITEX had signed an agreement with OCLC to maintain MULS on the OCLC Union Listing Subsystem.

The MINITEX programs are currently supported through direct appropriations to the Minnesota Higher Education Coordinating Board for service to educational and state agency libraries. In addition, the HECB contracts with the Minnesota Department of Education, North Dakota and South Dakota to provide service to Minnesota's public libraries and to designated libraries in North and South Dakota. Because MINITEX is a state program funded through a state appropriation to the HECB and housed at the University of Minnesota's Wilson Library, there are none of the overhead charges often associated with other regional networks; therefore, the costs to MINITEX members are modest when compared to the charges of many other networks.

MINITEX is first and foremost a document delivery/resource sharing system. The other services offered, including union listing of serials, OCLC, reference backup, and serials exchange, are designed to strengthen and to enhance resource sharing.[12]

NEW MEXICO—NEW MEXICO CONSORTIUM OF ACADEMIC LIBRARIES (NMCAL)

The critical impetus to the creation of the New Mexico Consortium of Academic Libraries (NMCAL) was the 1988 publication by the New Mexico Commission on Higher Education of a report entitled, *Planning for the Class of 2005*, which was a contextual analysis of higher education in New Mexico. One of the recommendations of that report was the establishment of consortia to meet specific needs and to encourage cooperation, resource sharing, and cost efficiencies. (The only other recommendation dealing with libraries advocated creation of a new funding formula for libraries.)

Action quickly followed, and today the members of NMCAL consist of both two-year and four-year colleges, a remarkable situation in view of historical events and the different missions of the two types of institutions that had initially rendered the two groups somewhat suspicious of each other. Also, the work of the consortium was made more difficult by the general lack of cooperative measures previously undertaken in the state; thus, NMCAL had to, and is still, breaking a lot of new ground. The initial work of the consortium was directed toward developing a new funding formula specifically for libraries (the old formula had lumped libraries into a general category of "academic support"). The new formula was approved by the New Mexico Legislature in its 1990 session with a three-year phase-in period.

NMCAL's current "front burner" project involves the cooperation aspect of the recommendations of the 1988 report, with the first step being a statewide retrospective conversion project. Being reluctant to wait for the completion of that project before any real benefits could be felt from resource sharing and coordinated collection development, the consortium is presently seeking grant funding for a CD-ROM union list of the bibliographic records of all members of NMCAL that are already available in MARC format.[13]

OHIO—OHIO LIBRARY AND INFORMATION NETWORK (OhioLINK)

A new academic network beginning operation in 1992 is OhioLINK, a partnership of seventeen academic institutions in Ohio plus the State Library of Ohio, to be operated under the aegis of the Ohio Board of Regents.[14] The emphasis of this consortium is collection sharing to improve access to information for the users of all the libraries. The history of OhioLINK begins in 1986 when the Ohio Board of Regents, at the request of the state legislature, formed a Library Study Committee. This committee was to consider the problems of library space to house rapidly expanding collections and increased and new services after the Regents had received combined funding requests from the state-assisted universities in excess of $120 million for construction and renovation of libraries. The Regents have emphasized to the Library Study Committee the need for a statewide system to support cooperative collection development.[15] The work and report[16] of the committee thus naturally led to the OhioLINK project.

Each OhioLINK member library has its own on-line library system (using Innovative Interfaces, Inc. software) that is connected to the others in OhioLINK by means of a central system which manages, in effect, a union catalog of all the bibliographic records collectively maintained by the seventeen participating libraries. The OhioLINK project calls for a reasonable level of uniformity among the library data bases in order to make it easier for patrons to negotiate the network.[17] The central system can retrieve detailed holdings and circulation information from each of the seventeen local systems and transmit this information to the person searching the system at any member library. The central system can also serve as a routing mechanism for sending and recording interlibrary loan requests among the participating institutions. Communication among the institutions and the central site takes place via a high-speed telecommunications network known as OARNet (Ohio Academic Resource Network), which also supports the state's supercomputer users. Current plans call for a delivery system that may include both electronic (fax and electronic full-text delivery) services for shorter items and truck delivery for larger items. In addition, the OhioLINK project, given adequate funding, anticipates providing funds to support a retrospective conversion project of the bibliographic data bases of all the participating libraries.

OKLAHOMA—OKLAHOMA NETWORK OF CONTINUING HIGHER EDUCATION (ONCHE)

The focus and stated goal of the Oklahoma Network of Continuing Higher Education (ONCHE) is to expand the opportunity for relevant higher education to everyone, everywhere in Oklahoma. The goals of the current aspects of the project include optimizing the use of educational resources of the state through interinstitutional cooperation and interagency collaboration and developing a cost-effective system whereby library resources can be shared through new educational technologies.[18]

The telecommunications backbone of the system is a statewide microwave network operated under the auspices of the Oklahoma Board of Regents. In an assessment of the network, Richard Millard stated that:

> It was undoubtedly this potential of the network not only to extend higher education opportunity to as wide a range of Oklahomans as possible but also to strengthen the Oklahoma State System of Higher Education through increased opportunities for interinstitutional cooperation and collaboration that led the W.K. Kellogg Foundation, the State of Oklahoma, and the Starkey and Noble foundations to support the network project. The telecommunications network provided the basis for achieving the project objectives in a cost-effective manner through extension of access to courses, to counseling, to information, and to continuing education throughout the state.[19]

Libraries are an important element in this project. In addition to the outreach services of the academic libraries, which are extensive, at least fourteen public libraries are part of the network.[21] To link all of the participating libraries required developing a means of linking nine different automation systems. Each library was provided with appropriate hardware and software for participation, telefacsimile equipment, and satellite downlinks, all of which provide the potential for wide bibliographic search packages. Some of the public libraries have earmarked special classrooms for teleconferencing and telecommunications instruction in their communities. The participating public libraries have, in effect, become an integral part of the total higher education system in Oklahoma.

In its control of the telecommunication network, the Oklahoma Board of Regents performs an essential coordinating function. By operationally making the resources of each institution available to all of the other institutions and students in the state, it provides a practical means of reducing unnecessary duplication and sharing of faculty, programs, and information resources throughout the state. [21]

PENNSYLVANIA—C. D. CAT: UNION CATALOG OF THE ASSOCIATED COLLEGE LIBRARIES OF CENTRAL PENNSYLVANIA

The seventeen college libraries plus the Dickinson Law School and the State Library of Pennsylvania that comprise the membership of the Associated College Libraries of Central Pennsylvania (ACLCP) tested in 1990 and later implemented a CD-ROM union catalog for the college library consortium.[22] The consortium had decided that the use of CD-ROM technology would be more convenient and less expensive than linking their public-access catalogs by means of dedicated telecommunication lines among members' sites. The union catalog, dubbed C. D. Cat, is updated periodically from the bibliographic records of member libraries. It is used at each member library for identifying needed materials, initiating interlibrary loan requests, and encouraging the use of reciprocal borrowing, a service which allows patrons of the member libraries to borrow directly from all libraries of the consortium.

Much earlier in its history, ACLCP established the Interlibrary Delivery Service, initially for just the members of the consortium but eventually evolving into a separate incorporated delivery service that transfers materials among more than 150 Pennsylvania libraries.[23] Somewhat later in 1983, the ACLCP organized telefacsimile communications among most of the Pennsylvania academic libraries.[24] The C. D. Cat is viewed as the culminating step in providing the technology and support services necessary for effective resource sharing among the Pennsylvania academic libraries belonging to ACLCP.[25]

As the above examples clearly show, state networks and library automation within a state have taken a variety of different forms and approaches. Many states with consolidated governing boards have concentrated on using the same automated system for all academic libraries in the state in order to make future linkages much simpler. This approach was taken in Florida (see chapter 9) where the university system was automated using a central system and NOTIS software, and the community college libraries were automated under a central system using DRA software with linkage through the Florida Center for Library Automation (FCLA). The same kind of approach was used in North Carolina, but because several of the large research libraries in that state were already automated and planning establishment of the Triangle Research Libraries Network (TRLN), the North Carolina Board of Governors became involved in setting up a network for the balance of that state's academic libraries (in public institutions). Their approach was to contract with a single vendor for an automated system, at that time OCLC's LS2000 system, to link these libraries, and to work toward further linking that system to TRLN. A somewhat similar situation developed at roughly the same time in Wisconsin where the two largest university libraries were automated but the other eleven joined in a cooperative manner under the auspices of the statewide governing board to select a single automation system for all of the other campuses.

Other states concentrated on linking existing automated systems, such as in Oklahoma. In some states, particularly those where not all the libraries were initially automated, academic library networks have typically concentrated first on building a state data base by means of a retrospective conversion project, such as in Alabama and New Mexico. Minnesota took a different approach, probably because their efforts began much earlier, and the MINITEX Consortium evolved into a regional and multitype network.

NOTES

1. Anne Lawhorne, "Missouri Research and Education Network: Catalyst for Change in Missouri Libraries," *Show-Me Libraries* 43 (Winter 1992), pp. 18–19.

2. National Commission on Libraries and Information Science 1975, *Toward a National Program for Library and Information Services: Goals for Action* (Washington, D.C.: Government Printing Office, 1975), pp. 82–83.

3. Huntington Carlile, "The Diversity Among Legal Structures of Library Networks" in *Networks for Networkers: Critical Issues in Cooperative Library Development*, edited by Barbara Evans Markuson and Blanche Woolls (New York: Neal Schuman, 1980), p. 194.

4. *Ibid.*, p. 190.

5. Richard DeGennaro, "The Role of the Academic Library in Networking" in *Networks for Networkers: Critical Issues in Cooperative Library Development*, edited by Barbara Evans Markuson and Blanche Woolls (New York: Neal Schuman, 1980), pp. 306–7.

6. Gerald R. Brong, "The State of Washington's Search for Intrastate Cooperation," *Library Trends* 24 (Oct. 1975), p. 267.

7. *Ibid.*, p. 270.

8. *Cooperative Library Resource Sharing Among Universities Supporting Graduate Study in Alabama* (Montgomery: Alabama Commission on Higher Education, 1983), ED 224 497.

9. Sue O. Medina, "The Evolution of Cooperative Collection Development in Alabama Academic Libraries," *College & Research Libraries* 53 (Jan. 1992), p. 10.

10. Medina, Sue O. et al., *Network of Alabama Academic Libraries Collection Assessment Manual* (Montgomery: NAAL, 1987).

11. For additional information, see Sue O. Medina, "The Network of Alabama Academic Libraries," *College & Research Libraries News* 51 (July/August 1990), pp. 640–43 and Sue O. Medina, "The Evolution of Cooperative Collection Development in Alabama Academic Libraries," *College & Research Libraries* 53 (Jan. 1991), pp. 7–19.

12. Michael J. LaCroix, "Minitex and ILLINET: Two Library Networks," *Occasional Papers of the University of Illinois, Graduate School of Library and Information Science* no. 178 (May 1987), pp. 3–15; Alice E. Wilcox, "Library Networks Circa 1984, or One Blind Person Touching the Elephant," *Resource Sharing and Information Networks* 2 (Fall/Winter 1984), pp. 33–34.

13. Susan Oberlander, "The New Mexico Consortium of Academic Libraries, 1988–1990," *College & Research Libraries News* 52 (June 1991), pp. 359–62.

14. The latest academic library cooperative network in a state becomes practically synonymous with the idea of cooperative networks—the establishment in 1967 by the college libraries in Ohio of the Ohio College Library Center, which became the world's largest bibliographic utility, OCLC Online Computer Library Center.

15. William J. Crowe and Nancy P. Sanders, "Collection Development in the Cooperative Environment," *Journal of Library Administration* 15, no. 3/4 (1991), p. 43; Carol Pitts Hawk, "The Integrated Library System: The OhioLINK Experience," *Library Resources and Technical Services* 36 (June 1992), p. 62.

16. Ohio Board of Regents, Library Study Committee, *Academic Libraries in Ohio: Progress through Collaboration, Storage, and Technology* (Columbus: Ohio Board of Regents, 1987).

17. Judith Sessions, Hwa-Wei Lee, and Stacey Kimmel, "OhioLINK: Technology and Teamwork Transforming Ohio Libraries," *Wilson Library Bulletin* 66 (June 1992), p. 45.

18. Richard M. Millard, *Today's Myths and Tomorrow's Realities: Overcoming Obstacles to Academic Leadership in the 21st Century* (San Francisco: Jossey-Bass, 1991), p. 14.

19. Millard, *Today's Myths and Tomorrow's Realities*, p. 229.

20. While technically multitype, the purpose is to aid higher education, not public library service per se.

21. Millard, *Today's Myths and Tomorrow's Realities*, p. 235.

22. Charles T. Townley, "College Libraries and Resource Sharing: Testing a Compact Disc Union Catalog," *College & Research Libraries* 53 (Sept. 1992), pp. 405–13.

23. Dwight Huseman, "Access to Materials in Pennsylvania: Interlibrary Delivery," *Wilson Library Bulletin* 59 (Dec. 1984), pp. 262–63.

24. Mark Wilson, "How to Set Up a Telefacsimile Network—The Pennsylvania Libraries Experience," *Online* 12 (May 1988), pp. 15–25.

25. Townley, "College Libraries and Resource Sharing," p. 412.

Chapter 7

Multitype Library Cooperative Networks—The Use of Overarching Agencies

One of the most significant national trends in the area of library development is the creation of multitype library systems. State library agencies are the primary advocates for multitype networking programs, and their program plans are usually viewed as the master plans for library programming in their respective states. These master plans are generally created through as comprehensive a study as possible of the state's libraries and their resources, and the library needs of the citizens of the state. While academic libraries are almost always included by state library agencies in such a master plan, secondary school and special libraries may be considered as well.

Multitype library networks are not a new idea. Their development can be traced back to the 1930s, but it is only since World War II that they have begun to flourish. The most common reasons cited in the library literature for creating multitype library networks are resource sharing, continuing education, and bibliographic purposes.

Although many multitype library organizations receive at least part of their financial support from members and users, ongoing funding from local or state tax revenue is often required in order to provide organizational continuity, basic administrative services, and the flexibility needed in order to serve a diverse group of libraries and users. As one commentator has written:

To achieve stable support from the public coffers, the multitype library organization must begin with the problem of getting on the political policy agenda of lawmakers on the local, state, and federal levels. Only a few items of the many proposed to legislators actually become part of the political agenda, still fewer are enacted. Multitype library organizations get on the political agenda by presenting to legislators an easily understood solution (cooperative effort) to a real problem (access to information sources) faced by large numbers of people.[1]

However, library problems may not seem so critical to legislators as those presented by crime in the streets, drugs in the schools, etc. It is an extremely important function of the multitype library organization's board, staff, and members to convince legislators and other decision makers of the worth of cooperative library programs.

The member libraries of a multitype library system by definition have diverse missions, goals, collection development policies, and responsibilities within their parent organization. Type-of-library differences are further complicated by the issues presented due to the members being only a component part of larger public or private institutions. The size, organizational structure, and the geographic location of members may also vary considerably. Although these differences are part of what makes a multitype library organization strong, they can also cause difficulties for individual members in terms of "fair and equitable" representation in the governance structure of the organization. Yet, despite differences and problems, most multitype library organizations have survived, many have flourished and been extremely successful, and a number of new ones have been established, primarily through state-level legislative action, in recent years.[2]

At least two factors make multitype library cooperation highly desirable. First, the expanding information needs and demands of users, and the explosion of information and knowledge wrought by technology, have created an environment in which all libraries are ultimately rendered inadequate. Cooperative library programs can reduce the level of this inadequacy, but it can never entirely eliminate it. Second, finite public dollars in all service sectors and at all levels of government require that librarians, as well as other providers of public services, find ways to be more efficient, and to do more with less.[3]

Multitype library cooperation requires that decision makers and those exercising administrative responsibility identify the range and scope of activity within which primary organizational goals and purposes can be fully supported, while at the same time meeting the needs of other, sometimes similar, though often very different, kinds of libraries. In analyzing multitype library cooperation in the state of Utah, one writer has correctly noted: "To be enduring, cooperation cannot be an end in itself; rather, it is a by-product of the organizational search for an enlightened self-interest. Cooperation ceases at the point at which the purposes, needs, and requirements of organizations trying to work cooperatively together come into conflict."[4]

Cooperation implies that all participating members contribute appropriately within their respective institutional roles, both giving and receiving benefits. The cooperative will inevitably break down if any single library or group of libraries consistently bears an inequitable portion of the burden of cooperation, or if the member libraries consistently fail to meet the legitimate expectations made of them within their institutional roles, or if they too opportunistically capitalize on cooperative relationships without making an appropriate contribution to the effort. Nor is this all since at a certain level of activity librarians do not have full decision-making power with regard to cooperative programs; library policy-making bodies and funding authorities must also concur in supporting the costs of cooperative interlibrary relationships.[5]

Cooperation within library-type networks (such as those discussed in chapter 6) is facilitated by the similarity of institutional contexts among the participants; similarity of institutional mission naturally makes it more likely that all of the cooperating libraries will share more or less compatible goals. However, the major complicating factor of multitype library cooperation is the existence of differences in institutional contexts that may not be fully understood or appreciated by all participants, thereby increasing the likelihood of conflict between organizational goals, and making cooperation more difficult to achieve.

Pennsylvania provides an excellent example of the efforts of a state library to support academic library and multitype library programs. A study[6] published in 1988 recommended that the State Library of Pennsylvania support academic libraries by developing programs to address five priorities perceived to be "high-need" in nature: (1) advocacy of academic library needs, (2) linked system protocols, (3) telecommunications development, (4) new technologies, and (5) coordination of preservation activity.

Since the funding of LSCA Title III, the State Library of Pennsylvania has made a number of grants for proposals that have involved academic libraries. As early as 1975, a clear mutual interest in fostering resource sharing was established when the State Library began using LSCA funds to encourage more than fifty Pennsylvania academic libraries to enter their holdings into the OCLC data base. In 1972, the State Library helped to subsidize the operations of the Interlibrary Delivery Service, a statewide multitype library courier service created in 1969 with a LSCA grant to the Associated College Libraries of Central Pennsylvania.[7]

In 1989, the State Library developed a mission statement dealing with the role of the State Library in providing statewide accessibility to all types of libraries:

[The State Library of Pennsylvania] will ensure accessibility to library resources and services to all residents of Pennsylvania; make statewide services available to meet educational, informational, and research needs; provide leadership to develop strong libraries and new programs; move toward the 21st century by using technologies to create and link networks; and promote interagency participation and support.[8]

The record shows that the State Library has worked toward the fulfillment of its mission and the academic priorities identified in the 1988 study mentioned above. The Oakland Consortium, the membership of which consists of the Carnegie Library of Pittsburgh, the University of Pittsburgh Library, and the Carnegie-Mellon University Library, received a LSCA Title III grant in 1987 that allowed the consortium to plan for a common automated system. When an agreement on a common system could not be reached, planning shifted to the creation and implementation of an interface among all three of the libraries' bibliographic data bases. A patron in any one of these three libraries can now access the data bases of all the libraries. The consortium also developed a five-year strategic plan that focused on issues in collection management and resource sharing, storage and preservation, staff development, automation, communication, and funding.[9] An additional LSCA Title III grant in 1991 funded a project to develop software for a cooperative collection development program. Initially the consortium used the Metadex Collection, a CD-ROM data base, to analyze their collections in the area of metals and materials science. The libraries of the consortium anticipate improving both bibliographic and physical access to the materials, and based on analysis of use patterns, will then be able to make cooperative decisions about titles to be added, canceled, or retained.

Another interesting Pennsylvania LSCA Title III project funded in 1991 is one in which Drexel University was provided with funding to study the effect of providing a gateway for access to the Internet and the Colorado-based UnCover system for data base searching and document delivery for librarians and school teachers in the Philadelphia School District and for professors of the sciences at Drexel. Other such projects include a grant to Edinboro University of Pennsylvania to establish and coordinate a CD-ROM network to provide remote access to ERIC and other bibliographic data bases for thirty-three school and public libraries, with the university library housing a multiple CD-ROM server which will have the ability to handle searches from many libraries simultaneously. In two other projects, community colleges are sharing their data base with local public libraries or, as in the case of Delaware County Community College, adding their holdings to an existing CD-ROM data base.

According to Thomas Duszak, Assistant Director for Academic Libraries and Networking of the State Library of Pennsylvania, "a major initiative of the State Library of Pennsylvania in 1992 will be providing access to BITNET and the Internet through PENN*LINK, which is the electronic mail system of the Pennsylvania Department of Education. The State Library initiative will extend to all types of libraries."[10]

In view of the many and varied approaches to multitype library cooperative programs, a further review of these programs will help to clarify the depth and variety of these programs. Library cooperation is never so fervently discussed as when there is a shortage of money. Given the financial difficulties in which state governments have recently found themselves, nothing seems more appropriate than a discussion of library cooperation in a multitype environment.

UNION LISTS OF SERIALS

The development of union lists of serials is perhaps the most common library project undertaken by libraries of various types within a particular state. In many such states, LSCA Title III moneys have been used to fund or partially fund union lists.

As an example, an ongoing project of the Alabama Public Library Service (APLS) is the *Alabama Union List of Serials* (AULS), which is partially supported by LSCA Title III funds. AULS includes the holdings of approximately 115 libraries of all types: public, school, academic and special. Over 20,000 unique titles are represented in the list, giving access to more than 150,000 local data records. In addition to paper and microfiche versions, AULS is also accessible through the OCLC Union List Subsystem.

Tennessee also has a union list of serials project, funded by the Tennessee State Library and Archives, with approximately sixty- five participating libraries. Delaware has recently begun a union list of serials as has New Mexico. Utah is working toward an OCLC-based state union list of serials, which is being partially funded through LSCA funds. In 1992, Vermont brought its Union List of Serials online as a component of the Vermont Automated Libraries System (VALS), and Maine began the planning for an automated state union list of serials.

Several of the Florida multitype library cooperatives have serials union listing projects that are available in the OCLC Union List Subsystem, including the Central Florida Library Consortium, the Panhandle Library Access Network, and the Tampa Bay Library Consortium. The Southeast Florida Library Information Network (SEFLIN) also has a union list of serials available on CD-ROM.

UNION CATALOGS

Statewide union catalogs are also a common project, and are also often funded with LSCA grant money from the state library. As an incentive to libraries to contribute their holdings, many state libraries have provided LSCA grant funds for the retrospective conversion of a library's holdings and tape loading into OCLC, if the union catalog is a subset of the OCLC data base.

One of the oldest, if not *the* oldest, of state union catalogs is the one that was begun in Nebraska in the 1930s as a card-based union catalog. Since that time, Nebraska's union catalog has been brought online as NEON, the state data base to identify Nebraska holdings in the OCLC Online Union Catalog. The Nebraska Library Commission, along with its other responsibilities involved in the coordination of library services, is also a full service OCLC network through its NEBASE program.

The Alabama Public Library Service (APLS) coordinates the production of ALICAT, a state union catalog with contributions of bibliographic records from public, academic and special libraries. ALICAT is available on microfiche and on the OCLC Union Listing Subsystem. As an incentive to academic libraries to include their holdings and provide interlibrary loan service to public libraries in Alabama, APLS negotiated a net-lending program with the Network of Alabama Academic Libraries (NAAL) to reimburse academic libraries for the number of loans to public libraries over the amount lent by public libraries to the academic library. The funds for this program are provided from LSCA funds.

The Division of Libraries, Archives and Museums of Alaska uses LSCA Title III moneys to provide a statewide, microfiche union catalog of the holdings of libraries in Alaska belonging to the Western Library Network (WLN). LSCA money is also used to pay the costs associated with out-of-state interlibrary loans for all of Alaska's libraries.

According to Duszak, Assistant Director for Academic Libraries and Networking at the State Library of Pennsylvania, one of the backbones of resource sharing in Pennsylvania is the ACCESS PENNSYLVANIA data base, a CD-ROM union catalog which is issued annually with the 6th edition produced in 1991. At that time there were 2.5 million unique titles accessible by author, subject, title and keyword. A total of 747 libraries had their collection on ACCESS PENNSYLVANIA in 1991–1992 (482 school libraries, 215 public libraries, 32 academic libraries, and 18 special libraries).

Access Colorado has connected all of the automated library catalogs into one statewide catalog. It is rapidly accomplishing its three goals: 1) to install local dial-in lines so that local citizens and librarians can connect toll-free to the basic CARL/MARMOT network of about sixty libraries' on-line catalogs, 2) to add an additional seventeen major libraries to this data base, and 3) to add non-bibliographic data bases to the network.

One variety of union catalog involves more than just access to a union data base but also actually sharing an automated system. This type of arrangement has become more prevalent in recent years. In Oregon there exist several library cooperatives involving public libraries and community college libraries in using a shared automated system, and there is also one consortium of public libraries, community college libraries, school libraries and state college libraries where they share a CD-ROM catalog. All of these ventures in Oregon have been very successful to date. A growing number of the members of the Tampa Bay Library Consortium, a multitype library consortium of seventy-one public, academic, school, and special libraries in the ten counties of the Tampa Bay Region of Florida, share a CLSI automated system, a cooperative venture that has also been very successful.

The State of Wyoming has been funding a shared statewide computer system for over six years. This system is a shared data base of about 50 percent of the public library records, five of seven community colleges libraries, the University of Wyoming Library and the State Library. LSCA funds have supported most of the personnel, travel/training, and peripheral costs while state funds support most telecommunications, equipment and software service contracts, and retrospective conversion. Jerry Krois, Deputy State Librarian of Wyoming, has stated that:

This project has been successful in its ability to strengthen interlibrary cooperation among all types of libraries in the state and build sensitivity for other types of libraries as resolution of issues are needed. While being successful in developing a 900,000 record database and supporting automated circulation, delays in expanding the state's new telecommunications network to provide dedicated access to the remaining colleges and public libraries has existed as a problem since 1984. This access will hopefully be resolved in 1992.[11]

REFERENCE NETWORKING

The State Library of Connecticut has funded through LSCA grants the Reference Network (RefNet) which promotes regional cooperation among all types of Connecticut libraries. LSCA funds have been provided to underwrite the cost of fax machines and expensive reference tools that might otherwise not be available at the local level. Both public and private academic libraries are included in the program. RefNet has had an aggressive publicity campaign involving videos and telephone book ads. Regional directories of CD-ROM data bases have been created and a reference networking philosophy statement and code have been established.

PRESERVATION

Preservation has fairly recently become part of the effort of some multitype library systems. The State Library of Pennsylvania is investigating ways for the State Library to coordinate preservation efforts among all types of libraries in Pennsylvania. Along a similar line, the Nebraska Library Commission received a grant in 1991 from the National Endowment for the Humanities to develop a statewide preservation planning agenda. Delegates from libraries, museums, county historical societies, archives, and the private sector are participating in strategic planning sessions. Libraries and the county historical societies were surveyed regarding their disaster preparedness plans. From the results of that survey emerged a planning document that included the publication of the tabulated survey data.[12]

In California a group of multitype libraries developed and field tested a preservation needs assessment tool that identifies priorities for the individual institutions and for resource sharing; they are currently experiencing great success in their efforts to implement the results of the needs assessment tool and preserving those items most in need of preservation for long-term resource sharing in the region.

STATEWIDE BORROWERS' CARD

Although more common among libraries of the same type (such as among academic libraries) a statewide borrower's card can also be a project of state libraries and multitype library systems. For example, Colorado recently implemented a statewide reciprocal borrowing program. All types of libraries are involved and their individual needs are being adequately accommodated. The State Library has paid expenses of the committee meetings involved in setting up the program and has allocated approximately $40,000 to provide for initial implementation. The State Library does not plan to reimburse libraries for the cost of loans, and therefore annual ongoing expenses are anticipated to be quite low, estimated at $5,000, which sum will likely come from LSCA funds.

INFORMATION NETWORKS

Reference and Research Library Resources Systems (3 R's). The New York Reference and Research Library Resources Systems constitute nine regional multitype library systems, all with the basic goal of sharing resources to meet the research and information needs of users of all types of libraries. The Reference and Research Systems offer interlibrary loan, continuing education for staff, delivery services, production of union lists and bibliographic control programs, microfilming and preservation programs, cooperative use of computer-based systems, reciprocal access, and interface with the New York State Interlibrary Loan System, a computerized library network established in 1967 to assure access to research libraries throughout the state. These systems also coordinate and administer state aid programs, such as New York's Coordinated Collection

Development program, which was established as a result of the 1978 Governor's Conference on Libraries. The program provides grants to public or nonprofit independent colleges or universities located in New York State that agree to share resources through the reference and research systems.[13]

While state grants are to be expended for library materials within the subject-area commitment of each library, no distinction is made in providing access between state-funded and locally funded materials. All resources are shared by members of the program. Coordinated collection development is simply viewed as the most cost-effective way to stretch finite public funds within the sharing environment of the Reference and Research Library Resources systems. The collection development program overlays a regional structure of support services that provides for its administration with minimal additional cost. At the same time, it strengthens the resource sharing for which the regional systems were created.[14]

No requirement exists that libraries must provide machine-readable bibliographic records to their collections, their subject area of collection responsibility, or even to the material purchased with grant funds. Most of the academic libraries, however, are members of one of the major bibliographic utilities (OCLC, RLIN, or UTLAS), and their records can be accessed by other members of the same utility, but there is no one source for all the system's resources.

ILLINET ONLINE. ILLINET ONLINE serves as an online catalog and circulation system for the forty members of the Illinois Library Computer Systems Organization (ILCSO). It is heavily state-subsidized, with 75 percent of the funding coming from the Illinois Board of Higher Education, 10 percent from the Illinois State Library (using a combination of state and federal funds), and the remaining 15 percent from the forty ILSCO libraries in the form of individual institutional assessments.[15]

The impetus for electronic resource sharing in Illinois came from the Library Committee of the Illinois Board of Higher Education in 1969, with the call for the establishment of a statewide automated network to support interlibrary activity. In the mid-1970s, the late Hugh C. Atkinson, then University Librarian at the University of Illinois at Urbana-Champaign, proposed the implementation of the Library Computer System (LCS) circulation system as the basis for a statewide resource-sharing network. Initially installed at the University of Illinois at Urbana-Champaign in 1979, LCS was extended in 1980 with Illinois Board of Higher Education funding to the library of the University of Illinois in Chicago and then to other colleges and academic libraries in the state. LCS, while extremely successful, had limitations since it is based on a short bibliographic record intended essentially only for circulation purposes.[16]

The second phase of the project involved the enhancement of the LCS system with full bibliographic records so that the system could replace local card catalogs and function as an on-line catalog. Grant funding was obtained from the Illinois State Library to purchase the Western Library Network (WLN) software with the condition that the money be used to research and to demonstrate the feasibility of a statewide union catalog. The River Bend Library System, a multitype library system in Illinois, was made a collaborator in the project. "This association provided an opportunity to show the practicality of cooperative bibliographic control between libraries of different kinds that also are separated geographically."[17]

In November 1986, ILCSO library directors began the third phase of the project by endorsing a multiyear proposal to expand the catalog data base for the University of Illinois at Urbana-Champaign and the River Bend Library System for use as a local on-line catalog and as a statewide union catalog. The proposal was subsequently endorsed by the Illinois Board of Higher Education and the Illinois State Library. Funding was made available by a combination of LSCA funds, funding from the Illinois Board of Higher Education, support from the Illinois State Library, and prorated contributions from each LCS member library.

The data base was created from OCLC archive tapes for Illinois libraries (academic, school, and public) from 1975 to 1989. The retrospective loading of bibliographic records and holdings was completed in March 1989 with current cataloging being added since that time. By August 1991, the ILLINET ONLINE data base contained over 5 million records representing over 20 million volumes in machine-readable form. Statewide level authority control is maintained by a system of shared authority work among several sites throughout the state.[18]

Currently, the success of ILLINET ONLINE is also causing problems for patrons and libraries because of the greatly increased demands for service due to popularity of ILLINET ONLINE at a time when the libraries are experiencing cuts in state funding. Some of the libraries have been forced to return requests that they cannot fill in the course of the normal workday or to initiate patron fees as an interim measure until state funding can be restored. Since patron fees are contrary to the spirit which created ILLINET ONLINE, most Illinois librarians hope that increased or renewed state funding will allow user fees to be discontinued.

North Carolina Information Network (NCIN). The purpose of the State Library of North Carolina is to serve as an information distribution system and resource center for state government and the citizens of North Carolina. To work toward fulfillment of this mandate, the State Library established the North Carolina Information Network (NCIN) in 1986 to function as a link between the geographically dispersed sources of information and local libraries of all types, using the latest computer telecommunications technologies. Funding for this network is from LSCA Title

III moneys. Some of the member services provided by NCIN include: access to the North Carolina Union Catalog and the North Carolina Union List of Serials; access to interlibrary loan and ERIC as part of the North Carolina OCLC Group Access Capability; access to AT&T Easylink electronic mail and to 850 third party data bases as well as North Carolina generated bulletin boards; access to the State Library's Dynix catalog; OCLC tapeloading of multitype library MARC holdings into OCLC; and gateways to both the University of North Carolina Education Computing Service and the State of North Carolina Computing Service telecommunications lines.[19]

NCIN has been constructed and promoted as the state's "information infrastructure" to provide information services to both urban and rural parts of the state, and to both corporate and individual citizens. In order to help assure political support for the network, it was also designed to support the role of the state's libraries in the educational processes at all levels, one of its main goals being to integrate the provision of information through libraries into the daily operation of businesses and local governments without confinement to the traditional library agenda.[20] NCIN thus attempts to make the provision of books and information services a basic part of the production of goods and services.[21]

When NCIN first began operations, its program offerings concentrated on the delivery of selected OCLC services and the construction of state on-line catalogs and union lists. However, in attempting to meet the challenges of serving small businesses and local economic development projects, the network moved from strictly bibliographic services to the data services that businesses typically need in daily operations. The State Library of North Carolina entered into cooperative agreements with several state agencies that work with the business community to establish electronic bulletin boards intended to assist in the publicizing of the work of these agencies. A good example is the Automated Purchase Directory, which lists state contracts in a wide variety of areas and includes a listing of state construction bids and the Department of Transportation contracts.

The State Library has also begun developing its own interactive data bases.[22] The State Library pays for all costs for use of the system except for the use of the commercial data bases accessed through the gateway service. In the latter case, the costs are billed back to the library.

NCIN was built with very little new money, but was instead constructed on past investments made in information materials by libraries of all types in the state and by state government agencies. The backbone of NCIN, however, is the University of North Carolina System, private academic libraries such as Duke University and Wake Forest University, the large urban public libraries, and the State Library. To date, the heaviest users of the network have been rural public libraries and corporate research libraries.[23]

NCIN has been built as a kind of umbrella network, purchasing services as needed from third party vendors and allowing its users to pick and choose services and products as needed; thereby, small and/or rural libraries are able to afford more sophisticated, computer- based information sources than might have ever been the case without NCIN.[24]

Vermont Automated Libraries System (VALS). The Vermont Automated Libraries System is a distributed network specifically designed to ensure that people in rural Vermont have the same access to information as those people in urban areas. In 1984, cooperative planning for what was to become VALS began among the University of Vermont, Middlebury State College and Vermont State College. Joined by the Vermont Department of Libraries, these libraries in 1986 signed a contract with Data Research for an on-line system. Other libraries, including academic libraries of private institutions, have since joined the cooperative effort, and now VALS connects a number of different automated systems. As of November 1991, there were eighty-two public libraries, twenty-four academic libraries, and sixty school libraries participating in VALS. The State Librarian and the Director of Library and Information Services assess VALS in the following way:

VALS is innovative on several levels and was one of the ten 1988 recipients of the Ford Foundation-Harvard/Kennedy School of Government Innovations in State and Local Government Awards. First, in a state with extremely limited information sources, it brings together the major public and private academic and state library resources and makes them available upon demand to rural libraries and individuals without limitation either in level, location or format of material or by age, economic status, location, or special needs of the user. The ultimate dream is to follow this first step to make all public state government data available at the local level, and provide the requested material in the format most convenient to the user, no matter how isolated he or she might be.[25]

VALS provides free access to public libraries; costs associated with access to other member's systems are shared with the major linked institutions. "Challenge" grant money supplied from the general fund along with funds from the Ford Foundation Innovations Grant helped to purchase necessary computer equipment to access VALS for the public libraries.

In addition to providing access to standard, national-level bibliographic data bases such as OCLC, VALS also provides access to state and local data bases such as a full text data base of Vermont session laws which can be searched by keyword and downloaded by lawyers all over the state. There is also a full-text data base of all General Assembly bills, both House and Senate.

Packet Radio Internet Extension (PRIE). A public (San Diego Public Library), an academic (San Diego State University Library), and a special

(San Diego Zoo Library) library have entered into a cooperative program to provide linkages for interlibrary loan and electronic mail and extended access to the Internet (through San Diego State University) via packet radio technology. This new type of network will allow the libraries to communicate with each other without the physical bonds of wires and telephone lines and amounts to a local area network (LAN) using radio transmissions.

The person most responsible for this innovative project, which has been in the planning stages for about ten years, is Dr. Edwin Brownrigg, who was quoted in *Library Journal* as stating:

The problems have been both technical as well as public policy in terms of getting this type of service into the library field. First of all, the amateurs have been restricted to very narrow bandwidth, which is really not useful for anything other than sporadic traffic such as you'd see between a terminal and an online catalog. But that's not what life is going to be all about in libraries in terms of electronic document delivery, which involves big bulk file transfer. So the problem has been in terms of public policy: How does the library avoid the hassle of applying for a license from the Federal Communications Commission (FCC), and then how do you build an affordable radio that can move data around at rates that are commensurate with Internet.[26]

All these problems have now been addressed if not absolutely solved through new technological developments and recent changes in federal regulations regarding radio transmission. The LAN in San Diego is just a beginning. While more research is still needed in such areas as routing protocol, this experiment opens up the possibility of new technological means of linking libraries.

The Virginia Library and Information Network (VLIN). A new state library network has been proposed for Virginia. According to John Tyson, State Librarian of Virginia:

The proposed Virginia Library and Information Network (VLIN), to be coordinated by the Virginia State Library and Archives, is an exciting new program initiative aimed at linking the information resources of all 3,042 libraries in the Commonwealth of Virginia into a single, unified, on-line database. Using the latest in modern technology, the VLIN ultimately hopes to provide all Virginia residents with speedy, electronic access to the vast and varied holdings of the state's public, school, university, corporate, medical, legal, and governmental libraries and research centers.

When fully implemented, the VLIN will enable Virginians to use the computer terminals in their homes, offices, schools, or community libraries to review the research materials available at any one or all of the participating institutions. Through this state-of-the-art electronic network, patrons will be able to identify readily all the information pertaining to their interests and needs and to request data, books, articles, films, and copies of selected documents from a wide range of repositories.[27]

Mr. Jefferson would no doubt be proud.

Libraries are established and funded by communities, counties, schools, colleges and universities, businesses and governmental agencies, but they do not exist in isolation. Although each library is responsible for serving a specific clientele, cooperative relationships enable each library to do a better, more cost-effective job. Cooperation, based on solid, adequately funded core library service, provides a true "plus" to library users. Improvements in access to library services, whether statewide, by region, or in any particular geographic area, yield major benefits to the general public, to business, to educational communities, and to state and local governments.

NOTES

1. Janet M. Welch, "The Multitype Library System and Its Political Environment" in *Politics and the Support of Libraries*, edited by E. J. Josey and Kenneth D. Shearer (New York: Neal-Schuman, 1990), p. 137.

2. *Ibid.*, pp. 140–41.

3. Douglas M. Adams, *An Organizational Analysis of Multi- Type Library Cooperation in Utah: A Consideration of Basic Issues for Laypersons and Librarians* (Salt Lake City: State Library Division, Department of Community and Economic Development, 1987). p. 1.

4. *Ibid.*, p. 2.

5. *Ibid.*, p. 5.

6. Charles T. Townley, Charles Peguese, and Kenneth G. Rohm, Jr., "Academic Library-State Library Agency Relationships: The Pennsylvania Needs Assessment," *College & Research Libraries* 49 (May 1988), pp. 239–50.

7. *Ibid.*, p. 240.

8. State Library of Pennsylvania, Advisory Council on Library Development, *Improved Access to Pennsylvania's Library Resources: A Review of the Comprehensive Plan and Governor's Conference Resolutions* (Harrisburg: State Library of Pennsylvania, 1991), p. 7.

9. Sylverna Ford, "Models of Access: The Oakland Library Consortium," *Resource Sharing and Information Networks* 7, no. 1 (1991), pp. 67–80.

10. Used by permission of Thomas Duszak, Assistant Director for Academic Libraries and Networking, State Library of Pennsylvania.

11. Quoted by permission of Jerry Krois, Deputy State Librarian of Wyoming.

12. Nebraska Library Commission, *1989–1991 Biennial Report of the Nebraska Library Commission* (Lincoln: Nebraska Library Commission, 1991), p. 4.

13. *Library Service to the People of New York State: A Long-Range Program* (Albany: University of the State of New York, 1987), pp. 9–10, ED 286 536.

14. Joan Neumann, "The New York State Experience with Coordinated Col-

lection Development: Funding the Stimulus," *Resource Sharing and Information Networks* 2, nos. 3/4 (Spring/Summer 1985), p. 117.

15. Bernie Sloan, "ILLINET Online and Lessons for Consortium System Design," *LITA Newsletter* 12 (Fall 1991), p. 21.

16. William H. Mischo et al., "University of Illinois at Urbana-Champaign" in *Campus Strategies for Libraries and Electronic Information*, edited by Caroline Arms (Bedford, Mass.: Digital Press, 1990), pp. 119–21; Michael Gorman, "The Online Catalog at the University of Illinois at Urbana-Champaign: A History and Overview," *Information Technology and Libraries* 4 (Dec. 1985), pp. 306–7.

17. Mischo, "University of Illinois at Urbana-Champaign," p. 123.

18. Barbara Henigman, "Networking and Authority Control: Online Catalog Authority Control in Illinois," *Information Technology and Libraries* 10 (March 1991), pp. 47–54.

19. "North Carolina Information Network," *Tar Heel Libraries* 14 (May/June 1991), p. 3.

20. To judge their success, after the announcement of the creation of NCIN at the governor's weekly press conference on October 2, 1986, Governor James G. Martin requested that his office become a Selective User of the state's union lists and that he be issued a password to the state electronic mail/bulletin board system. Both the governor and his advisors seem to have realized the economic development potential of the network.

21. Howard F. McGinn, "Electronic Services for Rural Libraries: Meeting the Challenge in North Carolina," *RQ* 29 (Summer 1990), p. 493; Howard F. McGinn, "Information Networking and Economic Development," *Wilson Library Bulletin* 62 (Nov. 1987), p. 31.

22. Howard F. McGinn, "Information and Development of Rural North Carolina," *Southeastern Librarian* 40 (Summer 1990), pp. 75–76.

23. McGinn, "Electronic Services," p. 493.

24. Howard F. McGinn, "The Role of Serials Location and Distribution in Economic Development in North Carolina," *Serials Review* 15 (Summer 1989), p. 16.

25. Information respecting the Vermont Automated Libraries System supplied by Patricia E. Klinck.

26. Quoted in Michael Rogers, "Automation News," *Library Journal* 117 (July 1992), p. 26.

27. Quoted by permission of John Tyson, State Librarian of Virginia.

Chapter 8

Program Review—Macromanagement or Micromanagement?

Program review has traditionally functioned primarily as an aspect of institutional self-assessment inaugurated locally for purposes of internal improvement, usually in conjunction with periodic accreditation review. As most states have recently been forced to become concerned with achieving optimal utilization of their limited resource bases, a perception has developed and persists in many states that state resources for higher education are now spread too thin over too many institutions and programs, and that too little attention has been paid to matters of quality, distinctiveness, and need. While decision makers in a few states are actively discussing the possibility that some need for downsizing public higher education may exist, a more common approach, though not always necessarily better than the meat-axe approach that the very word "downsizing" (obviously anathema to most university administrators) implies, to the problem of insufficient resources and "excess" institutional supply in relation to demand is program review[1] for both new and existing programs. By eliminating duplicative programs, particularly in low-enrollment or high-cost areas, it is felt that state resources can be more rationally conserved. Whether or not this is so in practice, program review can almost always be of value to the institution itself in terms of evaluating the quality of its programs.

Because of the collegial, or at least not so very rigidly hierarchical, nature of academic governance structures within most institutions, internal efforts at reallocation of effort and resources is often difficult and always time-consuming to achieve. Because of this fact of life, state coordinating agencies have had to become involved. Currently, most state coordinating agencies of higher education either undertake an advisory role or exercise regulatory authority over new programs in public institutions of higher education. A few coordinating agencies attempt to crack the tougher nut and conduct reviews of existing programs with an eye toward either their expansion or their elimination. The degree of attention to detail also varies; in some states, coordinating agencies review only major graduate programs involving requests for new funding, while in others the review process covers all new academic programs at all levels, as well as such matters as changes in degree designations and new majors or minors within degrees, sometimes regardless of whether or not new funding is involved.

In addition to state coordinating agencies, the role of legislators and governors in matters involving program reviews is also increasing (some would say metastasizing). Legislative involvement in program reviews varies from state to state, but all state legislatures have appropriations or education committees among whose tasks is the job of making recommendations regarding higher education funding in the state. These often very powerful committees can naturally become interested in program reviews, particularly if the reviews are statewide or involve institutions in the districts of key legislators. In several states, program reviews were initiated because the legislature was pressuring higher educational institutions to become more accountable for the funds they receive. The program reviews thus were a way of proving to the legislature that the institutions were operating efficiently.

With few exceptions, legislators rarely involve themselves directly in program reviews, but in their role of "reviewers of the reviews" they do act as highly interested bystanders. A notable exception to the "review only" role is in South Carolina, where applicable statutes provide for formalized appeal to the legislature of state coordinating agency program review decisions. At least one case where the South Carolina Commission on Higher Education had recommended termination of several associate degree programs was appealed by the University of South Carolina to the South Carolina House of Representatives, which found in favor of the university. Although South Carolina is the only state allowing institutional appeal to the legislature as a matter of statute, all state agencies that are not constitutionally formulated or empowered to allocate funds are subject to plenary legislative powers of intervention to the extent the legislature so desires to exercise those powers.[2]

In addition, almost every state governor has a staff member who is responsible for education policy in the state. These staff members typically research questions related to education and advise the governor on education issues at the state and federal level. These staff members can have influence on the program review process, but their influence is usually nominal. Sometimes the governor's staff member works closely with key legislative committees, such as the appropriations committee or the educational oversight committee. Likewise, some states have legislative staff members who may serve as educational advisers to the legislature. "Such advisers often become involved in statewide program reviews by negotiating changes in the process and influencing legislation affecting education budgets."[3]

Program reviews have multiple purposes. Program reviews are undertaken to assess a program's productivity, to discover ways to improve its quality, to ensure appropriate use of public and institutional resources, to ascertain the effectiveness of a program, to serve as an aid to planning, or to satisfy requirements of a state coordinating agency. Program reviews can be most useful when initiated in instances of duplicative programs, programs of questionable quality, programs producing graduates for a niche of the job market with either excess or slack demand, and in cases of imbalances between such things as public opinion and perceived need for the program.[4] Since about 1972, state coordinating agencies have moved aggressively in the area of program review, largely in an effort to stem the tide of new graduate programs being developed without adequate consideration of fiscal requirements or long-range institutional goals.

The purposes and objectives of program review concern both state and campus interests. In some areas, the state has a predominant concern such as in the formulating of statewide policies and plans and in identifying unnecessary duplication in programs across different campuses. The institutions have the biggest stake in making decisions about personnel, curricula, and requirements for admissions and graduation. Hines states that "[b]oth the campus and the state have a joint interest in balancing educational and economic interests, and it is in this area where conflict may arise between the state and the campus if, for instance, a campus views a program in educational terms and the state emphasizes its economic aspects."[5]

There is perhaps no other area in which the tensions between the state government and institutions of higher education are greater than in program review. Almost without exception, the review processes that governing and coordinating boards are using in the review of existing programs include lengthy negotiations and the extensive involvement of presidents, faculty, and others. They also tend to assign a high priority to initial institutional self-evaluations using time-honored procedures such as the use of highly respected external consultants in the program area under review.

In only a very few states is a program review undertaken primarily by the state coordinating agency staff. When this approach is taken (for example, in the State of Washington), the agency staff usually identifies programs with long patterns of low productivity and then requests the institution involved to develop reviews of the program and to make recommendations to the board on the program's continuation or termination.

The heart of the problem, however, is that few trustees, presidents, or faculty will volunteer to terminate their own institution or any of its programs. Almost without exception, recent gubernatorial or legislative initiatives to alter governance structures can be traced to pressure for (or opposition to) terminating or merging particular programs enjoying (or suffering from) a high level of political visibility. The issue facing state leaders and the academic community is how to accomplish retrenchment when necessary yet protect basic state interests and, to the extent possible, the time-honored prerogatives of campuses—and of presidents and faculty—to carry out basic academic functions free of governmental intrusion.

REVIEW OF NEW PROGRAMS

In most states, in one form or another seven basic factors are considered in the program review process for a new program: 1) description of the program itself, 2) delineation of the purposes and objectives of the program, 3) conduct of a needs analysis for the program, 4) conduct of cost analysis of the program, 5) conduct of resource analysis of what is needed for the program, 6) accreditation of the program (that is, consideration of what organization may accredit the program, its requirements for accreditation, and consideration of the present accreditations of related or expanded programs), and 7) consideration of the availability of adequate student financial aid.[6] Obviously, any analysis of the resources required for a program must necessarily include a consideration of library resources.

A potentially significant expense for the state in establishing any new or expanded programs is the cost of library materials to support both teaching and research in the new or expanded field of endeavor. For instance, initiation of a doctoral program, even in a field where a master's degree is already offered, will usually require significant library acquisitions of both retrospective and current materials; once students commence dissertation work even greater demands for resources will be placed on the library. For any state-level review, a major consideration must therefore be whether the institution's library possesses adequate resources to support the program in question. If it is determined that resources are truly adequate, the program review process must include both an evaluation of the library resources presently available and some consideration of the additional resources that will be needed in order to support the new program. Since by its very nature a new program proposal is for a program not previously offered on a campus and the institution's library will likely not have extensive holdings in the area unless some overlap exists with other program offerings, new program proposals should specifically indicate the additional resources needed and preferably should also include a budget for adding those resources over a reasonable length of time.

Of course, faculty and administrators wishing to establish a new program may feel that the consideration of library resources may hinder their chances of getting the proposal approved by the state coordinating agency or may even feel that the librarians are trying to obtain "veto power" over new programs. The latter is most certainly not the case. A quite different scenario is much more likely: a new program is established and the first time the library director and staff become aware of it is when the first students and the new faculty arrive at the library expecting, all too often in vain, to find the materials needed to support the new coursework.

REVIEW OF EXISTING PROGRAMS

A field-by-field or program-by-program review of all existing academic programs is an expensive and time-consuming process. Even a modest-sized state college will usually have more than fifty different program areas, and a large comprehensive research university may have hundreds. When fields are reviewed by degree level as well (bachelor's, master's, professional, and doctorate), the process becomes even more complex. Although there exists general agreement that the state should define the broad areas of program offerings of each institution (through general determinations of institutional role and mission), there is considerable disagreement among higher education experts about whether the state should even attempt to evaluate specific programs in all institutions. A middle ground seems to be that the state should require each institution to implement a procedure for the review of its programs and to take steps to assure that those programs meet state-determined standards of effective operation.[7]

State agencies can utilize incentives to encourage institutions to review their own programs without any assessment of statewide needs. Some states coordinate the institutional reviews through a planning process that also assesses statewide needs. In a few states, for example, Wisconsin, state coordinating agencies monitor the institutional reviews to ensure quality and, as much as possible, uniformity. The major problem with this kind of "middle ground" approach is that it does not readily provide for interinstitutional comparisons (desired by many legislatures and by state agencies as well for use in the budgeting process) in terms of either quality or duplication.

Where states require the review of existing programs, the purpose behind that requirement is usually one or more of the following: 1) financial (to cut back on expenditures), 2) efficiency (to enable more effective utilization of existing resources), 3) accountability (to assure that institutions effectively meet state goals), 4) quality (to upgrade the overall quality of programs by eliminating low-quality programs and reallocating resources to improve others), 5) consumer protection (to protect students from programs of questionable value), or 6) political (to demonstrate state coordinating agency response to political mandates).[8]

Currently, interest in state review of both new and existing programs seems to be increasing. If the primary concern is with the quality of programs being offered by state institutions, the hard work and expense of undertaking program reviews is well worth the effort. If, on the other hand, the primary motivation is simply control of costs, there are easier and less expensive methods of reallocating resources within the budgeting process itself.

LIBRARY-RELATED PROCEDURES IN PROGRAM REVIEW

In a study of library-related procedures for reviewing new and/or existing programs in a sample of six states, procedures ranged from what may be described as the complex to the extremely simplistic.[9] The most complex procedure in the states studied was in Alabama, where a collection assessment is required for the subject area of each proposed new graduate program, while the simplest was in Arkansas where nothing more than a simple statement is required in the new program proposal stating that the institution's library can support the new program. It was also noted, and was an area of concern for one Arkansas library director interviewed for the study, that the statement could come only from the particular department and was not required to come from the library, although some other library directors in the state indicated that on their campuses the departments had always consulted the library director even though they were not required to do so.

Program review procedures need to be structured so as to assure the involvement of the library directors in the institutional planning process. One library director in North Carolina pointed out that there is often an "innocent" assumption made that the institution's library is capable of supporting any program that the institution might want to add. This problem was also addressed in a study of Oklahoma academic libraries. The report stated:

A universal problem faced by many academic libraries is the addition of new programs on campuses without prior notification of the library and with no additional funding to purchase new materials in support of these programs. The library is placed in a difficult position because it cannot provide basic information resources required by faculty and students in new subject areas. It is difficult to acquire such materials quickly and many are simply not available at any price. In short, any new program should be carefully considered prior to implementation in terms of what support can be provided by the library, and institutional approval for new programs should always include the library as part of the review procedure.[10]

An examination of some of the program review procedures in a state where the library is actively involved will help to demonstrate how a library can be "tuned in" to both institutional and state-level planning.

ALABAMA—SYSTEM OF PROGRAM REVIEW FOR GRADUATE LEVEL PROGRAMS

One of the recommendations from the 1983 report of the Council of Librarians[11] (discussed earlier in chapter 6) was that a mechanism should be established for reviewing library collection adequacy as a portion of the program review for all new graduate programs. "This mechanism would ensure that collections adequate to support these programs are in place or will be funded within a minimum of five years from the program's approval."[12] The report also recommended actions to correct deficiencies in the existing library collections by means of a series of statewide collection analyses intended to identify the strengths and weaknesses of each academic library.

When NAAL was established in 1984, a Collection Development Committee was appointed and charged with implementing the recommendations of the report. First, it was necessary to decide upon a methodology for collection assessment, which was worked on and refined for several years. A preliminary draft was completed in 1985, which was then tested by use in the program reviews, and a final version was prepared in 1987.[13] The manual drew upon the strategies devised in the RLG Conspectus, including the use of similar collection level rankings.

Since the fall of 1985, the library of each Alabama institution proposing a new graduate program has been required to prepare an assessment of its holdings in the particular subject area of the program, using evaluative measures such as citation analysis and the checking of the library's holdings against standard, published lists of resources. The collection's strength is then rated according to the collection level codes of the RLG Conspectus. The library component of the new program proposal also includes a description of the kinds of additional resources needed to support the new program, along with a budget indicating the amount of additional funds necessary to purchase the needed retrospective resources on a one-time basis. In addition, the assessment form includes a section dealing with the amount of additional funds estimated to be required for ongoing acquisitions for the program during the first five years of operation. The library component of the new program proposal is given to the academic department to include in the overall new program request. However, there is no guarantee that it will be forwarded exactly as it was prepared by the library. The academic department can edit and modify the report as it feels is necessary or desirable. The library component of the new program proposal is then forwarded to ACHE where it is reviewed by a staff member and by appropriate outside consultants.

Because of the time required to conduct the assessment of the collection, the library director can be assured that s/he will be aware of and a part of any institutional program planning at least by the time that the institution gives its notice of an intent to plan to ACHE. Although the library component can involve a great deal of work if the new program proposal is in a subject area where no collection assessment has already been completed, its great value is that it puts the library director and staff right in the middle of the campus planning process.

NOTES

1. Some authors in the higher education literature distinguish between "program review" for existing programs and "program evaluation" for both existing and new programs. In this work the term "program review" will be used in the context of both new and existing programs.

2. Robert J. Barak and Barbara E. Brier, *Successful Program Review: A Practical Guide to Evaluating Programs in Academic Settings* (San Francisco: Jossey-Bass, 1990), p. 114–15.

3. *Ibid.*, pp. 115–16.

4. Edward R. Hines, *Higher Education and State Governments: Renewed Partnership, Cooperation, or Competition?* (College Station, Texas: Association for the Study of Higher Education, 1988), p. 89.

5. Hines, *Higher Education and State Governments*, p. 90.

6. Robert J. Barak and Robert O. Berdahl, *State Level Academic Program Review in Higher Education* (Denver: Education Commission of the States, 1978), p. 26.

7. John K. Folger, "Implications of State Government Changes" in *Improving Academic Management*, edited by Paul Jedamus, Marvin W. Peterson and Associates (San Francisco: Jossey-Bass, 1981), p. 54.

8. Barak and Berdahl, *State Level Academic Program Review*, p. 56.

9. Vicki L. Gregory, "The Academic Library in the Program Review Process," *Collection Management* 12, nos. 3/4 (1990), pp. 125–34.

10. *A Comprehensive Study of Academic Libraries in Oklahoma* (Oklahoma City: Oklahoma State Regents for Higher Education, 1985), p. 8.

11. *Cooperative Library Resource Sharing Among Universities Supporting*

Graduate Study in Alabama (Montgomery, Alabama: Alabama Commission on Higher Education, 1983). ED 227 497

12. *Ibid.*, p. 47.

13. Sue O. Medina et al., *Collection Assessment Manual* (Montgomery, Alabama: NAAL, 1987).

Part III

CASE STUDIES OF THE INTERACTION BETWEEN STATE GOVERNMENT AND ACADEMIC LIBRARIES

On the surface, resource sharing seems to involve a relatively simple and straightforward process.... However, to provide this service requires a variety of factors or components. The interaction of these components makes the efficient and effective processing of a request possible: policies and protocols, procedures and tools, staffing, collections and resources, roles of various participants, continuing education, funding, and administration....

—Virginia Boucher and Susan Fayad
Library Resource Sharing in Colorado
1988

Chapter 9

The Florida Center for Library Automation—A Relationship That Ultimately Succeeds

Margaret A. Hogue
Michele I. Dalehite

INTRODUCTION

This chapter will describe the establishment and governance of the Florida Center for Library Automation (FCLA) and its role in the state of Florida. The organization of public education in the state will be outlined to provide a context for the relationship between FCLA and state government. In addition, the counterpart organization for the publicly funded community colleges, the College Center for Library Automation (CCLA), will be discussed. Both organizations illustrate the emphasis placed on centralization of activities by Florida state government.

FCLA is part of the State University System (SUS) of Florida, established to support the shared on-line catalog and library management system to be used by the libraries of all nine of the State Universities. As a "public" agency, FCLA is strongly affected by the layers of state government above it. These layers include the publicly-funded universities, the SUS and its Board of Regents, the State Board of Education, and the Florida Cabinet and Legislature.

ORGANIZATION OF PUBLIC EDUCATION IN FLORIDA

In order to discuss the influence of government on the libraries in Florida (and FCLA), it is necessary to understand the basic structure of the state government. The system of public education in Florida is organized in an unusual way. Control resides in an ex-officio Board of Education, composed of the governor and the elected members of the cabinet (secretary of state, attorney general, treasurer/insurance commissioner, comptroller, and commissioners of agriculture and education). In most other states, members of the state education boards are appointed by the governor.[1] In a few others, the board is elected.

Since the Florida Board of Education is not typical of national practice, it is fair to ask how well it functions. An analysis of Florida's educational governance was done in 1973 by Frank DePalma as part of the Educational Governance Project.[2] The project, conducted by Ohio State University personnel, consisted of parallel studies of twelve states. DePalma reported unfavorably on the Florida Board.

The non-appointed members of the Florida cabinet are chosen in statewide elections. They provide administrative services in the areas of agriculture, banking and finance, education, and insurance. The cabinet sits as ten different boards with ten different agendas. In practice, the cabinet member responsible for a specific board's functions (e.g., education) prepares the agenda for that board. DePalma found the board meetings to be perfunctory and routine, because each member has special interests in obtaining positive action on agenda items. A kind of "I'll scratch your back if you scratch mine" practice prevailed at that time, and still does. Each member is given a great deal of autonomy in the government area that he/she administers. As a consequence, educational items on the agenda are heavily influenced by the commissioner of education. Practically all of the commissioner's recommendations are approved. Moreover, the large volume of cabinet business means that very little time may be devoted to the agenda items, resulting in superficial examination of important educational proposals. With the exception of the commissioner of education, cabinet members usually avoid participating in educational matters.[3]

This system also means that the commissioner of education sits on many other boards and participates in many decisions completely outside the field of education. The power of the commissioner of education to sit as a voting member of the state Board of Education is a source of much political control over the administration of education in Florida. Since the commissioner must run for office, he or she must build a strong statewide political organization. This becomes another source of power. The commissioner also heads the state bureau for administering the state educational program, the Department of Education. Since the administrative process involves significant decisions, this is an additional source of influence because the commissioner dominates the politics of the bureaucracy.

The Department of Education is the administrative agency for the state program as established by the legislature and the state Board of Education. Within the department are specialists in every area of education (e.g., curriculum and instruction, finance and business services, school plant facilities, personnel, student services, and many others). Thus the department is charged with the administration of many large and complex educational programs in Florida, and it is of necessity a very large and complex organization.

Much has been written about the wisdom of retaining the state's present system of education.[4] Various changes have been proposed, but few significant changes have been acceptable. In the 1978 Florida election, proposals to amend the constitution and make important changes to the system were overwhelmingly defeated. Among these proposals were a separate Board of Education, appointment of all cabinet members, and appointment of the commissioner of education. These changes were included in a long, complicated list of constitutional amendments, including a controversial referendum on casino gambling. Political analysts at the time felt that the Florida voters were confused and alienated by the long list of amendments, and so turned them all down, regardless of merit.

HIGHER EDUCATION IN FLORIDA

An addition to the educational system was made by Governor Bob Graham in 1980. The Postsecondary Education Planning Commission (PEPC) was charged with developing methods of coordinating various elements of higher education. This lay board has a small professional staff, which works with staffs of the Senate and House Education Committees, Senate and House Appropriations Subcommittees on Education, and other agency staffs. The outcome is that much of the legislation affecting both higher education and public schools and the appropriations for both are worked on by the house staff, the senate staff, the governor's education staff, and the presiding officers of the house and senate. This procedure somewhat lessens the influence of the state Department of Education, which was dominant in the 1960s and 1970s. In 1981, the legislature established PEPC by statute. The 1983 legislature assigned to it a number of special studies related to coordinating and controlling higher education and to coordinating adult education, vocational education, community colleges, and universities. PEPC is still active in the 1990s.

The needs of Florida's citizens relative to postsecondary education are met by two kinds of public institutions, community colleges and universities. Baccalaureate degrees and graduate study are provided through a system of universities under the operational and coordinating control of the Board of Regents. At this time (1992) there are nine universities, and planning is underway for the establishment of a tenth. There are twenty-eight community colleges located in all areas of the state, providing vocational-technical or occupational education, associate degrees, and a variety of continuing education courses. They are governed by local boards of trustees, and were coordinated by the state Board of Education until 1983. The 1983 legislature created a State Board of Community Colleges which has assumed the position of coordinator of these colleges.

STATE STRUCTURE FOR PUBLIC COMMUNITY COLLEGES

The state Board of Education is the top-level agency responsible for education in Florida. All four of the divisions (Vocational Education, Public Schools, Community Colleges, and Universities) operating under its supervision are concerned to some extent with postsecondary education. However, the Division of Community Colleges and the Division of Universities are the state agencies with major responsibility for higher education. (See chart 9-1, Department of Education organization chart.)

The Division of Community Colleges is under the direction of the State Board of Community Colleges established in 1983. It is comprised of eleven lay citizens appointed for five-year terms by the governor and approved by four members of the state Board of Education with confirmation by the senate in regular session. In addition, the commissioner of education is an ex officio member, as is one community college student who serves a one-year term.

The State Board of Community Colleges is responsible for establishing and developing policies that will assure the operation and maintenance of a State Community College System subject to the approval of the State Board of Education. It appoints an executive director of the system who is in charge of the board's office. The executive director and the staff are responsible for conducting system-wide program reviews and preparing a proposed legislative budget, including a multi-year priority list for fixed capital outlay projects. The role of the staff of the Division of Community Colleges is to provide leadership for the twenty-eight institutions. Other staff in the Department of Education may also work with the community colleges in special areas such as buildings, vocational and technical education, and special services.

Unlike the state universities, which have had a long history of centralized management, the community colleges have a very short history in this regard. Although completely funded from state appropriations, their budgets are transferred to their local governing boards with virtually no strings attached. The community college employees are quasi-state employees in that, technically, they are employed by these local boards, which are separate corporate entities with no direct attachment to the Department of Education. The establishment of the state board was the legislature's attempt to tighten its control over these autonomous units in a way similar to its control of the universities.

Chart 9–1
Florida Department of Education Organizational Structure. Adapted from Florida Office of Secretary of State. *Florida Administrative Code* **(Tallahassee, Fla., 1963–).**

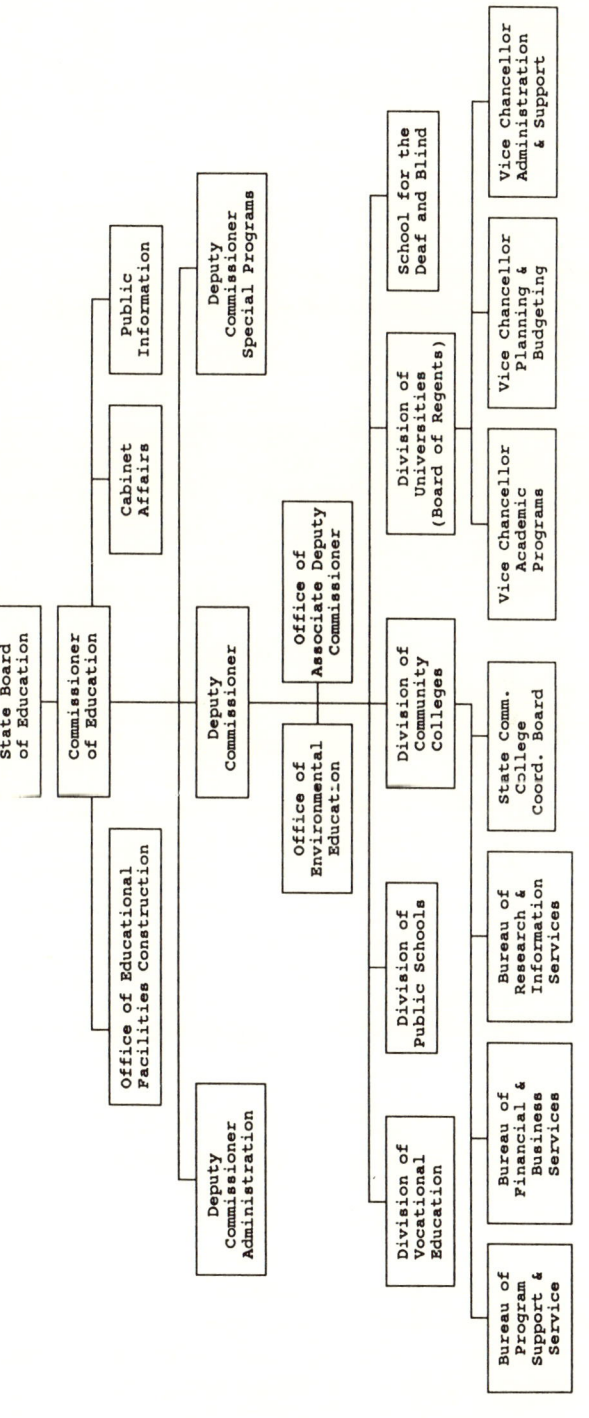

THE STATE UNIVERSITY SYSTEM

The Division of Universities is under direction of the Board of Regents (BOR) (see chart 9-2). The BOR consists of ten members who are appointed by the governor and approved by the senate. Nine regents are appointed to six-year terms; the tenth, a student member, is appointed to a one-year term. The commissioner of education is also an ex officio member. The regents employ a chancellor as the chief executive officer of the State University System (SUS). Each of the nine universities is under the immediate leadership of a president, also appointed by the Board of Regents.

The BOR staff serves in a consultive role to the operational activities of the nine universities, which in turn operate under the Board of Regents' policies and state Board of Education regulations, as well as statutes. The universities generally are referred to far more explicitly in the Florida Statutes than are the community colleges. University budgets have been much more constrained by legislatively imposed conditions and categories than the community colleges. For example, the SUS must get legislative approval for all new staff positions regardless of the availability of funds. The community colleges are not limited in this way; if there are sufficient funds in their budgets, they can define a new position and fill it without approval from a higher level entity.

The expansion of Florida's publicly-funded university system was guided by several long-range studies, the first of which was completed in 1957. Each new unit added to the SUS has been established under a plan approved by the Board of Regents and implemented by the state legislature. For example, the extension of university level opportunities for training into urban areas and the selection of specific roles for each institution have been matters of continuing, heated discussion, sometimes over long periods of time. These decisions are embodied in role-and-scope statements. The development of role-and-scope assignments for each university in the SUS (and the community college system) is recognized as a major responsibility of the state level leadership.

FLORIDA CENTER FOR LIBRARY AUTOMATION

The Florida Center for Library Automation (FCLA) is a small unit within the State University System (SUS), attached to the University of Florida. FCLA was established in 1984 as a result of a legislative appropriation to fund the implementation of a library automation system that would both support the internal operations of the SUS libraries and insure that the resources of all of those libraries would be known to all of the faculty and students within the SUS, as well as to the general citizenry. The extent of support for other libraries in Florida has been an area of

Chart 9-2
Florida Board of Regents Organizational Structure. Adapted from Florida Chamber of Commerce. *Inside Florida Government* (Tallahassee, Fla.: Price Publications, 1989) p. 141.

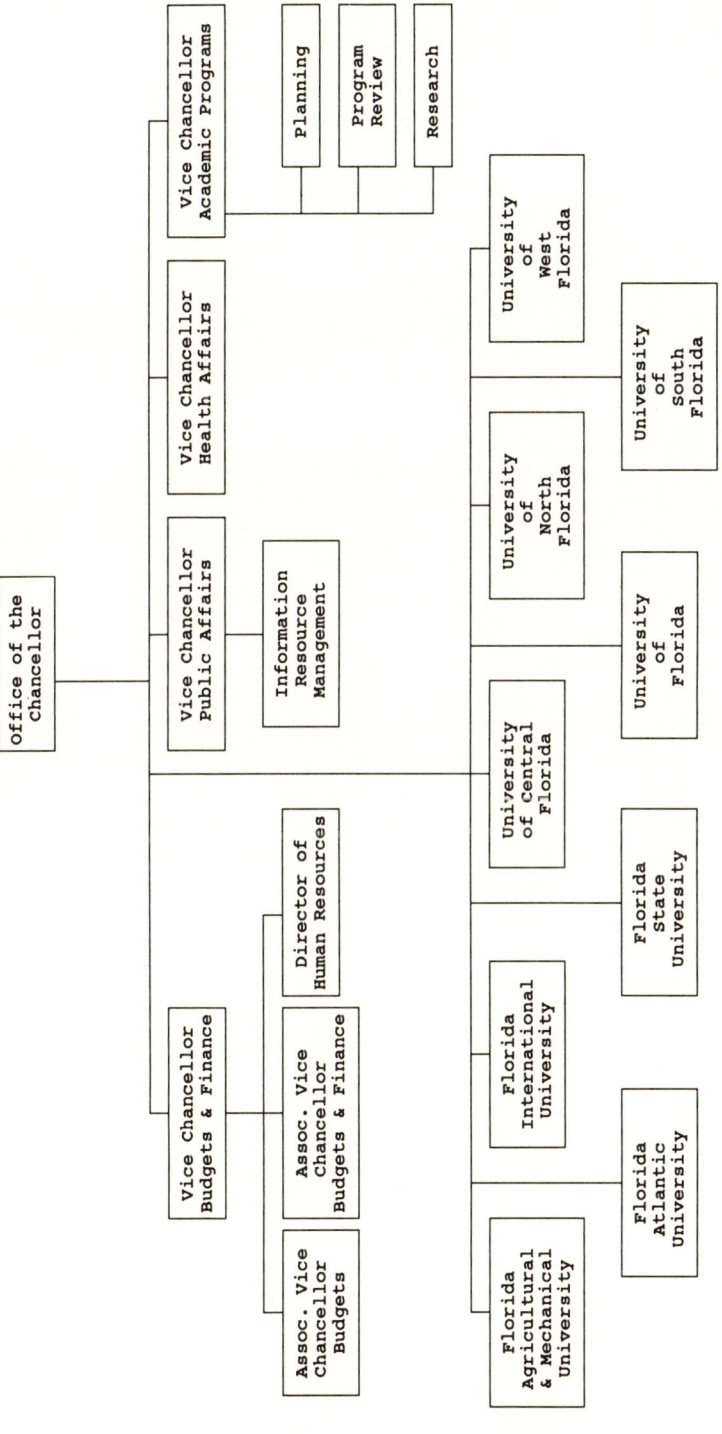

Table 1
SUS Data Bases

Florida A&M University	330,000
Florida Atlantic University	495,000
Florida International University	525,000
Florida State University	1,350,000
University of Central Florida	443,000
University of Florida	1,840,000
University of North Florida	388,000
University of South Florida	1,245,000
University of West Florida	384,000
Total	7,000,000

confusion since FCLA's inception. This issue will be discussed in greater detail below.

FCLA uses modified NOTIS software to manage the automation of all nine state university system libraries and their branches. There are a total of about fifty libraries, including twenty large libraries and about thirty smaller branches. All libraries are using the system for the major functions of cataloging, authority control, the on-line public catalog, and circulation. All but one are using the acquisitions module.

Most of the libraries have the majority of retrospective conversion done. Only the largest and oldest institutions (Florida State University and University of Florida) are still working on retrospective conversion projects, and the gaps in those two catalogs are very small. Because all nine institutions have separate and independent catalogs (linked by union author/title and standard number indexes), the total number of bibliographic records in the system is now over 7 million. The libraries also have access to several citation data bases through the online catalog: ERIC (1966-present); the IAC Expanded Academic (1980-present) and Business (1982-present) indexes; and two H. W. Wilson science indexes—Biological/Agricultural and Applied Science/Technology (both 1988-present). At this time, the heaviest on line usage of the system is in the public catalog, called LUIS, which is averaging about 2 million searches per month. Table 1 identifies the nine universities and their data base sizes.

The mainframe hardware needs of FCLA are supplied on a cost basis by a service contract with the Florida Northeast Regional Data Center (NERDC), another agency affiliated with the University of Florida. The software runs on a large IBM processor, using MVS and CICS. FCLA currently uses over 50 billion bytes of on-line disk storage. NERDC supplies all personnel support for the hardware and operating systems, so that FCLA staff need only be concerned with the application programming and support. This has worked out very well for both NERDC and FCLA (and therefore the state of Florida) in allowing both groups to benefit from the economies of scale resulting from the large installation.

FCLA has a staff of only fifteen, consisting of the director, two assistant directors (for computer services and library services), four librarians, five programmers, and three administrative support staff. This is supplemented by on-site support on a part-time basis by one or two staff librarians at each university.

FCLA Governance and Operations

As an agency of the Florida SUS, FCLA is technically known as a Type I center, which is SUS jargon meaning that it serves more than one of the nine universities. There are other types of centers which may serve only one or a few universities. FCLA is one of the few centers that serves all nine. Other Type I centers include the University Presses of Florida and the Florida Solar Energy Center. It is interesting to note that some of the established Type I centers (and smaller semi-independent units of the SUS) are included in the Florida Statutes as legal entities. Others, like FCLA, are not, and their establishment and continuation are based mainly on the inclusion of a line item for each in the state budget.

All centers, including Type I centers, are administratively attached to one of the universities to take advantage of that university's resources for providing administrative support, and to minimize the number of staff assigned to the SUS headquarters in Tallahassee. The University of Florida (UF) serves as host to FCLA, and provides administrative services such as purchasing, payroll, and personnel. In other words, UF insures that FCLA conforms to the rules and regulations of the SUS and the State of Florida. The FCLA director reports to the UF vice president for academic affairs. The University of Florida addresses its responsibility to the other eight universities through the SUS Council of Academic Vice Presidents, a nine-member body which reviews budgets and plans for multi-university activities. As an example of the close administrative link FCLA has to UF, the FCLA librarians are required to pursue tenure and promotion through the same channels and following the same criteria as the UF library faculty.

The FCLA director also responds to a twelve member advisory board that includes a representative from each of the nine universities, appointed by their respective academic vice presidents. These representatives are the directors of the main libraries at each university. In addition to the library directors, the board includes a vice-chancellor of the Board of Regents, a representative from the community colleges (the director of the College Center for Library Automation—CCLA), and the state librarian. The board is strictly advisory, does not elect officers, and the chair is appointed by the SUS Council of Academic Vice Presidents.

There are four standing committees of the FCLA board. These committees do much of the work of the board and provide the opportunity for opinions to be expressed and for the participants to ratify projects. Sharing a single copy of library software necessitates cooperation and the reaching of consensus on many issues. Two of the committees are composed of board members and two of library middle managers.

The first two committees, the Priorities and Budget (P&B) Committee and the Equipment Committee, are composed of three board members each, with their chairs appointed by the chair of the FCLA advisory board. The latter two committees, the Technical Services Committee (TSC) and the Public Services Committee (PSC), are composed of library middle managers from the thirteen administratively independent (that is, including the law and health sciences units as well as the "main") libraries. The members choose a chair by consensus.

The P&B Committee usually meets two to three weeks before the FCLA board which, in normal circumstances, meets quarterly. The responsibility of this committee is to review the status of FCLA's budget, to evaluate the progress of various projects, and to make recommendations to the full Board about situations which may affect either project priorities or the budget. One of its primary responsibilities is to review the FCLA's annual work plan, which is developed jointly by the Technical and Public Services Committees.

The Equipment Committee decides how the monies budgeted for equipment purchases will be allocated across the SUS. In past years, this amount has fluctuated between $1.8 million in the first year and less than $100,000 in later years. A formula was developed that attempted to factor in variables such as the student body size, collection size, number of physical locations (branches), number of technical processing centers and other special needs. The committee also tries to anticipate technological changes that could produce demands not yet being considered by the libraries. Legislative policy for funding state agencies includes regular infusions of monies to replace equipment, but in practice, the funds allocated are not adequate to the formula accepted as legislative policy. Nor are agencies, including universities, allowed to depreciate aging equipment or build a fund for replacement. Consequently, requests for new appropriations must be made with no assurance that monies will be available.

The Technical Services Committee (TSC) was the first operational committee formed by the FCLA board. It began its work in 1984 with the consideration of the issue of single versus separate data bases for the different institutions. The members of the committee are mostly heads of technical services or cataloging at the nine main libraries plus the two law and two health sciences libraries in the SUS. This committee examines issues related to cataloging, authority control, acquisitions, and serial check-in functions of NOTIS, and makes recommendations to the FCLA staff and the advisory board on appropriate actions to take.

Similar in function and makeup to the TSC, the Public Services Committee (PSC) is involved in the areas of the on-line catalog, circulation, and reference functions of the automated library system. The first year, the committee spent a great deal of time in developing printed user guides and a manual for SUS reference staff. Since each university has its own data base and could establish independent circulation policies within the NOTIS software framework, the circulation function has not required the same degree of coordination. Recent projects to acquire and mount journal citation data bases has provided new opportunities for cooperation and consensus-building for the PSC.

Once a year, under normal conditions, the TSC and PSC meet together for the purpose of setting priorities for enhancements, developing the annual FCLA work plan, and making recommendations to the advisory board in these matters. The members of these two committees share perspectives on the system and discuss alternative strategies in a statesmanlike manner. The character of these committees has done much to make the FCLA project the success it is.

From time to time, ad hoc committees and subcommittees have been formed to deal with specific issues. For example, a subcommittee on interlibrary lending drafted a policy statement for the use of telefacsimile devices for interlibrary loan, and the Reference Database Subcommittee conducted a comprehensive study of the use of electronic reference data bases within the SUS. Whenever it is necessary to bring in functional expertise in a particular area, the FCLA board will, if possible, approve an ad hoc committee to do the job.

FCLA Funding

FCLA is funded as part of the SUS, through the University of Florida. When the center was first established, a separate line item existed in the state budget for the first three years of funding. Now FCLA's budget requests are included as separate items in the University of Florida's educational and general (E&G) budget. There are four components to a university's budget: salaries, general expense, electronic data processing (EDP), and operating capital outlay (OCO). FCLA's budget has this same breakdown. In the first two years of operation, as the SUS libraries were gearing up, OCO was the predominant budget component. The purchase and installation of terminals, printers, control units, and modems was going on while the FCLA staff worked on getting data processed and loaded, phone lines installed, and users trained. After those first two years, as might be expected, EDP became the major expense item. This budget category supports disk storage; costs to manipulate data during loading, indexing, archiving and reporting; and the interactive online use costs for staff and patrons. Of the current budget, salaries represent 18 percent; general expense, 22 percent; OCO, 1 percent; and EDP, 59 percent. Almost 40 percent of the expense category is earmarked for Research Libraries Group (RLG) membership and use fees. The FCLA budget has averaged about 5 percent of the total budget for all of the SUS libraries.

Chronology of Centralization

The SUS has an established history of centralized planning and funding for automation that has affected the libraries. Since six of the nine universities were founded in the last thirty-five years, this is not surprising. The university libraries and many of the community college libraries were provided with necessary funding in 1973 to become members of SOLINET and use OCLC. Shortly thereafter, most of the major libraries (public and academic) in Florida received funding from the Florida Division of Library Services (Florida's State Library) to begin a retrospective conversion project called COMCAT. This project had a long-range impact on the universities because it was the first of a series of projects that resulted in the libraries having a substantial portion of their cataloged collections in MARC format when FCLA began. At FCLA's inception, the portion of the card catalog holdings available in MARC format ranged from 99.6 percent at Florida International University to 45.5 percent at the University of Florida. The average over all the SUS institutions was 71.3 percent for all monographs and serials.[5]

In 1978, the larger SUS libraries were in need of automated support for circulation activity. After receiving several independent requests for such systems, the SUS decided that a single request for proposal (RFP) would be written. This would be used to acquire separate, stand-alone systems of the same type for all of the SUS libraries. CL Systems, Inc. was awarded the contract and seven of the nine libraries installed CLSI systems in 1979 and 1980. There was no coordination of implementation parameters. The systems were different from the beginning and there was no attempt to link them. Two of the universities, UF and the University of South Florida (USF), did not acquire CLSI systems. In 1981, UF purchased software (now marketed as NOTIS) developed by Northwestern University. USF decided to postpone its decision and re-examine the options later.

During the 1983/84 fiscal year, the SUS again received budget requests for library automation support (hardware and software) from several of the libraries. USF was in desperate need of a system to replace an obsolete batch automated circulation system since the hardware could no longer be maintained. Some of the CLSI users needed upgrades and wanted to expand functionality of their software to provide such things as on-line catalogs. Some wanted a completely new, fully integrated system to replace their CLSI circulation systems. UF wanted funds to expand the NOTIS system to include more of the branch libraries and to implement additional functions of the system. All of these requests reached the BOR at the same time. The result was the decision that there should be an SUS-wide plan which would provide economies of scale and facilitate SUS-wide resource sharing. During that year, rapid plans were made, which culminated in a budget request to the state legislature for $4 million in initial funding to establish FCLA and to expand the NOTIS system running at UF to the other eight universities. After the legislature appropriated $3.1 million, the SUS prepared a revised plan to fit the allocation. At its request, a five-year plan with a budget was submitted to the BOR within a month after funds were appropriated.

Somewhere along the way, the SUS plan was interpreted to be the first phase of a broader plan to include other Florida libraries. What was not clear was just which libraries and what functions should be supported. Over the next few years, several attempts were made by the legislature to get clarification on this issue.

THE PROVISO WARS

When the Florida legislature allocates money for a specific purpose, it normally attaches strings to that money by using "proviso" language in the line item. For example, the proviso for the FCLA funding in 1984 was:

Funds in Specific Appropriation 507B for developing an automated library system shall be expended based on a plan to be approved by the Division of Library Services of the Department of State. The plan shall include the State University System, private institutions, community colleges, public libraries, and other library resources available within the state and by interstate cooperative agreements. Provided further that all university libraries will be supported by single software systems for principal library functions, that files will be available through FIRN for other educational units of the state and that required computer systems will be located with and operated by the State University System Regional Data Centers and be an integral part of FIRN. Up to nine positions may be established associated with this appropriation; however, no funds shall be used for salary adjustments for existing positions. Funds in this appropriation may be used for Research Libraries Group memberships.[6]

The multitype library plan referred to in the first sentence was in development at the time of FCLA's creation, so release of the first year's funding was delayed until the state librarian submitted a letter of approval for the SUS five-year plan that had been submitted to the BOR. The above quoted sentences are relevant to the university libraries and they dictated what FCLA could do. In the first year, nine positions were filled and the SUS libraries were connected to the host system via the SUS component of the Florida Information Resources Network (FIRN), a telecommunications network funded by the state Department of Education. The single software system (NOTIS) remained at the Northeast Regional Data Center (NERDC) on the UF campus while the other data centers assisted with the telecommunications link and network support. The last sentence mandated that approximately 10 percent of the FCLA budget at that time would be used for RLG. The original intent was an SUS-wide membership for all nine universities, but this was not acceptable to RLG. This attempt by the legislature to promote system-wide activities met resistance in the form of the RLG's membership criteria. Consequently, only FSU and UF became full member/partners of RLG. The remaining seven have had search access only.

FCLA was not exempt from proviso in later years as the legislature worked on accomplishing its goal of centralization of library automation for all higher education. The 1985 proviso stated:

Funds in Specific Appropriation 519 for developing an automated library system shall be expended based on a plan to be approved by the Division of Library Services of the Department of State. The plan shall include the State University System, private institutions, community colleges, public libraries, and other library resources available within the state and by interstate cooperative agreements.[7]

The language describing the conditions imposed on the universities was omitted, presumably because those conditions had or were being met. The multitype library plan was still unformed; no definition of its extent had been documented nor had a budget request been made.

The 1986 and 1987 FCLA proviso was the same, but the specific appropriations were spread across several budget components, reflecting the move of the FCLA budget from a single category to separate categories within the SUS' total budget. In addition, the 1987 proviso included a charge to the Postsecondary Education Planning Commission (PEPC):

From funds provided in Specific Appropriation 537A, the Postsecondary Education Planning Commission shall conduct an evaluation of the Florida Center for Library Automation. The evaluation shall include an analysis of the following issues: program mission, governance, scope of the project, and short term and long term fiscal implications. The Commission shall submit a report...[8]

This charge to PEPC resulted from a legislative dissatisfaction with FCLA's progress in expanding service to other libraries. There was confusion in interpretation of intent. When the SUS libraries sought funding for internal automation, there was much rhetoric thrown out about resource sharing, access, and benefits to the general citizenry. The conflict lay in whether the legislature envisioned a limited-function statewide data base (i.e., a union catalog with some type of interlibrary lending function) or a single system supporting all library functions: cataloging, acquisitions, serials control, circulation, and the on-line public access catalog. The former might have been feasible. The latter would have been daunting given the existence of over 500 libraries in Florida, excluding the more than 2,000 K-12 schools. The SUS, understandably, became very protective of the resource that FCLA had become.

In February, 1988, the PEPC produced the results of its study of FCLA and Florida libraries' automation and networking.[9] Within the thirteen recommendations PEPC made were several that attempted to clarify FCLA's role as an agency of the SUS. In addition, PEPC strongly advocated a separate automation program for community colleges and for the State Library, with appropriate funding.

Frustrated in its first attempt, the legislature tried again. The 1988 FCLA proviso reads:

Expenditures in funds in Specific Appropriations 528, 529, 530, 531, and 545 for further development of library automation by Florida Center for Library Automation (FCLA) and the FCLA plan for 1989–94 shall reflect the findings of the FIRN Applications Development Group as reported to the Legislature December, 1988.[10]

FIRN was now assigned to study FCLA, "evaluate the progress made by . . . [FCLA] in pursuit of its objectives in accordance with its approved plan" and to determine the feasibility of a statewide on-line catalog to include the SUS and community college libraries. FIRN was also to address technological obstacles, recommend strategies, and produce a schedule and cost estimates for the proposed catalog.[11] To cover all the bases, the legislative staff had also added a proviso to the community college appropriation. Approximately $23,000 was allocated to the State Board of Community Colleges for the development of a plan for automating the college libraries. The report was to be done in consultation with FCLA and the state librarian, and was to incorporate the FIRN study. This plan was also to include a time line and cost estimates.[12]

All of this proviso upheaval reflects the legislative desire to find a solution to the problem of getting comparable support of library automation for the community colleges. Thus, in the summer and fall of 1988, FCLA was the subject of another study: a project of the Senate Governmental Operations Committee (GOVOP) staff which was assigned by the senate president "to analyze the benefits, costs, and feasibility of expanding the State University System automated library network and data base to incorporate the holdings of, and to allow access by, other libraries in the state."[13]

The FIRN report, submitted in December 1988, recommended that FCLA be funded to expand its services to the community colleges, but did not address the issue of other libraries. It recommended that governance should be expanded to encompass equitable representation of SUS and community college libraries. FCLA participated in the development of the budget projections and time line. Charged with basing its resource estimates on the assumption of total parity with the SUS libraries for projected volume of use and level of support, the FIRN plan called for a five-year implementation schedule, an increase in the central support staff by nineteen people, and an additional $19 million between 1989 and 1993. These figures were based on extrapolating from the experience of supporting the nine SUS libraries and projecting them onto the twenty-eight colleges.

Concurrent with the FIRN and GOVOP studies of FCLA, King Research, Inc. conducted the study assigned to the Division of Community Colleges. Its plan, produced in January 1989, called for a separate system with its own support center and governance. This was a departure from the FIRN report and the community colleges' original position that strongly called for inclusion in the FCLA program. The King plan also provided a budget and implementation schedule requested by the legislature. A new community college library automation center would acquire a turnkey system through the bid process, install the central site and library hardware, load the data bases, and train the library staff in all twenty-eight colleges between July 1989 and June 1992. This would require a staff of eight FTE and a total five year budget of $14.3 million. The study was based on the responses from several library automated systems vendors to an request for information (RFI) issued by King. Unlike the FIRN study, the RFI did not require parity with the SUS or estimates based on extrapolations of actual SUS usage.

The GOVOP report released in April 1989 was, perhaps, the most comprehensive analysis and delineation of the history of FCLA and the issues surrounding its existence. The essence of this report's recommendations was the creation of the Florida Commission for Library Automation, the transferral of FCLA's staff to the new commission, the development of a plan for a statewide computer-based library network and data base, and the approval of plans and budgets for all libraries and other entities intending to participate in this new statewide network.

The net result of all these studies was the creation and funding of a separate automation project for the community colleges. While two of the four studies had strongly recommended expansion of FCLA services, apparently the unresolved issue of governance equity, in combination with the newly awakened but clear message from the community colleges for autonomy and an independent system, swayed the legislature. That body may have just finally grown tired of the issue. The 1989 appropriations provisos for the various bodies called for the establishment of a separate community college library automation agency, the acquisition of a vendor supplied library turnkey system, a three-year implementation plan, networking via FIRN, and an annual budget of approximately $3 million. The new agency is called the College Center for Library Automation (CCLA). The Legislature interjected its desire for statewide access by mandating that CCLA and FCLA systems be linked to one another. By June 1992, the Data Research Associates system had been chosen, CCLA had a staff of twenty-one, central site hardware was installed, and the data bases of five libraries were loaded, with staff trained and the system operational in the cataloging and on-line catalog components. The CCLA system is called LINCC (Library Information Network for Community Colleges).

In 1991/92, the Division of Library and Information Services (DLIS, a renamed DLS) received funding to upgrade its in-house system. It chose the same vendor that CCLA chose (DRA) and installation was complete by the end of fiscal 1992. The expectation is that the three systems, FCLA's LUIS, CCLA's LINCC and DLIS' as-yet-to-be-named system, would be able to link, thus forming a large portion of the statewide network desired by the legislature.

AFTER THE PROVISO WARS

During these years of being studied, FCLA was continuing to implement its original plan for the SUS. At the end of the first five-year plan (June, 1989), the SUS data bases had almost 5.5 million catalog records loaded, over 1,000 library terminals were installed, a union author/title index was in place, all libraries were operational on all desired subsystems, and the FCLA staffing plan was complete. Several features of the FCLA/SUS system were a direct result of legislative influence. Besides the creation of a centralized service, the decision to have nine separate data bases was largely driven by the expectation that there would be an operational system by the end of the first year of funding. Given that the staff had to be hired and the archive data of eight libraries had to be acquired and processed, there was not much time for negotiating the types of operational agreements that a shared data base would require. Since NOTIS does not allow a "master record" structure, a single data base still requires redundant catalog records in order to adequately support the holdings and item data. That amount of redundancy is not significantly less than what is needed for separate data bases.

Separate data bases allowed each university to have its own indexes, which meant that the students could search their own university's catalog

Table 2
FCLA System Statistics

	1985/1986	1992/1993
SUS catalog records	3,600,000	7,000,000
Article citation records	0	5,600,000
On-line transactions	12,000,000	170,000,000
Circulations	0	3,000,000
Student FTE	90,000	113,000
FCLA staff	8	15.5

and did not have to search a combined or union index of the entire SUS. NOTIS did not support limiting search results by location during this period. The legislature, however, did want users to be able to find a publication through a single search, so FCLA created a merged or union catalog of all the author and title entries in the individual catalogs. Only the index entries are replicated; the actual data records (cataloging, circulation, etc...) are not. Another feature that FCLA developed was a menu system that enables users to switch data bases easily. This too was not offered by NOTIS at the time.

With the completion of its first phase of operations, FCLA was ready to begin a new five-year plan for the SUS. This new plan encompassed the development of keyword/Boolean search software, expansion of the union catalog to include subject access, journal citation data bases such as ERIC and other commercial products, support for document delivery, and linking the SUS automated system to other systems. All these new ventures required new funding. Two events have resulted in FCLA not only getting no new funding, but actually having a budget reduction. The legislature initially zero-funded the new FCLA projects until the community colleges reach parity with the SUS. Then, the economic recession of 1990–1992 caused budget cuts that affected all agencies. Despite the reductions, FCLA continued to move forward with keyword/Boolean and the loading of the ERIC and other journal citation data bases. This was accomplished with the financial help of the libraries and negotiation of new pricing algorithms with NERDC for disk and on-line use costs. Table 2 illustrates the changes that have occurred in resource requirements and usage since the first year of operation.

COPING IN A PERIOD OF BUDGETARY RESTRAINT

The economic recession of 1990–1992 caused budget cuts for all state agencies. Florida law requires a balanced state budget, in other words, no deficit spending. With state revenues decreasing in 1990/91, the Florida cabinet made budget cuts to the Department of Education. The cuts were passed down the line, through the BOR, SUS, UF, and finally to FCLA. Although the Florida Supreme Court ruled that the cabinet did not have necessary authority to cut budgets, a special legislative session resulted in the same action. For education, an erosion in funding had begun earlier than 1990/91 as the proportion of general revenue funds for DOE started decreasing in inverse proportion to the income produced by the Florida Lottery. Originally sold to the public as "enhancement" funding, lottery income gradually began to supplant general revenue funding. This has meant a reduction in "enhancement" programs as money was shifted to cover the gaps in funding for basic services. It has also meant less stable budgets since lottery money is often doled out late in the fiscal year but still with the stipulation that it be spent within that year. Consequently, DOE agencies have more difficulty forecasting their budgets and making spending commitments.

Between June 1989 and June 1992, the FCLA budget was reduced by 10 percent. The reduction was felt in many areas. Student population continued to grow during these years, resulting in increased usage of the system at a time when there was no new money to cover that increased usage. The new keyword/Boolean function and the journal citation data bases were financed out of cost reductions based on upgrading to newer hardware technology, realization of some economies of scale, and volume discounts from NERDC, the SUS data center used by FCLA. While FCLA did not lose any positions in the cuts, when one of its User Services Librarians resigned, the position was frozen and the salary monies for that fiscal year had to be returned to the state.

For the libraries, positions were not just frozen, they were permanently cut from the budget. This means that it will take years to recover those positions once economic conditions improve. The effect of this reduction in library staff (while student body sizes have continued to increase) was a greater demand for system functionality to replace activities previously performed manually. With no increase in FCLA staff over several years, the ability to meet this demand has been limited. Adding to the staff reduction stresses, by order of the legislature, there were no salary raises for state employees in fiscal years 1991/92 and 1992/93. Retention of staff was difficult under such conditions, thus causing further stress on existing staff trying to cope with a larger user population and no reduction in the pressures to provide new library services.

Travel by FCLA and other SUS employees was restricted as well. The FCLA advisory board had a hiatus of almost two years because travel restrictions and political considerations prohibited the members from meeting in fiscal years 1990/91 and 1991/92. The review and approval of plans and budgets was conducted via conference calls. The consequence of this hiatus has been a paucity of long-term and strategic planning for resource sharing and cooperation by the libraries and FCLA. The Equipment Committee was disbanded due to the fact that FCLA received almost no equipment monies since fiscal year 1989/90. This situation combined with the fact of aging peripheral equipment is creating a potential problem for ongoing support of libraries. The PSC and TSC could not meet individually or jointly in 1991 again due to the lack of travel funds and a moratorium on statewide meetings for political reasons. A meeting was finally authorized for mid-1992 which enabled FCLA library staff to map out a plan of operation for the 1992/93 fiscal year. Restrictions on travel and meetings led FCLA to find an alternative to face-to-face meetings for communicating among the libraries. An electronic mail discussion list was created to broadcast information from FCLA and to gather input from the liaisons and representatives from the two operational committees. The list, open to all library staff, provides the added benefit of broadening the base of users who are kept informed of issues and system changes. The list is a great benefit, but it is not a complete substitute for meetings and on-site training. Face-to-face meetings are needed to allow the give and take of the discussions to mold a plan and to develop a consensus for ongoing development and direction.

CONCLUSION

In 1991, the SUS successfully lobbied the legislature for changes in how monies are allocated to the BOR and then distributed to the universities. Rather than strict budget categories and inflexibility in determining how the monies could be spent, the universities were given authority to move money from one category to another without requiring the approval of the Cabinet. In exchange for this new authority, the SUS is expected to define performance measures and to report on how they are meeting those measures on an annual basis. There are still a number of restrictions, such as requiring legislative approval for all new positions. The budget cuts of 1991/92 have meant that this new flexibility has mostly been used to try to patch the holes in the dike and shore up the defenses against the ongoing erosion of resources. Once Florida is in a more positive financial position, the real benefit of increased flexibility in managing the budgets may be realized.

For FCLA, there will be a continuation of the present course toward expanding the functionality of the NOTIS software and the support of additional data bases. Because the SUS libraries agreed to sharing the cost of site licenses, FCLA has been able to load ERIC, IAC's Business and Expanded Academic Indexes, and Wilson's Applied Science/Technology and Biological/Agricultural Indexes. These have proved to be enormously popular and have resulted in increased pressure to provide more such data bases on-line. The development of a keyword/Boolean function has enhanced access to these data bases and the on-line catalogs, thus providing users with increased abilities to find their desired information.

New funding would not only allow FCLA to acquire more data bases, but also enable the replacment of terminals with more powerful workstations. This will be needed for two reasons: the age of the existing peripheral equipment and the need for the central system to provide access to full-text and image data bases. This latter function requires a network that can support greater bandwidth and workstations that can display images. Access to more sources of information will be a key aspect of FCLA's services in the next few years as well. The libraries are being expected to link to their respective campus-wide information systems (or CWISs), which means that FCLA must make it possible for the central system to provide that link. In addition, there is increasing expectation that the on-line catalog will provide access to the wider world envisioned by the National Research and Education Network (NREN). Again, FCLA will have to be prepared to support that connectivity.

One way FCLA is planning to provide connectivity is through a project funded by a federal Department of Education Title IID grant. FCLA is developing the ability for its NOTIS system to support the Z39.50 Computer to Computer Link Protocol. With this software, the SUS library system could link to any other information system that also supported Z39.50 in a seamless manner that would not require its users to interact with the other system's user interface. This will make it much easier for users to move from one system to the other without needing to know how the other system works. It is expected that the CCLA DRA system will be enhanced similarly.

Another area of opportunity only beginning to be explored is the pending creation of a 10th university in the southwestern area of the state. The BOR is interested in building a university for the 21st century. Included in this concept is the "electronic library." It remains to be seen just what this will mean for the services expected of FCLA, but the opportunities are endless. Would that the resources will match them.

NOTES

1. Ralph Kimbrough, Kern Alexander, and James Wattenbarger. "Government and Education" in *Florida's Politics and Government*, edited by Manning J. Dauer (Gainesville: University of Florida Press, 1984).

2. Frank DePalma, *The Governance of Education in Florida* (Columbus: Educational Governance Project, Ohio State University, 1973).

3. Kimbrough, "Government and Education."

4. *Ibid*.

5. Michele Dalehite. "Florida Center for Library Automation: the Organization" in *Advances in Library Automation and Networking*, vol. 3 (Greenwich, Conn.: JAI Press, 1989).

6. Florida. "Session Law Chapter No. 84–220, Specific Appropriation 507B," *1984 Supplement to Florida Statutes, 1983* (Tallahassee, Fla., 1984).

7. Florida, Legislature, *Laws of Florida, 1985*, Chapter 85–119, Specific Appropriation 519 (Tallahassee, Fla., 1985).

8. Florida, Legislature, *Laws of Florida, 1987*, Chapter 87–98, Specific Appropriation 537A (Tallahassee, Fla., 1987).

9. Florida, Department of Education, Postsecondary Education Planning Commission, *Automation and Networking for Florida Libraries* (Tallahassee, Florida: 1988).

10. Florida, Legislature, *Laws of Florida, 1988*, Chapter 88–555. Specific Appropriation 528 (Tallahassee, Fla., 1988).

11. *Ibid.*, Specific Appropriation 366.

12. *Ibid.*, Specific Appropriation 496.

13. Florida, Senate, Committee in Governmental Operations, *A Review of the Benefits, Costs, and Feasibility of a Statewide Network Linking the Libraries in Florida* (Tallahassee, Fla., April, 1989).

Chapter 10

Public Academic Libraries in Massachusetts— Reorganization Redux

Janet Freedman

The former President of the university where I am employed was known for his frequent use of aphorisms. One of his favorites was "Life is what happens when you're planning it." After just a few months as library director in a Massachusetts university, I had discovered firsthand how apt this expression was to our circumstances.

Massachusetts considers itself the education state. Its proud claims in this regard include the birthplace of private higher education with the establishment of Harvard University in 1636 and the founding of the first public school. Such noble achievements coexist with more dubious distinctions, including a statistic that is relevant to the topic of this chapter. Within the state that boasts some of the richest private academic library collections in the world, the expenditure per student for public academic libraries is the lowest in the nation.[1] The public colleges and universities struggle for recognition among the world-renowned private institutions and within an environment in which political influence plays as important a role as academic excellence.

Perhaps the most dramatic example of how politics takes precedence over planning is the way in which Massachusetts public higher education was reorganized in 1984. A committee had been appointed to conduct a detailed study and make recommendations for a revised structure. At the time I was Vice President and Program Chair of our association of public academic librarians and was immensely proud of the fact that I had recruited the Chair of the study committee to address the group at its annual conference. A few days before the conference, however, the state legislature passed a higher education reorganization plan as a sidebar to the state budget appropriation bill, completely ignoring the established structure that had been charged with the task. Rumor was that the legislation had been drafted shortly before its passage by two politicians on a plane returning from a business trip.

The legislature established a Board of Regents to consolidate the three segments of public higher education—community colleges, state colleges, and universities—under one governing agency. Although each institution still retained its own Board of Trustees, the new governing board had strong budgetary and program authority.

In June of 1991 the public higher education system was overhauled again and further centralized. Throughout the 1991 academic year, the business of higher education was nearly suspended while a variety of scenarios for reorganizing the public community college, college, and university system were reviewed. Legislators, educators, and lay people responded to several competing visions of a system for delivering postsecondary education. The plan that was finally enacted by the legislature in June 1991 dismantled the Board of Regents and put in its place a Higher Education Coordinating Committee (HECC) that reported to a newly created Cabinet post of Secretary of Education. That office became responsible for all public education in the Commonwealth from kindergarten through graduate school. Along with the creation of an additional layer of bureaucracy, the legislature created a five-institution university. Two regional universities, the University of Lowell, and Southeastern Massachusetts University, which had previously existed with their own Boards of Trustees, were incorporated into the University of Massachusetts under a single "superboard."

What happened to the public higher education libraries during these machinations?

Happily, the library directors have maintained remarkably cordial and effective working relationships, so that there usually has been concerted effort in the interest of all the libraries. A statewide organization of public academic library directors, the Massachusetts Conference of Chief Librarians in Public Higher Education Institutions (MCCLPHEI), has existed since 1968. The body has served as the principal vehicle for discussion and action on a number of fronts.

MCCLPHEI's initial activism was in response to the large gaps in the collections of the public academic libraries that threatened the general accreditation of a number of institutions (see charts 10–1, 10–3, 10–4 and 10–5). Chart 10–6 illustrates the inferior level of the acquisitions budget of one Massachusetts public academic library in relation to peer institutions in the northeast. That crisis was met through a sizable bond issue

Chart 10–1
Library Expenditures Per FTE Student

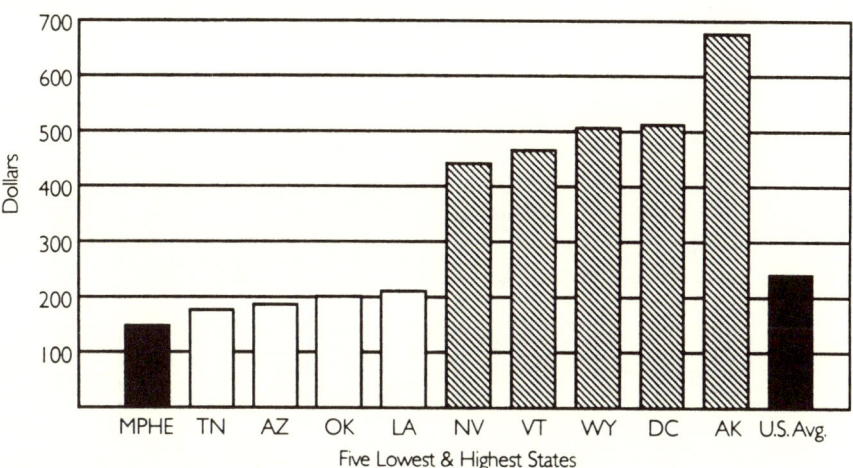

for the Books for College Libraries (BCL) Project whereby funds were distributed on a formula basis (recommended by MCCLPHEI) to each institution, which could then choose the resources to support the needs of its curriculum from the Books for College Libraries list developed in California. From fiscal year 1969 to fiscal year 1975, $1,500,000 per year was provided for materials and $175,000 for operating costs, plus an extraordinary outlay of $2,400,000 in fiscal year 1975, for the state college segment that had been the target of particular criticism. The materials were purchased centrally and cataloged at the University of Massachusetts at Amherst.

The BCL Project was followed by the establishment of a special line in the state budget for library materials for the public higher education libraries. The Educational Reference Materials (ERM) line was intended to assure that there is stable funding to maintain and build library collections. In a state where support for public higher education is particularly vulnerable to vicissitudes in the economic and political climate, an annual appropriation earmarked for the libraries has been essential. No matter how needy the parent institutions have been for funds for other campus projects, the ERM monies can be used only for collection development. The funding for library materials has varied widely from year to year, making planning extraordinarily difficult, but even when the amount has been small, each library is assured of some funds to continue journals and other serials publications.[2]

A Standards Committee within MCCLPHEI, representing librarians within each of the public higher education segments, has been charged with recommending a distribution formula. The distribution plan is dis-

Chart 10–2
ERM Purchasing Power (in FY 1979 Dollars)

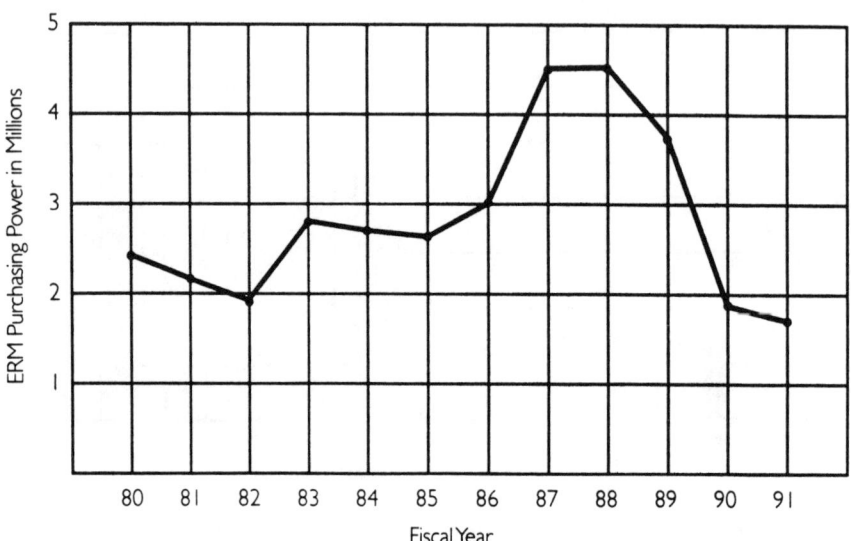

Chart 10–3
Number of Titles Per FTE Student

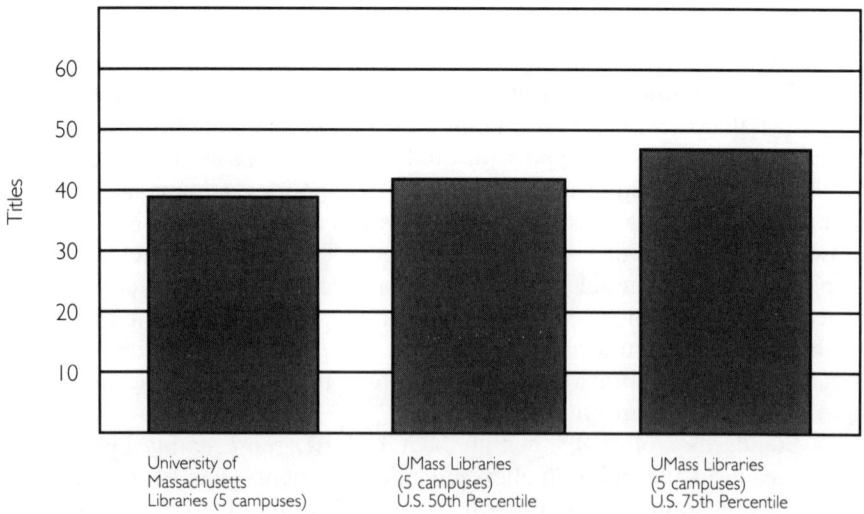

Chart 10–4
Current Serials Subscriptions

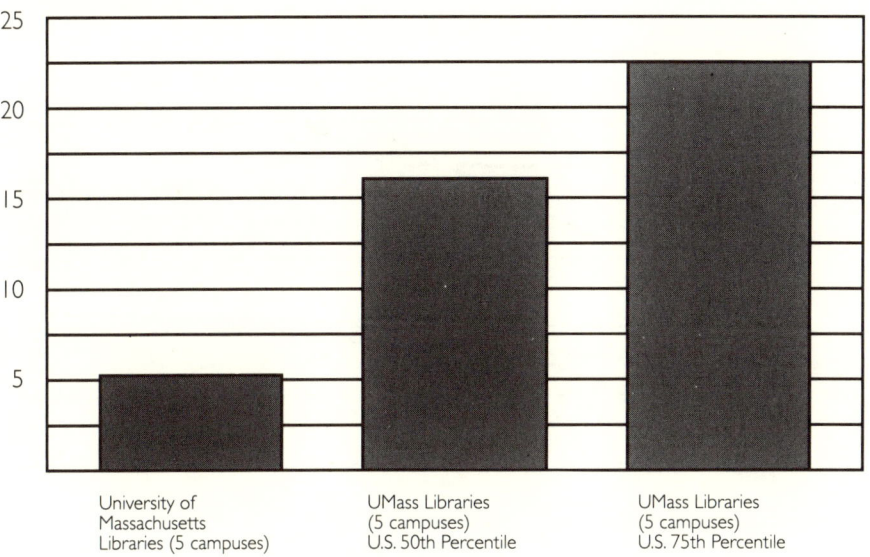

Chart 10–5
Library Staff Per FTE Student

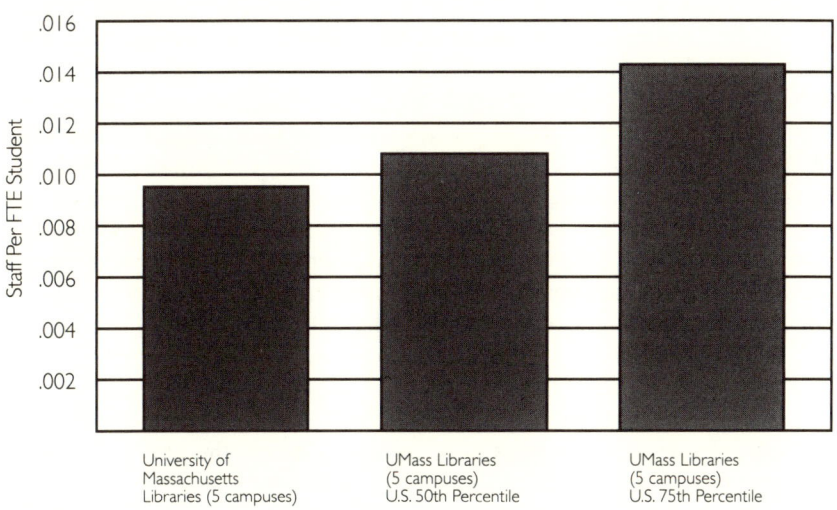

Chart 10-6
Library Budget UMass Amherst vs Ten Northeast Peers

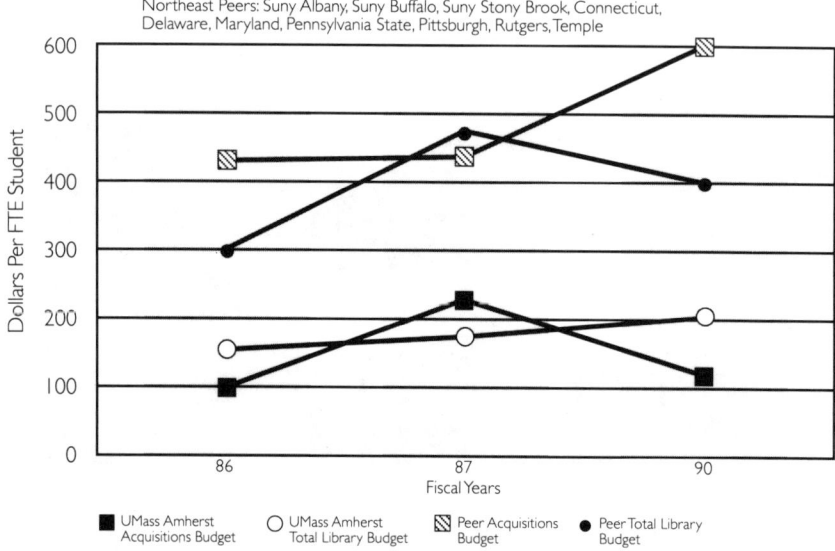

cussed and approved by all members annually. The formula has been adopted by the system's governing bodies, with the exception of one year when a local legislator adjusted the distribution plan to provide additional funds to the community college in his district based on his belief that there was an error in the initial data on which the allocation was based that disadvantaged that institution.

Because the total amount of ERM funding was never adequate to support all the needs of the libraries (see chart 10–2), and in response to the sharp reductions beginning in fiscal year 1989,[3] the members of the MCCLPHEI determined that a plan was needed to guide the future of the twenty-nine public academic libraries. A letter was written to the Vice Chancellor for Academic and Student Affairs of the Board of Regents proposing that a task force be authorized to study current conditions and propose an action plan to address them. After several months delay, a Statewide Academic Library Planning Committee was appointed and charged with conducting a needs assessment and enumerating recommendations to respond to its findings. The delay was caused, in part, by MCCLPHEI's failure to address its request through the Council of Presidents rather than directly to the staff of the Board of Regents. In retrospect, it is difficult to assess whether this innocent circumvention of protocol was negative or positive; it is possible that the charge to study the libraries actually received a more immediate response because of the attention drawn to an apparently inappropriate process.

The Statewide Planning Committee was created by soliciting nominations from Presidents, Chancellors, MCCLPHEI and the Massachusetts State College Association, the collective bargaining agency for the majority of higher education faculty and professional staff. The Committee was composed primarily of library directors, but included an academic vice-president, who served as Chair, an academic dean, a representative of the Board of Regents Academic Services staff, the Director of the Regents' computer network and a media center director.

Several months of meetings took place to determine the approach to the study. A number of documents, most emphasizing new technologies and library resource sharing, were circulated to provide the committee members with a common background for the study. Models of other state planning processes were gathered and studied, and detailed discussion took place on how best to assess and meet the expectations of the audiences for the final document. There was lengthy debate on how much information should be collected and presented, some committee members arguing for what they believed should be a very thorough, well-documented report, others arguing that an overabundance of information would obscure the clarity of the message that the committee wished to impart.

Eventually, the decision was made to begin the process of gathering information and set aside, for the time, the details to be presented in the final report. Four subcommittees were formed in the areas of collections, services and staffing, resource sharing, and facilities. Each subcommittee devised its own mechanism to collect information. The IPEDS survey was used as a template and expanded to include more detail and additional questions that committee members felt to be appropriate. Although much more information was collected than was reported in the final document, this data has proved useful to most of the libraries for planning on their own campuses. The Planning Committee Chair, together with the chairpersons of each subcommittee and a staff representative of the Board of Regents formed a Steering Committee that monitored the information-gathering process with regard to established time lines and did the final writing and editing of the report.

That report, *Learning at Risk: Long Range Plan for the Improvement of Massachusetts Public Higher Education Libraries*, was transmitted in April 1990 to the Interim Chancellor of the Board of Regents of Higher Education after review earlier in that month by the Presidents and Chancellors and the membership of MCCLPHEI. The letter of transmittal that accompanied the document attributed the weak condition of collections, facilities, and staff in the public academic libraries to "the intermittent attention and sporadic infusion of resources over time [that] has produced an inevitable deterioration of the ability of our educational institutions to provide high quality instruction, research and service to the citizens of the Commonwealth." The letter called on the Board to respond with "conviction and commitment: conviction in the principle that libraries are central to the educational process and commitment to achieve the tangible goal of providing our new society of lifelong learners with strong library collections housed in functional buildings, and staffed at realistic levels by an appropriate number of well-trained librarians and support personnel."[4]

The report outlined appropriate remedies to the crisis in the libraries, which are summarized below.

1. Increase funding for Massachusetts public higher education libraries to recover from critically low levels of support provided in the past and to strengthen collections, personnel, facilities, and interlibrary cooperation.
2. Establish standards for Massachusetts public higher education libraries that are consistent with national norms for professional and clerical employee staffing levels and ratios and provide a safe workplace.
3. Develop and implement institutional and statewide coordination efforts to facilitate access and delivery of information services throughout Massachusetts public higher education libraries.
4. Increase resource sharing capabilities and improve information services at Massachusetts public higher education libraries by automating and networking all applicable library functions.
5. Require acquisition of information search skills as an integral part of the educational experience for students at Massachusetts public higher education institutions.
6. Ensure active involvement of Massachusetts public higher education libraries in institutional and statewide academic planning and decision-making processes.
7. Establish institutional and Board of Regents standards for Massachusetts public higher education libraries which are consistent with national norms for adequate space, environmental conditions, and equipment.
8. Establish a process at the Board of Regents for the implementation of recommendations of this Plan, for the continuous development and monitoring of the condition of Massachusetts public higher education libraries, and for the coordination of statewide resource sharing.[5]

The report placed these recommendations within the context of the current and future library environment. The authors acknowledged major changes in the way information is now packaged and accessed, but emphasized that the primary function of the library as collector, organizer, and repository remains vital. It was further stressed that libraries are at the vanguard in acquiring and managing learning resources acquired via computer and telecommunications and are the central access point to the world of information on our campuses. The report reviewed the use of computers for cataloging, interlibrary loan, searching distant data bases, downloading searches, delivering content from other locations and reaching out to commercial sources of information while emphasizing that:

Even though these capabilities are increasing, it is essential that libraries possess the information resources that are needed on a continuing basis by its users. If libraries cannot fill the needs of even their own users then resource sharing is little more than the sharing of poverty. The library of the future will act as the repository of resources needed frequently by learners and faculty; however, the computer, automation systems and telecommunications connections and other information processing technology will turn the library into a window on the world of information for the user. It is critical that the libraries gear up for the new information access.[6]

Regrettably, both the Chancellor of the Board of Regents, who had commissioned the report, and the Vice Chancellor of Academic Affairs, who had overseen the creation of the Committee, had resigned from their positions before the final document was presented. Although the precise reasons for the departure of these two talented senior officials are not known, it is clear to those within and outside the system that the lack of support for their initiatives and the rumblings that the Board itself might be replaced in a reorganized Massachusetts public higher education system were obviously strong factors in their resignations. The document was received with appreciation and praise by the Interim Chancellor of the Board of Regents who spent time with representatives of the Committee in exploring strategies and next steps to move the recommendations forward. But simultaneously with the transmittal of the report, the debate over the reorganization of higher education in the Commonwealth became the focus of energy for all involved in and concerned with public higher education. As it was fighting for its continued existence, the Board of Regents that had authorized the study and report could do little more than give lip service to the issue of library planning and support. Within a short time, the expected reorganization occurred and MCCLPHEI members were faced with the need to develop new strategies to assure that the urgent needs of the public academic libraries would be addressed.

The President of MCCLPHEI immediately sent *Learning at Risk* to the new Secretary of Education and established contact with officials of the Higher Education Coordinating Committee (HECC). At the same time as the university, college, and community college libraries began working to make a united case for the implementation of the recommendations in *Learning at Risk*, the university librarians became aware that the legislation creating the newly structured public higher education system in Massachusetts left some room for speculation regarding the autonomy of the university segment in relationship to HECC. Thus one of the first tasks of the library directors of the newly organized University of Massachusetts was to place library needs on the agenda of that institution's new Board of Trustees. Thanks, in part, to the vocal concern of faculty at the University of Massachusetts, Amherst, the Chair of the Board of

Trustees of the University of Massachusetts was contacted early in that entity's formation and, through the President's Task Force on Academic and Student Affairs, a committee was charged with preparing a report on the five university libraries.

A Vice Chancellor at the University of Massachusetts, Boston, was appointed to coordinate the work of the committee, composed of the library directors and a faculty representative from each of the universities. The faculty members were helpful in articulating a vision for the report, while the library directors appropriately were assigned the function of gathering and analyzing data pertinent to their institutions to present within the two-month time frame assigned.

The charge from the Task Force enumerated five areas the Committee was to assess: 1) "Current Strengths and Weaknesses of the Libraries as a System." This charge requested information on the relationship of collections to the mission of the University as a whole and to the mission of each campus, how subject strengths complemented one another and the five-campus University, and how gaps affected each institution and the system; 2) "Potentials for Improved Access to Library Materials across the Campuses" sought to determine the potential benefits and limitations of interlibrary loan and electronic information sharing with attendant technical requirements and "possible costs, including cost savings" resulting from cooperation within the university system, with the twenty-four other public higher education institutions, and through other consortium relationships; 3) "Comment on the Issue of 'Selective Acquisitions' " was a request for recommendations for "principles to be used in determining whether campus libraries can be designated as principal repositories for the University as a whole in particular subject areas;" 4) "Addressing Fiscal Strictures as they Affect the Libraries" sought "reasonable estimates" of costs to maintain current collections at minimal levels, and a tentative plan to restore library funding to desirable (not luxurious) levels over a three year period, including strategies to allocate funds among the campuses and to "develop non-appropriated funds;" and 5) "Addressing the Goals/Accountability Imperative," called for "[r]ecommendations concerning appropriate response for the libraries to demands for goal definition and accountability measurement on the basis of those goals."[7]

Obviously, fulfilling these demanding charges proved difficult, not only due to the limited time frame, but also to the fact that the mission of the new system and of the institutions within it that were to be the foundation for defining library goals had not yet been determined (and were still not finalized as this report was prepared five months later). As work progressed, most committee members experienced increasing discomfort with the very premise of the charges that had been given. This feeling was expressed pointedly by the faculty representative from Amherst.

Rereading the drafts, I have grown uneasy about one key premise that lurks behind the charges put to the committee. I think we need to address directly assumptions about the apparent benefits conferred on each library by the new five campus reorganization. By making five libraries— hitherto separate and totally autonomous— part of a single system, do individual campuses necessarily gain anything?[8]

Indeed, since their inception the messages from the new University "superboard" and from the Higher Education Coordinating Council (HECC) have been that consolidation and centralization *will* save money. The elimination of duplication of books, journals— and instructional programs—is a clear goal, although the process for achieving the expected streamlining has not been outlined. Nor is there a sense of how effective the Secretary of Education, HECC, or the University Board of Trustees will be in countering the political opposition that is likely to accompany program cuts in particular institutions that serve local needs and interests.

Despite the feeling that the findings would not be heeded unless they conformed with the assumptions underlying the charges, the university committee devoted considerable time and energy to preparing the report. As with the earlier report, *Learning at Risk*, the work was divided among the library directors, who gathered data, prepared, and circulated for comments and revisions a draft for a particular section. The Chair integrated the separate sections into a complete report that went through several reviews by the entire Committee.

On February 25, 1992, the "Preliminary Report of the Libraries Committee" was presented to the Chair of the Academic and Student Affairs Task Force. As the Chair of the Libraries Committee explained: "In the course of drafting [the] report, the committee members recognized that several of these issues call for more detailed attention than could be accomplished in the two months of work available to the committee."[9]

This "preliminary report" contained six recommendations:

1) The Committee should continue to exist and be charged with preparing another report "to address the library system strengths and weaknesses, long term funding standards, appropriate funding mechanisms, measures to enhance resource sharing, and appropriate staffing levels."

2) The University invest in the technology that will enhance resource sharing among the five campus libraries. It was estimated that a minimum of $2.9 million will be required for equipment during the next two fiscal years in order to share resources effectively, and it was also recommended that about $100,000 per year be spent for membership in the Boston library Consortium.

3) The University include restoration of library appropriations among the highest of budget priorities for the University as a whole and for each campus. It was estimated that a minimum of $4 million would need to be added to the University library budgets during fiscal year 1993 and $12 million by 1995. These amounts

were based on the assumption that funding levels equivalent to the fiscal year 1992 Education Reference Materials appropriation will be maintained in the University budget whether or not there is a specific higher education line item.

4) The University support acquisition of information search skills as an integral part of the educational experience for students at all campuses of the University.

5) Each campus take specific measures to ensure that budget and planning procedures provide for integral participation of library representatives at senior levels.

6) Each campus ensure that libraries are involved in the work of ongoing relevant task forces, for example, the infrastructure and information systems working groups.[10]

Contrary to what were known to be hopes of the Board of Trustees that the five-university system could yield savings, the report emphasized that the libraries were in a state of crisis due to recent declines in what has never been adequate funding. The report reiterated the message of *Learning at Risk*, that the "functions of the libraries will be enhanced and modified by emerging technologies for information storage and retrieval" but noted that "access to the wide range of such technological systems is not currently available on our five campuses."[11] There was a re-emphasis, too, of the point that new technologies, even if they were available on the campuses, would not obviate the need for collections. The fact that the technologies, while expanding access and efficiency, would not cost less and might cost more was also put forth in the early pages of the report.

The body of the report revealed that, during the years of rapid expansion at each of the universities, library collection development had not been able to keep pace with academic program development. Funds began to be cut before any library could fulfill plans to build the required core collections to support new programs or, for that matter, to sustain long-established offerings. Where collection strengths existed, these had eroded due to recent budget cuts.

The present situation finds all the libraries with fewer journals than required and making few book purchases (in one case, a 90 percent cut from usual levels of book purchasing) in order to maintain serial subscriptions. Conditions at the flagship institution, Amherst, are offered to exemplify: staffing and acquisitions budgets at mid-1960s levels, standing among the 107 member Association of Research Libraries fallen from 49th in 1987 to 93rd in 1992, and hours of operation cut by 14 percent.[12] The report suggested that an additional $12,000,000 be added to the system's current level of spending over the next three years.[13]

At its meeting of March 1, 1992, the Academic and Student Affairs

Task Force included in its final report to the President a response to the Libraries Committee report:

> The Task Force strongly endorses the general goals detailed in the document for the strengthening of the university library system and campus libraries as critical elements of the university. However, the specific fiscal goals must be evaluated within the context of the entire university budget and in consultation with the Budget Task Force. The Task Force also requests that the Five Campus Libraries Committee explore university policy with regard to the purchasing of journals as opposed to books in collaboration with faculty in diverse subject areas and report to the Academic Advisory Council. The Five Campus Libraries Committee has been asked to prepare a report on the libraries for June, which will address, among other issues, the issue of selective acquisitions and specialized library resources based on campus mission, and the networking and sharing of library resources both electronically and otherwise.[14]

The President then cited library concerns as the first in his "Action Goals" recommended to the Academic and Student Affairs Committee of the Board of Trustees. Predictably, another deadline was established to study and report on the following charge by May 31, 1992.

> "Sharing of library services will be emphasized.
> *Use of existing intercampus courier services will be explored to facilitate greater sharing of books and other materials from the several collections.
> *A decision will be reached as to the location of specialized collections.
> *An attempt will be made within the current budget request which we have made to HECC and which they have approved (but is not in the Governor's recommended budget at the moment) to secure a 'shot in the arm' allocation for purchasing badly needed books and library materials.
> *Guidelines will be developed to indicate priorities in books/materials to be purchased in these tight budget times."[15]

Accordingly, the Libraries Committee reconvened to prepare responses to each of the requests and to explore mechanisms to distribute a special allocation for the libraries, should such be approved by the legislature.

A brief document drafted by Richard Talbot, Director of the University of Massachusetts Amherst Libraries, outlined a program for resource sharing and selective acquisitions predicated on the assumptions that there will be 1) an adequate core collection on each campus. 2) a means of determining what each campus holds, such as a union list for journals, 3) a process for making collection decisions, and 4) an effective delivery system.[16]

The draft reiterated once again the need for adequate core collections on each campus, pointing out that the average cost for an interlibrary loan is $16, thus making it not cost effective for the libraries to share a single book that would be used by more than three students on any one campus.

Yet some resources can and should be shared. To discover what these might be, the librarians proposed a three-year process to review, with extensive faculty participation, the journals lists at each institution, establish a union list, and implement an improved system for document delivery. Although the full-scale project will require several years to complete, benefits will accrue as decisions are reached in various subject areas. The creation of a mechanism for a union list and improved delivery, perhaps through the new scanning technology, Ariel, will be implemented as soon as possible.

The formula for distributing among the five campuses the potential supplementary allocation has proven difficult. In concert with the Governor's agenda, the University Board of Trustees is attempting to institute formula budgeting for the system's five campuses that will include a library component. In preparation for instituting the formula in fiscal year 1994, an educational consultant has been hired to identify peer institutions for each campus. The initial review of the peers that have been chosen suggests that, while the choices for the medical school and flagship campus at Amherst seem appropriate, the choices for Dartmouth, Lowell, and Boston may be less suitable as models for determining needs and distributing funds. Clearly, considerable work will need to be done to establish a library formula acceptable to all the campuses, but it is heartening that the directors are attempting to resolve differences without rancor in keeping with their history of positive working relationships.

Massachusetts' poor record of support for its public academic libraries is at sharp odds with the frequent expressions of the state's educational excellence and the recently articulated goal to build a "world-class" public university. Given the repeated insistence that resource sharing can precede or obviate the need for the development of resources, a sense of incredulity remains on the part of the faculty, librarians, students, and community supporters of the libraries. Yet the public academic librarians are taking advantage of every opportunity to respond to requests for information in a thorough and thoughtful way.

STATEWIDE LIBRARY PLANNING EFFORTS

Unlike many other states, Massachusetts has not been successful in developing a statewide plan that brings all types of libraries together to deliver services to residents. This chapter would not be complete without at least a brief overview of statewide library planning efforts, or the lack thereof, in the Commonwealth of Massachusetts and how this has affected the public academic libraries.

Most of the state's twenty-nine public academic libraries belong to one or more regional and statewide consortia. The five college libraries consortium that links the University of Massachusetts Amherst with four private colleges—Amherst, Hampshire, Mt. Holyoke, and Smith—clearly enriches the scholarly resources available to support teaching and research. This is true, too of the membership by the Amherst and Boston campuses of the University of Massachusetts to the Boston Library Consortium, which includes Northeastern University, Boston University, Boston College, Wellesley College, Boston Public Library, MIT, Brandeis, Tufts, and the Massachusetts State Library. (Since the merger of the five universities, Lowell and Dartmouth also have applied for membership in the Boston Library Consortium.)

However, many of the twenty-nine public academic libraries are involved in consortia that are less relevant to their primary missions. The impetus for a number of these consortia was funding from LSCA monies for multitype library cooperation. Throughout the last two decades, a large portion of LSCA funds was awarded for the creation of automated circulation systems throughout the state. Examples of public academic library involvement in these include the participation by the University of Massachusetts Lowell, Salem State College, and two community colleges in a partnership with a number of public libraries in the northeast part of the state. Framingham State College is the single public college in a network joining it to a small private college and many public libraries west of Boston. Worcester Cooperative includes a more balanced mix of public, academic, private academic, and public libraries in the center of the state.

During the same period the Board of Library Commissioners also provided LSCA funds for union lists of periodicals. In southeastern Massachusetts, there is a union list of serials of public and private academic libraries, public libraries, and a veterans hospital library. Some of these institutions are linked by a delivery system; others rely on patron referral or mailed interlibrary loans. One of the unlikeliest union lists created during this period joined the holdings of the Marine Biological Laboratory Library at Woods Hole, one of the world's largest and most unique marine collections, with the holdings of a number of public libraries on Cape Cod.

The most troubling aspect about these collaborations is that they did not develop as components of a cogent, carefully articulated plan to provide Massachusetts residents access to what, collectively, are among the richest library resources in the world. Nor has it ever been clear how the multitype library networks, which have received federal support through the Massachusetts Board of Library Commissioners, link to yet another state system for providing and delivering library services, the state-funded Regional Library System. There have long existed three regions, Eastern, Western, and Central, each with subregions through which interlibrary loan requests are made and facilitated by means of a truck delivery service. The regional libraries are given state dollars to support richer collections and, when they are unable to meet the needs of area residents, the Boston Public Library functions as the "library of last resort." Over the years, many new cooperative entities have been established that coexist, and even compete, with the regional system. Some have delivery trucks that, on a given day, are likely to pass another vehicle heading for the same library.

Another disturbing aspect of the failure of statewide library planning in the Commonwealth is that technical considerations for expanding cooperation were seldom taken into account when the automated circulation systems were instituted. For example, in the 1970s when most academic libraries were joining OCLC, the Board of Library Commissioners was funding a variety of regional library automation projects among libraries that were not using a common standard for entering records. The shared circulation systems have enhanced joint borrowing within particular regions, but many of the members did not have access to the wider resources offered through OCLC. (Over time, most systems have developed this valuable capacity.) Disparate systems for entering records have also made it difficult to broaden linkages—for example, for on-line catalogs.

As indicated above, many of these cooperating library networks have public academic library participants that play a major role in resource sharing with small public libraries. Many of the public academic libraries also play an important role in servicing the school library populations who have been left out of statewide planning altogether. Indeed, some of the best examples of cooperation may receive no recognition or support. They have developed from the concern of the librarians involved, in spite of, rather than because of, the leadership provided by the Board of Library Commissioners, the regional public library system, Nelinet (New England's regional link to OCLC), or any other agency, for a cogent, statewide connection. In retrospect, it would probably have been wiser for the public academic libraries to have been more thoughtful in the consortium arrangements they joined. The lure of LSCA funding for the institutions that had so little may have turned the focus away from other cooperative ventures, perhaps a system linking all twenty-nine higher education institutions that could have reached out to other libraries.

There was some hope that the comprehensive study commissioned by the Board of Library Commissioners in 1990, at the very time that the public academic librarians were preparing *Learning at Risk*, would produce alternatives to the hodge-podge of cooperative library arrangements in the Commonwealth. Yet, King Research, Inc., a Tennessee library consulting firm contracted to assess "the current state of library services and library cooperative activities in Massachusetts," and to recommend "strategies to develop an action plan for the improvement of library services for the residents of Massachusetts"[17] focused, as do most of the projects of the Massachusetts Board of Library Commissioners, on public libraries.

The recommendations of the King Report appeared to be a mechanism for subsuming the independent regional library system, in which the Boston Public Library is the central player, into six to twelve "library cooperatives" under the Board of Library Commissioners. Although it appears that public academic libraries are being viewed as key participants, the report was seriously flawed for its lack of effort to gain representative or adequate input from the public higher education libraries, or for that matter, from private academic, school, and special library constituencies. The response from efforts of MCCLPHEI for meaningful inclusion was a tag-on recommendation in the final version of the King Report that "The institutional and special library communities should develop similar working documents (as *Learning at Risk*) for their libraries."[18]

Such gratuitous gestures, along with the feeling that the entire report was deficient in many ways, have led to some reactions that may, finally, bring about systematic multitype library planning in the Commonwealth. Several useful meetings of public and private academic librarians have been held with a staff member of the Board of Library Commissioners and more recently, some of these librarians have formed an even more diverse grouping under the auspices of the Massachusetts delegates to the White House Conference on Libraries. Indications are that this group will develop a model that expands the King Report to include a vision of a statewide system that includes all library constituencies in the Commonwealth, especially since the newly hired Director of the Board of Library Commissioners is an enthusiastic participant.

Obviously, the drama of public academic libraries in Massachusetts has a large cast of players. This chapter began with a revelation of the power of politics in the Commonwealth of Massachusetts. If the political climate has been the reason for some of the problems of the Massachusetts public academic libraries, it has also been the reason for some of the successes, so it is important to revisit this arena before concluding.

Public academic libraries in Massachusetts have been fortunate in receiving some directorial suggestions from key legislators. Former State Senator John Olver, once a chemistry professor at UMass Amherst, and former State Representative Stanley Rosenberg, were strong advocates for the public higher education libraries in the Massachusetts Legislature. Public academic librarians like to think that it is because these legislators were "on the side of the angels"—us—that their political fortunes have risen. John Olver was elected in 1990 to the United States Congress, and Rosenberg was chosen to fill his vacated state senate seat. However, the career advancement of these strong supporters, coupled with the reorganization of higher education, has meant that the statewide library directors group, MCCLPHEI, must find new advocates in appropriate positions of influence to champion the cause of public academic libraries.

While MCCLPHEI can be assured of Rosenberg's support, his state senate committee assignment is to the agriculture committee—and we have yet to identify a supporter with seniority and power to replace Rosenberg's advocacy in the House of Representatives. This is particularly serious at a time when the Republican governor is attempting to reduce the size of state government and privatize services. It is clear that the underlying assumptions beneath the creation of the new higher education system is to realize savings through consolidation within and across all segments. The university librarians are the first to discover this. In writing the recent reports, the faculty and librarians on the committee received gentle but persistent advice from the vice chancellor who was appointed as chair that we were to emphasize the financial benefits of consolidation. This was a difficult task at a time when UMass Amherst, to cite an example that applies across the higher education system, is buying fewer than one fifth of the books it should be purchasing. All of the librarians look forward to further collaborative efforts to improve service to our users, but know that the predictions for next fiscal year of level funding, at the abysmal figure received last year, will further devastate these possibilities. Further—and most alarming—the monies that were formerly in the special line designated for Educational Reference Materials have been rolled into each institution's total budget. For the first time in nearly twenty-five years, it may be that even this small pocket of funding can no longer be relied upon for collection maintenance and development. Since the formula for determining and distributing budgets that is a goal of the Governor has not been determined, library allocations could fall through the cracks unless the legislature is alerted to the problem.

The backdrop for the struggle to provide the library support that is the foundation for teaching and learning in the public colleges and universities is not an attractive one. Faculty and students are demoralized by the cutbacks that have affected every institution. Employees in Massachusetts have not had a pay raise in four years. On top of that, they received furloughs, *i.e.*, forced, unpaid "vacation," or the withholding of wages until retirement, resignation, or death, and have been assessed additional contributions to health insurance. "Public" higher education is moving from a state-funded to a state-supported (barely) system. Students are bearing the burden of this with raises in tuition and even larger increases in fees. In many of the institutions, including the one I serve, some fees have been instituted ostensibly for library services, but these do not always get to the library. In fact, the library fee at UMass Dartmouth was rolled into a broader "Academic Services Fee" that places the library in a competitive position against computing services, admissions, remedial programs, advising, the Registrar's office, and other groups. Despite the fees, library budgets continue to decline, furthering disappointment and anger.

Although students and staff who are faced with the difficulties of meeting expenses have little time left to organize, the withering of library services has engaged the attention of a number of groups. During the past academic year, special committees at the Amherst and Lowell campuses of UMass formed to raise the issue of the impoverishment of the libraries. MCCLPHEI has been building on this awareness. Librarians have been active participants in lobbying efforts with other campus groups and MCCLPHEI's own Legislative Watch Committee has engaged in an active campaign of letter-writing and phone calls followed up by a day of lobbying at the State House. The message to the legislators is that the designated line for library materials must be restored and funded at a reasonable level if Massachusetts public higher education is to be credible.

So I conclude this overview of public academic library planning in Massachusetts on a note of optimism. Although, at times, it has appeared that the requests for still more information were delaying tactics to avoid addressing an obvious reality, the substantial data that has been and continues to be gathered has placed the libraries in a proactive position. In contrast with previous periods in the recent history of Massachusetts higher education, it is clear that the legislature, governing boards, institutional leaders, faculty, students, and community users are united in their concern about the libraries. If not all the words we have produced have been read by those to whom they were addressed, the existence of *Learning at Risk* and the subsequent university reports seem to have had an influence in pushing the issue to the fore. It is too soon to know if the strong case for special funding for the colleges and universities will translate into the desired response that is to fund all the libraries in fiscal year 1993 through the reinstitution of the ERM line. It is also possible that the university will receive increased support in addition to, or perhaps in place of, the ERM.

In any case, Massachusetts public academic libraries will keep planning within their individual institutions and through the statewide organization, MCCLPHEI, and will participate actively in the new statewide planning initiative that was described above. And they will attempt to find audiences and advocates for their reports. Planning is integral to a profession that has the obligation to meet the information and research requirements of current scholars— and also must look ahead to the future generations whose understanding depends on the choices we make today.

NOTES

1. *State Higher Education Profiles, 1988 edition: a Comparison of State Higher Education Data for FY86*. Washington, D.C.: U.S. Department of Education, 1988.

2. Thanks to Margaret Howland, former Director, Greenfield Community College Library, for supplying some of the history of public academic library funding.

3. The charts are drawn from *Statistical Norms for College and University Libraries*, derived from the *U.S. Department of Education 1985 Survey of College and University Libraries* (Boulder: John Minter Associates, 1987) and from the fiscal year 1988 Integrated Postsecondary Education Data Surveys (IPEDS).

4. Margaret Soderberg, Letter to Randolph W. Bromery, 17 April 1990.

5. *Learning at Risk: Long Range Plan for the Improvement of Massachusetts Public Higher Education Libraries*, Report prepared for the Massachusetts Board of Regents of Higher Education (1990), p. 5.

6. *Ibid.*, pp. 10–11.

7. University of Massachusetts, Academic and Student Affairs Task Force, Charge for libraries Committee, 3 December 1991.

8. David Paroissien, Letter to Donald Babcock, 9 February 1992.

9. Donald Babcock, Letter to Richard O'Brien, 25 February 1992.

10. "Preliminary Report of the Libraries Committee: Report prepared for the Academic and Student Affairs Task Force of the Board of Trustees," University of Massachusetts, 14 February 1992.

11. *Ibid.*

12. *Ibid.*, p. 2.

13. *Ibid.*, p. 7.

14. Academic and Student Affairs Task Force, "Final Report to the President," 1 March 1992.

15. E. K. Fretwell, "Report to the Academic and Student Affairs Committee of the Board of Trustees of the University of Massachusetts," 1 April 1992.

16. Richard Talbot, "Memorandum to the University Librarians on Selective Acquisitions and Resource Sharing," 22 April 1992.

17. Jose-Marie Griffiths and Donald W. King, *Massachusetts Libraries: an Alliance for the Future* (Knoxville: King Research, 1991).

18. *Ibid.*, p. 48.

Chapter 11

Networking in the University System of Georgia—A Case Study in Successful Interaction

Ralph E. Russell

The University System of Georgia (USG) is comprised of two year, senior college, and university level institutions. Governed by a Board of Regents appointed by the governor, it is a statutory authority defined in the Georgia Constitution. The University System and its Board of Regents came into existence on January 1, 1932, as a result of an earlier state survey committee report which stated that "possible friction or rivalry between the higher institutions and some duplication of work could be eliminated, and much better results for all obtained, if there were one Board of Trustees or Regents...."[1]

The legislature appropriates money to the Board of Regents. The Regents, acting upon the advice of the Chancellor and his staff, allocate money to the USG institutions. Among the publicly supported systems of higher education in the United States, it is the opinion of the author that the USG is more highly decentralized than most state systems with much autonomy resting with the individual institutions. This has been a controlling characteristic when discussing the development and evolution of library networking within the system. The difference in institutional library funding, the variability of local policies, even the variability of local interpretation of state law or Board of Regents policies—all add to the complication in any system or statewide library development effort, whether it be networking or something as straightforward as data collection for annual compilation of standard measures of library growth.

The University System of Georgia is comprised of thirty-four institutions: five universities, fourteen senior colleges, and fifteen two year colleges. The settings for these institutions vary from the most rural to the urban. Consistent with much local autonomy, the mission, resource base, and community vary widely for each institution within the system. As one would expect, the librarians working within the USG libraries vary widely in their professional expertise, professional outlook, and personal skills. The concerns of a senior college located in a metropolitan area are not identical to those of a two year college located in the most sparsely populated county in the state; or, from another perspective, a specialized university such as Georgia Tech or the Medical College of Georgia may have relatively few common library issues to discuss with a rural senior college.

The diversity of mission, population served, resource base, and expertise level of individuals employed is a factor in addressing common library issues. As the ensuing chapter is developed, those diversities emerge again and again as elements which may retard progress at times and, at other times, actually stimulate and promote progress. In his study of the University System of Georgia, Cameron Fincher said that "In its quest for academic excellence, one of the University System's best investments can be seen in its campus libraries."[2] In a succeeding comment, he added that "... the library holdings of institutions within the University System are among its most impressive accomplishments."[3]

There is no record of a formalized, continuing group of library administrators within the USG until 1968. The University System Advisory Council (USG institution presidents who advise the System's chancellor) authorized the establishment of an Academic Committee on Libraries (ACL). The name and structure of the group is parallel to other advisory committees, for instance, for home economics, history, and the like. Each of these committees advises the Administrative Committee on Academic Affairs, a group comprised of the chief academic officers from each of the USG institutions. The authority and characteristics of all the USG academic committees rest in the Statutes and Bylaws of the University System Advisory Council (July, 1963).

The organizational meeting of the Academic Committee on Libraries (ACL) was guided by Vice Chancellor Mario J. Goglia (who remained the friend and guiding light for USG librarians through his tenure as Vice Chancellor) and Dr. William R. Pullen, Librarian at Georgia State University, who chaired the initial meeting. The topics discussed at the initial meeting on January 15, 1968, are a laundry list of library issues which reappear on ACL agendas through the committee's history to the present. The topics included:

1. Computer applications for library processes and information retrieval. What directions might be expected from the Board of Regents? More importantly, what funding might be expected from the Board of Regents?

Networking in the University System of Georgia 145

2. Education for librarianship.
3. Shortage of librarians.
4. Telecommunications. Use of WATS lines, teletype, and telefacsimile.
5. Standards for library services and collections.
6. Impact of new academic programs on libraries.
7. Standards for library buildings.
8. Librarians' salaries, faculty status, promotion, tenure.
9. Audiovisual materials and equipment.
10. Purchasing procedures.
11. Federal grants to libraries.
12. Communication among USG libraries.
13. Master plan for library use. Who should be allowed to use USG libraries? Could library cards be issued to USG students to enable them to use any USG library?

For the purpose of this chapter, two issues are most relevant to networking within the USG and which, when tracked over the past twenty-four years, most clearly demonstrate the evolution of that networking: (1) automation of USG libraries and (2) resource sharing. They clearly blend into each other in that it is only through library computerization and the application of telecommunications technology that we effectively share resources. From an historical standpoint and a review of the minutes of the Academic Committee on Libraries (ACL), however, it is clear that the two issues are important, are crucial to networking, and dominate the ACL minutes.

The first topic discussed at the first meeting of ACL was automation; judging from the minutes the topic quickly segued into what directions library automation might take and what funding might be expected from the central source, the Board of Regents. The answer throughout the committee's history has been indeterminantly negative; the actions of the USG Board of Regents clearly demonstrate that the Board funds institutions, not special projects, special interests, or programs. Once funds are allocated to an institution, it is up to that institution to allocate them for library development. So, from the beginning, the ACL was destined to be a group of haves and have-nots. Those librarians with political acumen, ability to conceptualize solutions to address needs and to articulate those solutions, and the good fortune to work on a campus with funds to allocate above subsistence level, were the haves. Everyone else was a have-not.

By 1969, the ACL had begun to review and report on progress within the system as individual libraries worked toward automating their processes. Georgia Tech, as a leader in the use of emerging technology, was described as putting " ... the entire card catalog of the Institute on microfische (sic) thus making available to all departments in the Institute a complete library card file" (October 29, 1969, p. 2).[4] There are also occasional queries within the committee about the use of teletype/telefacsimile between libraries.

There was a surge of interest in library automation in 1972 because of the Association of Southeastern Research Libraries (ASERL) committee working toward replicating OCLC in the Southeast. A representative of the ACL met with the ASERL committee and reported back favorably. Again, a survey was mounted of automation efforts within the USG to compare with a national survey and analysis of major cooperative library computer applications in operation or development. There was a call for specific plans to be developed to implement a library computer network for USG libraries, either independently or in conjunction with a regional system (February 28, 1972). In the latter part of the year, a meeting was called to discuss the ASERL feasibility study of a regional library computer processing center. There continued to be momentum for supporting a regional approach rather than a state-based system. No definite action followed.

In 1974, library automation issues jumped back to the front burner because the ASERL committee's work was about to come to fruition with the inception of Solinet. One benefit from ACL was the sharing of information and the spreading of good sense and enthusiasm for a sound idea. It is within the context of such a group that the concept of a regional network to broker on-line cataloging services is sold and people "get on board." New ideas may be more palatable when propounded by a neighbor or friend: after all, they have to live with you and your ire if you've been led down the garden path . . . ! All were encouraged to attend the initial Solinet membership meeting in March, 1974, to adopt bylaws. The ACL representative from the University of Georgia announced plans to automate UGA's shelflist and expressed concern that Solinet's inception might be too slow to accommodate their plans for automation. The early ACL members realized that the machine-readable bibliographic record is the basic building block for library automation and, ultimately, resource sharing. The group encouraged each institution to create those records, most reasonably through a bibliographic utility. That encouragement is a theme which continues throughout the records of the ACL. All of the larger institutions, university and senior colleges, joined Solinet. The newer, smaller senior colleges and the two year colleges were much slower to join and to enjoy the benefits brought by library automation.

By 1978, Solinet/OCLC was an established method of cataloging for many libraries; furthermore, they were eagerly awaiting the advent of interlibrary lending request transmittal via electronic communication. Searching of reference data bases had been done for USG libraries by the systems staff at the University of Georgia Computer Center. Because of the rising overhead costs (and prices) of the UGA Computer Center, the

ACL discussed the proposed costs as opposed to individually subscribing to services which provided access to what were primarily bibliographic data bases for periodical and report literature. Although the group took no collective action, this increase in costs forced the advent of on-line searching of reference data bases in USG libraries, except for Georgia Tech. As in many other instances, Georgia Tech was already providing the access. The University of Georgia Libraries were continuing to work toward developing an in-house integrated library system, and there was continuing discussion of what the implications might be of such automation for the other USG libraries.

The Academic Committee on Libraries was interested by 1980 in the means to produce computer output microfiche (COM) catalogs. After some study and discussion, it was proposed that ACL jointly fund a computer analyst position to produce COM catalogs with a goal of enhanced resource sharing among USG libraries. A letter from the ACL chair went out describing what the analyst would accomplish and detailing the cost per institution for the position (letter from Mary Emma Henderson dated April 4, 1980). An analyst was hired, but the USG institutions who wanted COM catalogs produced them in ways other than through ACL and most did not share the costs of funding the analyst position. This cooperative venture did not go very far.

During the latter years of the 1970s and the early years of the 1980s, reports and discussion at ACL meetings dealt with Solinet/OCLC activities, products, services, and pricing issues. The ACL serves a very important ongoing function in providing a more intimate group (of "home folks") with whom to hash out and discuss issues of networking and Solinet/OCLC. In 1983, the first mention of a statewide telecommunications network surfaces in a description of a planning document submitted to the USG Chancellor and the Georgia Superintendent of Public Instruction (March 3, 1983). This foreshadowing is important because it is the element in the nineties that is making resource sharing feasible. It was announced at the same meeting that the University of Georgia Libraries had purchased Blackwell North America software to produce COM catalogs for interested institutions. This is an example of one institution moving ahead to do something for the group which the group had faltered in doing. Subsequently, the University of Georgia Libraries produced COM catalogs for several USG institutions.

A continuing theme of ACL meetings is the urging and encouragement of the smaller institutions to join Solinet/OCLC so that their cataloging records could be in machine readable form. The continuous cheerleading and exhortation paid off, because by 1992, only five institutions out of thirty-four were not generating machine readable catalog records.

In 1985, the ACL received a proposal from the General Research Corporation to accomplish retrospective conversion of cataloging records and produce COM catalogs for USG libraries (November 7–8, 1985, page 7). The company proposed using OCLC tapes to create files against which non-member libraries' data would be searched. There was much discussion but also reluctance to commit resources. Ultimately, everyone was in favor of accomplishing the proposal's goals. The ACL finally determined to reject the proposal and to support and advocate sufficient funding for all USG libraries to join OCLC.

The issue of a statewide telecommunications network emerged again in 1986. A member of the Board of Regents staff met with ACL to seek their support for the funding of Peachnet, the proposed telecommunications line. The ACL endorsed Peachnet.

By 1986, all the senior colleges and universities in the USG were Solinet/OCLC members and creating machine-readable cataloging records. Many of the two-year colleges were not members and some of their representatives felt that they needed help in convincing their presidents that Solinet membership is desirable and viable.

The ACL sent a recommendation to the USG Administrative Committee on Academic Affairs (the chief academic officers from each of the 34 institutions in the USG) that focused on resource sharing. In essence, it said that in order to share resources, we first must have machine-readable cataloging records produced for each institution's library bibliographic file. In other words, all institutions should be Solinet/OCLC members. This was formulated to address the plight of two year colleges.

The director of the state library agency described to ACL a statewide data base of monograph holdings that he hoped could be produced from our Solinet/OCLC tapes. Again, ACL endorsed the concept.

At the Fall 1986 meeting of the ACL, the Administrative Committee on Academic Affairs reported that a committee had been appointed to "look into" ACL's recommendation for resource sharing. Conceptual information on a statewide union list of monographs and serials was disseminated; the group was positive but no steps toward implementation were reported.

The ACL 1987 meetings generated additional information on (still proposed) Peachnet. Some of the larger institutions had leased lines for transmission of serials information back and forth to Faxon. By using Peachnet and a node with a single line to Faxon, communication costs could be lessened considerably and shared.

Georgia State University offered its on-line library system as a host system for other institutions that had not yet automated their libraries. After some discussions of costs and benefits, one institution (several years later) began using both the on-line public access catalog (OPAC) and the circulation subsystem. Out of that offer came a multi-institutional union catalog. Twenty institutions, public and private, contributed their bibliographic files, which are mounted and accessible on a mainframe via dial-up or dedicated port. The state library agency director continued to describe again the option of having a statewide bibliographic data base using OCLC. He was ready to begin; the ACL expressed concern that serial holdings be included initially.

By 1989, there was progress to report for the statewide union catalog, christened GOLD (Georgia OnLine Database); 136 libraries were profiled by Solinet/OCLC for inclusion in the project. A major event was the creation of the position and the appointment of the first USG Vice Chancellor for Information Technology; that individual met with ACL to describe the nascent Peachnet and predicted that it would be fully operational within three years. Not only was he sensitive to library technological needs, he saw USG libraries as appropriate and immediate users of Peachnet. He expressed the need for some help in looking at library automation vendors on a system level rather than on an individual level. He urged that librarians be involved in planning for the informational technological development within the USG. The ACL chair appointed a subcommittee to advise the Vice Chancellor for Information Technology (hereafter referred to as the subcommittee).

The subcommittee went right to work. They represented two year colleges, senior colleges, and universities; they were experienced librarians and were eager to play their projected role. They were charged specifically to determine:

1. The necessary functions of an automated library information management system.
2. The levels of service categories for the libraries in USG.
3. A match of the required automated functions with the commercially available software/hardware so that a recommended automated library system(s) could be chosen.
4. Other options in information technology which could be supported or developed centrally. (October 3, 1989, page 1).

As they reported at the fall meeting, the subcommittee provided the requested recommendations. In 1990, the subcommittee began writing a paper to the Chancellor, advocating increased funding for libraries for collections resource sharing, and that perennial favorite topic, the need for all libraries to generate machine-readable cataloging records.

By 1990, all four universities, 29 percent of senior colleges and 33 percent of two year schools had integrated library systems in place. The automation theme of the May 1990 ACL meeting was the critical need for each USG institution to build machine-readable cataloging records with the goal of sharing resources and participating in the statewide data base, GOLD. The subcommittee had articulated a goal of any USG student having access to the data base of all USG libraries and being able to reap the benefit of resource sharing; the ACL adopted that goal.

The subcommittee met with the USG Chancellor on April 19, 1991, to present their paper and recommendations. They recommended that the Chancellor:

1. Fund a program through the Vice Chancellor for Information Technology to encourage development and sharing of machine-readable bibliographic data bases among USG libraries.
    a. Create a realistic timetable for:
        (1) producing MARC bibliographic records for all USG libraries;
        (2) including all USG libraries in Solinet/OCLC;
        (3) providing on-line or automated access to primary clientele at each USG institution; and
        (4) providing on-line or automated access to every USG library from any other USG library.
    b. Encourage/support use of Peachnet.
    c. Negotiate and purchase site licenses for selected on-line and CD-ROM data bases and equipment for all USG libraries.
    d. Provide central library support as requested.
2. Provide special initiative funding for libraries. This will be used to:
    a. create accurate machine-readable cataloging records;
    b. purchase new library technology;
    c. implement or upgrade integrated library automated systems;
    d. develop high quality collections; and
    e. replace outdated equipment.

Unfortunately, within four months of the meeting with the Chancellor, the state experienced a budget shortfall, which necessitated cuts to budgets for all state agencies; thus, attention was diverted from quality improvement to survival.

Tangible progress is evident in the automation of USG libraries in mid 1992. Peachnet is a reality, and by the end of 1992, all institutions will be connected. Several institutions have offered the use of their library systems as host systems for other institutions. A number of institutions are investigating and considering such sharing. Most libraries in the state, public and private, are members of GOLD.

As with automation, library resource sharing was on the agenda at the initial meeting of the ACL (January 15, 1968). It was focused on a library card for all USG students which would be used to check out books at any USG institution. It is so simple in statement and yet it took so long to achieve! There has been much progress in the process, however.

One of the initial tasks for a subcommittee was to compile a handbook of circulation policies, hours of library opening, and photocopying charges for each institution. The handbook was disseminated to all institutions. They also developed a proposed statement on referring students and faculty from one institution's library to another institution's library to check out books. A policy was approved at the November 11, 1968, meeting to provide an interlibrary use card for all USG faculty and students. The implementation would take some time, however. Because of the differences in local setting (rural, suburban, metropolitan) and the subsequent differences in demand from students at other institutions, the ACL decided that each library would decide its own policy of service to the public. Although there was mention in most ACL committee minutes of the interlibrary use borrowers' policy, in 1974 the ACL coined an official term for the card and policy—the joint borrower's card.

Resource sharing was discussed at a 1977 meeting and the conclusion reached that it be considered on a statewide basis with special attention to document delivery.

A subcommittee on resource sharing presented a four point report:

1. a proposal for requesting materials;
2. priorities (recommended);
3. sanctioned telephone requests for rush materials; and
4. recommended shipping via UPS (subcommittee minutes October 21, 1977).

By late 1977, the subcommittee on resource sharing had broadened its view to include cooperative book purchasing, cooperative book storage, centralized 16mm film collection, and a staff development program. Aside from the staff development program, the other elements were greeted with underwhelming interest on the part of ACL. Specifically concerning cooperative storage facility, the subcommittee wrote "Although earlier some consensus existed as to the question of centralized storage; arguments in opposition were advanced, with the result that the committee agreed that this matter should be restudied" (February 2–3, 1978, p. 4).

The issue of cooperative book purchasing was raised at least once in the ensuing years but never got beyond the general discussion stage. In 1981, the ACL met with the Assistant Director of State Purchasing to discuss a group contract for the purchase of library books; at the conclusion of that discussion the ACL voted not to work towards a statewide purchasing contract.

By 1982, the continuing discussion of the joint borrower's card had yielded progress to the point where one card permitted faculty and graduate students to borrow from any USG institution; prior to this point, the card was issued for use at only one institution. The policy was extended to include undergraduates in 1985 (November 7–8, 1985), and further extended to include vocational/technical schools in 1987 (October 15–16, 1987). In 1989–90, a subcommittee was appointed to consider borrowing privileges for all citizens but concluded that such was not feasible. As outlined earlier in this chapter, the automation developments were undertaken, usually with enhanced resource sharing as their goal. Certainly the machine-readable cataloging records, the GOLD, and OCLC's data bases have resource sharing as their purpose.

As described earlier, the paper submitted to the Chancellor from ACL in April 1992 was focused on resource sharing. It clearly described automation as a means towards that end, but the objective ultimately was access to all USG libraries for all USG students and faculty.

The Academic Committee on Libraries has existed for twenty-four years. Its primary benefit has been that of a discussion and cheerleading group. The group has encouraged its membership to learn and do—with new technology, with Solinet, with the 1978 copyright law. Automation has been an individual institutional action until the 1990s. Because of the static or diminished resources available to colleges and universities, resource sharing will be the only option for development in some instances. That means sharing an automated system as well as a journal article or videotape. On the immediate horizon for ACL is negotiation for statewide access to periodical indexing data bases. If not that, a price for access by multiple institutions must be negotiated. Without central funding, it is clear that the incremental costs for multiple institutional access will be paid by those institutions benefitting.

With or without the joint borrower's card, students and faculty are using whatever library suits them. The question of access to proprietary data bases mounted on the local library system at a neighboring institution but not available to students and faculty at a sister institution is not going to fade away. It will be dealt with successfully. The goal still remains maximum access for all USG students and faculty—and after that, the citizens of Georgia. The ACL is experiencing momentum as a result of clear opportunity and financial necessity. The technology such as Peachnet is available to facilitate progressive resource sharing. These opportunities will be seized—as well as those coming in subsequent years.

NOTES

1. Cameron Fincher, *Historical Development of the University System of Georgia: 1932–1990* (Athens, Ga.: Institute of Higher Education, University of Georgia, 1991), p. 2.

2. *Ibid.*, p. 118.

3. *Ibid.*, p. 119.

4. Minutes of the Academic Committee on Libraries, letters from the ACL chair, and occasional references to minutes of ACL subcommittees are cited within the text by date enclosed in parentheses.

Chapter 12

Colorado Alliance of Research Libraries: The Role of the State

George R. Jaramillo
Helen I. Reed

OVERVIEW

The Colorado Alliance of Research Libraries (CARL) was founded by the library directors of seven Colorado institutions: Auraria Library, Colorado School of Mines, Colorado State University, Denver Public Library, University of Colorado at Boulder, University of Denver, and the University of Northern Colorado. These library directors were interested in developing a cooperative system of solutions to common problems that would result in: increased access by patrons to materials and research available in and outside of Colorado; the elimination of duplication of resources; and a system that could provide cooperative acquisition, management, and information processing.

Since CARL's beginning, four more full members have been added: University of Colorado Health Sciences Center, The University of Colorado Law Library, Denver University Law School, and the University of Wyoming. There are more than ten associate members, including community colleges, the Colorado State Department of Education, and several public and school libraries. Colorado State University dropped out as a full member in 1984 and rejoined as a full member in 1992.

CARL is a nonprofit corporation organized in 1974 and incorporated in 1978. CARL derives its authority from Articles of Incorporation first filed in 1978 and most recently amended and restated on December 7, 1990. CARL currently operates under bylaws dated May 1, 1991.

In 1981, CARL introduced "The CARL System," which currently supports over 2,065 dedicated terminals at the 53 libraries of CARL members and CARL associate members. The CARL System is a comprehensive information access and delivery network. It includes an on-line public access catalog and an integrated support system for all major library management needs, including circulation, acquisitions, serials access and control, and bibliographic maintenance.

CARL Systems, Inc. (CSI), is a for-profit corporation formed by CARL in 1988 to enhance, market and support the CARL System and to develop new products in the field of information access. CARL formed CSI to permit aggressive marketing of CARL products without the legal constraints of a nonprofit structure. CARL hoped to create an entrepreneurial environment which would encourage and financially reward CSI's principal employees, who in turn would generate profits which could be used for the benefit of the CARL members. Since its formation CSI has successfully marketed the CARL System and currently supports over 3,690 terminals in 289 libraries coast to coast in the continental United States and in Hawaii.

COMMITMENT

The initial support for CARL came from those institutions sharing in the cost of developing a shared on-line system. The establishment of CARL could not be done without a public/private partnership between private and public universities and city supported libraries. In an article by Patricia Culkin and Ward Shaw[1] it was stated:

These members (CARL) represent a variety of kinds of organizations—state supported, city supported, private, or viewed another way, large general academic, large public, small special academic. They differ in size from the University of Colorado—Boulder Library, a member of ARL, to the School of Mines Library, serving a specialized academic clientele, to the Denver Public Library serving a large metropolitan public. The members are diverse, but they are alike in certain important ways. They all have, as a part of their reason for being, the need to support large numbers of general users. And they all have a commitment of one kind or another to serve a wider user population than that of their immediate campus or city.

This kind of resource sharing had never been done, and institutions had to be creative in establishing this public/private partnership. All institutions agreed that the sharing in the system would provide the impetus to develop resource sharing projects among the member libraries.

In a personal interview with Ward Shaw,[2] he states, "One of the things that I think is important to understand is that the six libraries involved have each made a major commitment to this effort, and made the hard budget decisions needed to ensure that this project went, that it was a success. And, needed to make it happen. They deserve a lot of credit for that. We did have a modest LSCA grant, which was very important to us in terms of some initial work. But overwhelmingly the bulk of the money has come right out of the operating budgets of these institutions."

STATE SUPPORT

The state structure in supporting institutions of higher learning has evolved over the last fifteen years since CARL filed its Authority of Corporation in 1978. In the 1970s the state operated on a line-item budgeting system. Each institution was provided a specific budget for specific categories. During this period the Colorado Association of Public College and University Presidents (APCUP) undertook an analysis of formula budgets as a means of appropriating funds for each line-item, including those for libraries. In 1977, the Library Formula Budgeting Subcommittee made recommendations for a formula to establish funding levels for library staffing and collections which would " ... assist the resource allocators of the State in devising more effective as well as efficient means of utilizing state resources to increase, subject to availability of funds, the over all (sic) quality of library resources."[3] These formulas were utilized to determine levels of appropriation of monetary resources among the twenty institutions of higher education.

Beginning with the 1981/82 fiscal year, the appropriation of the higher education budget was governed by a "Memorandum of Understanding"[4] developed between the Universities and the Joint Budget Committee of the Colorado General Assembly. The budget recommended by the Joint Budget Committee to the General Assembly and the Governor for each institution now included a single budget line and a narrative containing the assumptions used to arrive at the single line. The assumptions were based upon application of the APCUP formulas to the various segments of the budget.

In 1985, a new law was enacted that provided institutions of higher education with more flexibility in the internal management of their funds. The Colorado Commission of Higher Education (CCHE) was abolished and recreated under new guidelines and charged with overseeing the institutions of higher education in Colorado. The Colorado General Assembly House Bill No. 1187[5] stated:

The purposes of this article are to maximize opportunities for postsecondary education in Colorado; to avoid and to eliminate needless duplication of facilities and programs in state-supported institutions of higher education; to achieve simplicity of state administrative procedures pertaining to higher education; to effect the best utilization of available resources so as to achieve an adequate level of higher education in the most economic manner; and to continue to recognize the constitutional and statutory responsibilities of duly constituted governing boards of state-supported institutions of higher education in Colorado. In this article, express powers and duties are delegated to a central policy and coordinating board, the Colorado Commission on Higher Education. The ultimate authority and responsibility is expressly reserved to the general assembly, and it is the duty of the Colorado Commission on Higher Education to implement the policies of the general assembly.

In House Bill 1187, CCHE was mandated to establish a distribution system for funds. The APCUP budget formulas are still used as a basis for generating the appropriation for each institution although the institutions have latitude in allocating the funds within their own organization. After consultation with the university governing boards, the CCHE recommends a higher education budget to the General Assembly and the Governor. The General Assembly makes the final decision and decides the appropriation for each governing board.

Once an institution has received its allocation, it is responsible to distribute these funds to the various areas in an equitable and fair allocation. At the University of Northern Colorado, for example, the University President receives recommendations from the University's Vice Presidents, Deans, Directors, and the University Budget and Planning Committee. The President forwards the budget recommendations to the Board of Trustees for final approval before making allocations to each area.

Under line-item budgeting the appropriation for the learning materials budget of each library was generated by the state and managed by the institution. All expenditures for the library's collection at the University of Northern Colorado and several state institutions, including the majority of the costs for CARL, were expended from this line item. Thus, the learning materials budget, as it is today, supported the cost of on-line access.

As the cost for maintaining the on-line system grows, the various institutions have recognized that the cost for establishing CARL must come from a different source of revenue. A loan, backed by a public institution, was acquired and the money backed up an "interagency cooperative agreement" signed in November 1981 by the University of Northern Colorado, the University of Colorado, Colorado State University, Denver Public Library, and the University of Denver. The revenue provided the capital to create the foundation and provide the operating costs for the CARL system. This included the purchasing of equipment, office space, salaries, and overhead expenses, and the development of the CARL data base program.

CARL

In its early days CARL focused its efforts on developing an on-line catalog that would facilitate sharing the vast resources of Colorado libraries with its membership. As outlined in the 1984 "CARL Operating Plan"[6] the purpose of the organization was:

1. To manage for access the collections of its members as if they were one collection.
2. To create a single research resource for the people of Colorado.
3. To enable its members to more easily meet the transition from ownership to access in the management of the information resources.

To meet this end, CARL has evolved and expanded to include circulation, acquisitions, serials, and bibliographic maintenance.

Since CARL was founded in 1978, the committee structure has evolved to support the development of these modules. The directors of the original seven institutions formed the CARL Council. It was this council that led CARL to its current existence and set the foundation for what was to follow.

Because CARL was founded on the principle that it was to develop policies and plans to share all resources within the state, the CARL COLA (Colorado Organization for Library Acquisitions) Committee was formed. Its charge was to utilize the on-line system in a manner so that all resources from the state could be shared. The committee began by cooperatively purchasing materials that all CARL libraries could share. Each institution was assessed a fee that was placed in a special account. Each institution would request major purchase items that would be to the benefit of all. Because the CARL system was viewed as one catalog for its members, access to materials purchased was shared. It was agreed that there would be equal access by all participating institutions and no circulation restrictions would be placed on any one CARL purchase. As it evolved, the group collected collection data from each institution in the form of a "conspectus." The "conspectus" outlined the collection strengths and weaknesses for each institution. There was little question as to who was responsible for any particular area. For example, the University of Northern Colorado has its designation as an institution primarily concentrating in the field of education. Thus, the *Gray Education Collection* was purchased with CARL COLA funds and housed in the UNC James A. Michener Library. Through the COLA agreement, any institution that contributed to the collection could borrow the contents of the collection. Normally, a microfiche collection of this size would be restricted for in-house library use only.

As CARL grew, the committee structure also grew. The current structure is elaborate and parallels the major components that comprise the CARL system. There is currently a CARL Board, CARL Council, COLA, Users Group, Access Issues Committee, Bibliographic Issues Committee,

Acquisition/Serials Committee, Circulation Committee, Government Documents Committee, and Systems Group. The CARL Council is comprised of the Directors from the participating members and reports to the CARL Board. The Users Group is the coordinating group for all committee groups and is a recommending body to the CARL Council. The entire committee structure provides important input to the CSI staff in the development of the CARL software.

One of the goals since the inception of CARL was to produce revenue and to provide CARL System free to its original members. In the "CARL 1988–89 Operating Plan"[7] five objectives were set forth:

1. Develop and implement strategies to maximize the research resource of CARL.
2. Provide for its users access to a variety of computerized data bases.
3. Generate 50 percent of CARL's annual cost of operations by the sale of products and services by July 1989.
4. Complete the integration of the Colorado Library Network around CARL by July 1991.
5. Provide full test of documents as appropriate.

It was the third objective that provided the impetus for CARL to move from a not-for-profit organization to a profit making organization. The CARL organization worked under restrictive regulations as determined by its not-for-profit status. It was voted by the board that CARL form a subsidiary, for-profit organization not bound by tight restrictions. CARL's lawyer and auditors advised a subsidiary organization with majority ownership held by CARL. As a for-profit organization, the CARL subsidiary could freely sell its products to libraries and markets other than libraries with the profits returned to the member libraries. The for-profit subsidiary would be known as CARL Systems, Inc. (CSI). As CSI, the organization would sell to libraries and markets other than libraries. The revenues generated from sales would be used to offset expenses or funneled back to support more growth. In June 1988 CARL Systems, Inc., filed its Articles of Incorporation and became a for-profit organization. Becky Lenzini was hired as the President of CARL Systems Inc. and began marketing CARL to the library community. Immediately CARL began to receive numerous inquiries and to respond to "Request For Proposals" submitted. Several major contracts were signed and CARL became a national competitor in on-line information systems.

Since its incorporation, CARL Systems Inc. has generated profits that are currently being channeled back into research and development and upgrading existing equipment. Because of the demand and popularity of the products offered, over forty staff members have been added and CARL Systems, Inc., has moved to larger offices.

A major development for CSI, following its incorporation for profit, was the UnCover data base. Begun in late 1988, the UnCover database provides access to article records taken from the table of contents of all journals received by CARL's member institutions. In a paper written by Martha Whitaker, CARL Coordinator for Markets and Client Relations, she states that the "searcher can retrieve articles on any topic of interest, or recreate the table of contents of specific journals. Thus UnCover provides a user-driven current awareness service accessible in the comfort of the users home or office, or in any CARL member library."[8] A more thorough and technical discussion of UnCover can be found in two 1990 articles by George Jaramillo and Jan Squire,[9] and by Marie Kroeger.[10]

The primary checking-in of journal titles listed in UnCover takes place at a centralized location, the CARL offices in Denver. Member libraries, both public and private supported institutions, have agreed to have their journal titles mailed directly to a Denver post office box where a courier picks them up. CARL staff members enter in the data overnight and ship the journal to the library the next day. The UnCover data base is the most current on-line article retrieval system available to library users today. The state funded institutions support the UnCover project by supplying its journals to CSI for data input. In return, CSI provides the manpower to check in and record all institutional journals, relieving current staffing for other duties.

Currently, UnCover provides the user the ability to select an article from any participating library and have the article faxed to the individual. CSI has established sites at several institutions to retrieve requested articles from journals and input them directly into the CSI computer via phone lines. The article is faxed within twenty-four hours or it is provided free to the user. Once the article is captured in the computer it can be faxed within a matter of a few hours if requested again. The user pays a service fee plus all copyright charges. The average cost is between $8.00 and $12.00.

FUTURE DEVELOPMENTS

Currently, the state has developed a cooperative project among the Colorado Libraries, the Colorado Library Association, and the Colorado State Library, known as *Access Colorado*. The basic goals of *Access Colorado* as described by Susan Fayad,[11] Senior Consultant for Networking and Resource Sharing, are:

1. Establish a telecommunications network linking library and other databases.
2. Provide toll free dial access to the network for all residents so that they can search the network from home, school, business, or library computers.

The project was authorized by the Colorado General Assembly House Bill 1230[12] but received no start-up funding. The project was charged with raising funds for implementation and first year operations. However, once the project is viewed as a success by the state it is possible to return to the legislature and request continued funding. The outcome of *Access Colorado* is to improve access to information for all Colorado residents. Anyone with access to a microcomputer and modem will dial an 800 number and gain access to a network. A menu would be displayed allowing the user to select CARL from the various data bases. Gaining access to CARL will enable the user to search the CARL data bases of the 122-plus libraries, state and federal publications, ERIC, adult literacy materials, UnCover, and other non-library data bases.

The CARL COLA Committee is looking at ways to maximize the CARL system in an effort to share resources. In an effort to determine if UnCover can be used for resource sharing, COLA is currently analyzing periodicals holding data within its members in an attempt to identify titles that may be cancelled by one member, but held by a second member. As the inflationary costs for serials continue to spiral upward, and with minimal increases to the book budget, the sharing of resources becomes more crucial. As Gary Pitkin[14] stated, "Certainly the development of this effective article access (UnCover) and delivery mechanism will set the stage for the cooperative reevaluation of serials collection development—an effort that has long been discussed by library consortia but met with relatively little success."

CONCLUSION

CARL was founded in 1974 by the directors of seven public and private institutions in Colorado with the mission of developing a foundation for cooperation among the institutions, thus maximizing resources of all types. The CARL System grew from these endeavors and established itself as a competitor in the on-line system market. As CSI, it manages the marketing, sales and development of the automated system as a for-profit subsidiary adjunct to the alliance of CARL libraries. The alliance still serves to provide a foundation for cooperative efforts among the member libraries.

Funding for the formation of CARL and development of the CARL System generally came from the library budgets of the member libraries. The State of Colorado appropriates funds to the governing board of each institution and in turn the governing boards allocate funds within the institution. Separate state allocations were never made for CARL. Thus, of necessity, libraries used operating funds, or more often the learning materials budget as a source of funds for the CARL efforts. When CSI was formed it was intended that profits from sales would help offset costs of CARL to the institutions. While the profits do support development and thus, in part, offset the financial obligation of the institutions, each CARL member continues to pay an annual assessment for system maintenance and support.

The CARL System currently provides all CARL users access to over 122 library catalogs throughout the United States. With the advent of Access Colorado, the CARL system will become a resource available to any citizen of the state. The goal of the founding members of CARL, to provide increased access by patrons of materials and research in and outside of Colorado, will be furthered on a statewide level.

NOTES

1. Patricia Culkin and Ward Shaw, "The CARL system," *Library Journal* 110 (February 1985), p. 68.

2. Judith Rice-Jones, "An interview with Ward Shaw and Patricia Culkin of CARL PAC," *Colorado Libraries* 11 (March 1985), p. 9.

3. Colorado, Formula Budgeting Committee, *Report of the Association of College and University Presidents' Library Formula Budgeting Subcommittee* (1977), p. 1.

4. Colorado, General Assembly, Joint Budget Committee, *Appropriations Report 1981–82* (1981), pp. 61–65.

5. Colorado, General Assembly, House Bill No. 1187, An Act... Concerning the Reorganization of Higher Education (1985), p. 750.

6. Colorado Alliance of Research Libraries, *Operating plan* (Denver: CARL, 1984), pp. 1–16.

7. Colorado Alliance of Research Libraries, *Operating plan* (Denver: CARL, 1988), pp. 1–3.

8. Martha Whitaker, *The Colorado Alliance of Research Libraries: Building Systems that Inform* (Denver: CARL, n.d.), p. 3.

9. George Jaramillo and Jan Squire, "UnCover—Instant Article Access," *Serials Review* 16 (Fall 1990): pp. 29–37.

10. Marie Kroeger, "Using UnCover (Article Access) in a University Library," *Reference Services Review* 18 (Winter 1990): pp. 69–76.

11. Susan Fayad, "Update on the Access Colorado Information Network," *Colorado Libraries* 17 (December 1991): pp. 26–28.

12. Colorado, General Assembly, House Bill No. 1230, An Act... Concerning the creation of a computer information network in the charge of the Colorado Commissioner of Education, acting as the state librarian, and, in connection therewith, creating the computer information network fund and making an appropriation (1990), 1304.

13. Gary Pitkin, "Access to Articles Through the Online Catalog," *American Libraries* 19 (October 1988): p. 770.

Appendix A

Acronyms Used in this Work

ACHE	Alabama Commission on Higher Education
ACL	[University System of Georgia] Academic Committee on Libraries
ACLCP	Associated College Libraries of Central Pennsylvania
ACRL	Association of College and Research Libraries, a division of the American Library Association
APCUP	Association of Public College and University Presidents
APLS	Alabama Public Library Service
ARL	Association of Research Libraries
ASERL	Association of Southeastern Research Libraries
AULS	Alabama Union List of Serials
BCL	[Massachusetts] Books for College Libraries Project
BOR	[Florida State University System] Board of Regents
CARL	Colorado Alliance of Research Libraries
CCHE	Colorado Commission on Higher Education
CCLA	[Florida] College Center for Library Automation
CICS	[IBM] Customer Information Control System
CLSI	CL Systems, Incorporated
COMCAT	[Florida] Computer-Output-on-Microfilm Catalog
CSI	CARL Systems, Incorporated
CWIS	Campus (Community, Company)-Wide Information System
DLIS	[Florida] Division of Library and Information Services (the State Library, formerly DLS)
DLS	[Florida] Division of Library Services (now DLIS)

DOE	[Florida] Department of Education
DRA	Data Research Associates (CCLA systems vendor)
ERIC	Educational Resources Information Center
ERM	[Massachusetts] Educational Reference Material
FCLA	Florida Center for Library Automation
FIRN	Florida Information Resources Network
FTE	Full-time equivalent
GOLD	Georgia OnLine Database
GOVOP	[Florida Senate] Government Operations Committee
HECB	[Minnesota] Higher Education Coordinating Board
HECC	[Massacusetts] Higher Education Coordinating Committee
IAC	Information Access Corporation
ILCSO	Illinois Library Computer Systems Organization
LAN	Local area network
LCS	Library Computer System
LINCC	[Florida] Library Information Network Community Colleges
LSCA	Library Services and Construction Act
LUIS	Library User Information Service [on-line catalog for Florida State University System Libraries]
MARC	Machine-Readable Cataloging
MCCLPHEI	Massachusetts Conference of Chief Librarians in Public Higher Education Institutions
MINITEX	Minnesota Interlibrary Telecommunications Exchange
MOREnet	Missouri Research and Educational Network
MULS	Minnesota Union List of Serials
MVS	[IBM] Multiple Virtual Storage
NAAL	Network of Alabama Academic Libraries
NCIN	North Carolina Information Network
NCLIS	National Commission on Library and Information Science
NERDC	[Florida State University System] Northeast Regional Data Center
NMCAL	New Mexico Consortium of Academic Libraries
NOTIS	Northwestern Online Total Information System
NREN	National Research and Education Network
OARNet	Ohio Academic Resource Network
OCLC	Online Computer Library Center
OhioLINK	Ohio Library and Information Network
ONCHE	Oklahoma Network of Continuing Higher Education

Acronyms Used in this Work

PAC	Public Access Catalog
PEPC	[Florida] Post-Secondary Education Planning Commission
PRIE	[San Diego] Packet Radio Internet Extension
PSC	[FCLA] Public Services Committee
RefNet	[Connecticut] Reference Network
RLG	Research Libraries Group
SEFLIN	Southeast Florida Library Information Network
Solinet	Southeastern Library Network
SUS	[Florida] State University System
TRLN	Triangle Research Libraries Network
TSC	[FCLA] Technical Services Committee
UF	University of Florida
UMass	University of Massachusetts
USF	University of South Florida
USG	University System of Georgia
VALS	Vermont Automated Libraries System
VLIN	Virginia Library and Information Network
WLN	Western Library Network

Appendix B

State Coordinating Agencies of Higher Education

Alabama	Alabama Commission on Higher Education One Court Square, Suite 221 Montgomery, AL 36104
Alaska	Alaska Commission on Postsecondary Education 400 Willoughby Avenue Box FP Juneau, AK 99811
Arizona	Arizona Board of Regents 3030 North Central Avenue, Suite 1400 Phoenix, AZ 85012
	Arizona Commission for Postsecondary Education 3030 North Central Avenue, Suite 1407 Phoenix, AZ 85012
	State Board of Directors for Community Colleges of Arizona Century Plaza, Suite 1220 3225 North Central Avenue Phoenix, AZ 85012
Arkansas	Arkansas Board of Higher Education 1220 West Third Street Little Rock, AR 72201
California	California Postsecondary Education Commission 1020 12th Street, 3rd Floor Sacramento, CA 95814

California (continued)	Board of Governors Chancellor's Office California Community Colleges 1107 Ninth Street, 6th Floor Sacramento, CA 95814
Colorado	Colorado Commission on Higher Education 1300 Broadway, 2nd Floor Denver, CO 80203
Connecticut	Connecticut Board of Governors for Higher Education 61 Woodland Street Hartford, CT 06105
Delaware	Delaware Postsecondary Education Commission 820 North French Street Wilmington, DE 19801
District of Columbia	District of Columbia Office of Postsecondary Education Research and Assistance 2100 Martin Luther King Avenue SE Suite 401 Washington DC 20020
Florida	Florida Postsecondary Education Planning Commission Florida Education Center Tallahassee, FL 32399 Florida University System Board of Regents 1514 Florida Education Center Tallahassee, FL 32399 Florida Board of Community Colleges 1314 Florida Education Center Tallahassee, FL 32399
Georgia	Georgia Board of Regents University System of Georgia 244 Washington Street SW Atlanta, GA 30334
Hawaii	University of Hawaii Board of Regents Bachman Hall, Room 209 University of Hawaii 2444 Dole Street Honolulu, HI 96822
Idaho	Idaho State Board of Education 630 West State Street, Room 307 Boise, ID 83720

State Coordinating Agencies of Higher Education

Illinois	Board of Higher Education 500 Reisch Building 4 West Old Capitol Springfield, IL 62701
Indiana	Indiana Commission for Higher Education 101 West Ohio Street, Suite 550 Indianapolis, IN 46204
Iowa	Iowa State Board of Regents Old State Historical Building Des Moines, IA 50319 Iowa Department of Education Division of Community Colleges Grimes State Office Building Des Moines, IA 50319
Kansas	Kansas Board of Regents Suite 609, Capitol Tower 400 Southwest Eighth Street Topeka, KS 66603-3911
Kentucky	Kentucky Council on Higher Education 1050 U.S. 127 South, Suite 101 Frankfort, KY 40601
Louisiana	State of Louisiana Board of Regents 150 Riverside Mall, Suite 129 Baton Rouge, LA 70803
Maine	University of Maine System Board of Trustees 107 Maine Avenue Bangor, ME 04401
Maryland	Maryland Higher Education Commission Jeffrey Building 16 Francis Street Annapolis, MD 21401 State Board for Community Colleges Georgetown Plaza, Suite 210 914 Bay Ridge Road Annapolis, MD 21403
Massachusetts	Massachusetts Higher Education Coordinating Committee One Ashburton Place Boston, MA 02108
Michigan	Michigan State Department of Education P.O. Box 30008 Lansing, MI 48909

Minnesota	Minnesota Higher Education Coordinating Board 400 Capitol Square Building 550 Cedar Street St. Paul, MN 55101
Mississippi	Board of Trustees of State Institutions of Higher Learning 3825 Ridgewood Road Jackson, MS 39211
	State Board for Community and Junior Colleges 3825 Ridgewood Road Jackson, MS 39211
Missouri	Missouri Coordinating Board for Higher Education 101 Adams Street Jefferson City, MO 65101
Montana	Montana University System 33 South Last Chance Gulch Helena, MT 59620
Nebraska	Nebraska Coordinating Commission for Postsecondary Education State Capitol, 6th Floor P.O. Box 95005 Lincoln, NE 68509
Nevada	University of Nevada System 2601 Enterprise Road Reno, NV 89512
New Hampshire	New Hampshire Postsecondary Education Commission Two Industrial Park Drive Concord, NH 03301
	University System of New Hampshire Office of the Chancellor Dunlap Center Durham, NH 03824
New Jersey	New Jersey Board of Higher Education 20 West State Street, CN 542 Trenton, NJ 08625
New Mexico	New Mexico Commission on Higher Education 1068 Cerrillos Road Sante Fe, NM 87501
New York	New York State Education Department Cultural Education Center Room 5B28 Albany, NY 12230

State Coordinating Agencies of Higher Education 171

North Carolina	University of North Carolina General Administration P.O. Box 2688 Chapel Hill, NC 27515
	Department of Community Colleges 200 West Jones Street Raleigh, NC 27603-1337
North Dakota	North Dakota University System State Capitol Building Bismarck, ND 58504
Ohio	Ohio Board of Regents 30 East Broad Street 3600 State Office Tower Columbus, OH 43266
Oklahoma	Oklahoma State Regents for Higher Education 500 Education Building State Capitol Complex Oklahoma City, OK 73105
Oregon	Oregon Office of Educational Policy and Planning 225 Winter Street, N.E. Salem, OR 97310
Pennsylvania	Pennsylvania State Department of Education 333 Market Street 5th Floor Harrisburg, PA 17102
	Division of Postsecondary Education Services Pennslyvania Department of Education 333 Market Street 9th Floor Harrisburg, PA 17102
Rhode Island	Rhode Island Independent Higher Education Association Charles-Orms Building, Suite 120 10 Orms Street Providence, RI 02904
South Carolina	South Carolina Commission on Higher Education 1333 Main Street, Suite 300 Columbia, SC 29201
South Dakota	South Dakota Board of Regents 207 East Capitol Avenue Pierre, SD 57501
Tennessee	Tennessee Higher Education Commission Parkway Towers, Suite 1900 4404 James Robertson Parkway Nashville, TN 37219
	Tennessee State Board of Regents 1415 Murfreesboro Road, Suite 350 Nashville, TN 37217

Texas	Texas Higher Education Coordinating Board P.O. Box 12788 Austin, TX 78711
Utah	Utah System of Higher Education 355 West North Temple 3 Triad Center, Suite 550 Salt Lake City, UT 84180
Vermont	Vermont Higher Education Planning Commission Department of Finance and Management 109 State Street Montpelier, VT 05602
Virginia	State Council of Higher Education James Monroe Building 101 North 14th Street Richmond, VA 23219
Washington	Higher Education Coordinating Board 917 Lakeridge Way, GV-11 Olympia, WA 98504
West Virginia	University of West Virginia System 1018 Kanawha Boulevard East Suite 700 Charleston, WV 25301 West Virginia State College System 1018 Kanawha Boulevard East Suite 700 Charleston, WV 25301
Wisconsin	University of Wisconsin System 1720 Van Hise Hall 1220 Linden Drive Madison, WI 53706

Appendix C

State Library Agencies

Alabama Public Library Service
6030 Monticello Drive
Montgomery, AL 36130

Alaska State Library
State Office Building
P.O. Box G
Juneau, AK 99811-0571

Arizona State Library
State Capitol
1700 West Washington
Phoenix, AZ 85007

Arkansas State Library
One Capitol Mall
Little Rock, AR 72201

California State Library
914 Capitol Mall
P.O. Box 942837
Sacramento, CA 95809-2037

Colorado State Library
201 East Colfax
Denver, CO 80203-1704

Connecticut State Library
231 Capitol Avenue
Hartford, CT 06106

Delaware Division of Libraries
43 South DuPont Highway
Dover, DE 19903

State Library of Florida
R. A. Gray Building
Tallahassee, FL 32399-0250

Georgia Department of Education
156 Trinity Avenue
Atlanta, GA 30303-3692

Hawaii State Public Library System
465 South King Street
Honolulu, HI 96813

Idaho State Library
325 West State Street
Boise, ID 83702-6072

Illinois State Library
Centennial Building, Room 275
Springfield, IL 62756

Indiana State Library
140 North Senate Avenue
Indianapolis, IN 46204-2296

State Library of Iowa
Des Moines, IA 50319

Kansas State Library
State Capitol
Topeka, KS 66612

Kentucky Department of Libraries and Archives
300 Coffee Tree Road
P.O. Box 537
Frankfort, KY 40602-0537

State Library of Louisiana
760 Riverside Mall
P.O. Box 131
Baton Rouge, LA 70821-0131

Maine State Library
LMA Building
State House Station 64
Augusta, ME 04333-0064

Maryland State Department of Education
200 West Baltimore Street
Baltimore, MD 21201

Massachusetts Board of Library Commissioners
648 Beacon Street
Boston, MA 02215

Library of Michigan
717 West Allegan Avenue
P.O. Box 30007
Lansing, MI 48909

Minnesota State Library Agency
440 Capitol Square Building
5550 Cedar Street
St. Paul, MN 55101

Mississippi Library Commission
1221 Ellis Avenue
P.O. Box 10700
Jackson, MS 39209-0700

Missouri State Library
2002 Missouri Blvd.
P.O. Box 387
Jefferson City, MO 65102

Montana State Library
1515 East Sixth Street
Helena, MT 59620

Nebraska Library Commission
1429 P. Street
Lincoln, NE 68508-1683

Nevada State Library and Archives
Capitol Complex
401 North Carson Street
Carson City, NV 89710

New Hampshire State Library
20 Park Street
Concord, NH 03301

New Jersey State Library
185 West State Street
Trenton, NJ 08625-6200

New Mexico State Library
325 Don Gaspar
Santa Fe, NM 87503

New York State Library
Cultural Education Center
Empire State Plaza
Albany, NY 12230

North Carolina Department of Cultural Resources
109 East Jones Street
Raleigh, NC 27611

North Dakota State Library
Liberty Memorial Building
Capitol Grounds
Bismarck, ND 58505

State Library of Ohio
65 South Front Street
Room 510
Columbus, OH 43215

State Library Agencies 177

Oklahoma Department of Libraries
200 NE 18th Street
Oklahoma City, OK 73105

Oregon State Library
State Library Building
Summer & Court Streets
Salem, OR 73105

State Library of Pennsylvania
P.O. Box 1601
Harrisburg, PA 17105

Rhode Island Department of State Library Services
300 Richmond Street
Providence, RI 02903

South Carolina State Library
1500 Senate Street
P.O. Box 11469
Columbia, SC 29211

South Dakota State Library
800 Governors Drive
Pierre, SD 57501-2284

Tennessee State Library and Archives
403 Seventh Avenue North
Nashville, TN 37219

Texas State Library
1201 Brazos Street
P.O. Box 12927 Capitol Station
Austin, TX 78711

Utah State Library
2150 South 300 West
Salt Lake City, UT 84115

Vermont Department of Libraries
111 State Street
State Office Building Post Office
Montpelier, VT 05602

Virginia State Library
Richmond, VA 23219

Washington State Library
Capitol Campus
Olympia, WA 98504

West Virginia Library Commission
Science and Cultural Center
State Capitol
Charleston, WV 25305

Wisconsin Department of Public Instruction
125 South Webster Street
Room 325
P.O. Box 7841
Madison, WI 53707

Wyoming State Library
Supreme Court and Library Building
Cheyenne, WY 82002

Selected Bibliography (Arranged by Broad Subject)

HIGHER EDUCATION AND GOVERNMENT

Almanac of Higher Education 1991. Chicago: University of Chicago Press, 1991.

Atkins, Stephen E. *The Academic Library in the American University*. Chicago: American Library Association, 1991.

Baldridge, J. Victor et al. *Policy Making and Effective Leadership*. San Francisco: Jossey-Bass, 1978.

Berdahl, Robert O. "Public Universities and State Governments: Is the Tension Benign?" *Educational Record* 71 (Winter 1990): 38–42.

Berdahl, Robert O. *Statewide Coordination of Higher Education*. Washington, D.C.: American Council on Education, 1971.

Blumenstyk, Goldie. "Massachusetts Reorgnization of Public Higher Education Gives Wide Powers to Secretary, 11-Member Council." *Chronicle of Higher Education* 37 (July 24, 1991): 17A-18A.

Blumenstyk, Goldie. "The Outlook for Higher Education in 50 State Legislatures this Year." *Chronicle of Higher Education* 37 (Jan. 9, 1991): 21A.

Carnegie Commission on Higher Education. *The Capitol and the Campus: State Responsibility for Postsecondary Education*. New York: McGraw-Hill, 1971.

Caruthers, J. Kent and Joseph L. Marks. *State Funding of Higher Education for Quality Improvements in the SREB States*. Atlanta: Southern Regional Education Board, 1988.

The Control of the Campus. Washington, D.C.: Carnegie Foundation for the Advancement of Teaching, 1982.

Dauer, Manning J., ed. *Florida's Politics and Government*. Gainesville: University of Florida Press, 1984.
DePalma, Frank. *The Governance of Education in Florida*. Columbus: Educational Governance Project, Ohio State University, 1973.
Education Commission of the States. *Challenge: Coordination and Governance in the 1980s*. Denver: Education Commission of the States, 1980.
Enarson, Harold H. "Quality and Accountability: Are We Destroying What We Want to Preserve?" *Change* 12, no. 7 (1980): 7–10.
Fincher, Cameron. *Historical Development of the University System of the University of Georgia: 1932–1990*. Athens, Ga.: Institute of Higher Education, University of Georgia, 1991.
Glenny, Lyman A. *Autonomy of Public Colleges: The Challenge of Coordination*. New York: McGraw-Hill, 1959.
Glenny, Lyman A. et al. *Coordinating Higher Education for the '70s*. Berkeley, Calif.: Center for Research and Development in Higher Education, University of California, 1971.
Gregory, Vicki L. "Library Cooperative Programs and Coordinating Agencies of Higher Education." *Library and Information Science Research* 10 (Sum. 1988): 305–29.
Gregory, Vicki L. "State Coordination of Higher Education and Academic Libraries." *College & Research Libraries* 49 (July 1988): 315–24.
Hines, Edward R. *Higher Education and State Governments: Renewed Partnership, Cooperation, or Competition?* College Station, Texas: Association for the Study of Higher Education, 1988.
Jedamus, Paul; Marvin W. Peterson and Associates. *Improving Academic Management*. San Francisco: Jossey-Bass, 1981.
Johnson, Thomas E. *Role of the State in Planning and Coordination of Autonomous Institutions of Higher Education*. Lansing: Michigan State Department of Education, 1977.
Jones, Dennis P. *Higher Education Budgeting at the State Level: Concepts and Principles*. Boulder, Colorado: National Center for Higher Education Management Systems, 1984. ED 256 625.
Keefe, William J. and Morris S. Ogul. *The American Legislative Process, Congress and the States*. 2nd ed. Englewood Cliffs, N.J.: Prentice-Hall, 1968.
Kerr, Clark. *The Great Transformation in Higher Education 1960–1980*. Albany: State University of New York Press, 1991.
Littleton, Isaac T. *State Systems of Higher Education and Libraries*. Washington, D.C.: Council on Library Resources, 1977.
McGuinness, Aims C., Jr. *The Search for More Effective State Policy Leadership in Higher Education: Recent State Higher Education Studies and Trends in Coordination and Governance*. Denver: Education Commission of the States, 1986.
McGuinness, Aims C., Jr. *State Postsecondary Education Structures Handbook, 1988*. Denver: Education Commission of the States, 1988.
McKeown, Mary P. "The Use of Formulas for State Funding of Higher Education." *Journal of Education Finance* 7 (Winter 1982): 277–300.

Meisinger, Richard John. *State Budgeting for Higher Education: The Use of Formulas*. Berkeley: Center for Research and Development in Higher Education, University of California, 1976.

Millard, Richard M. *Today's Myths and Tomorrow's Realities*. San Francisco: Jossey-Bass, 1991.

Miller, James L., Jr. *State Budgeting for Higher Education: The Use of Formulas and Cost Analysis*. Ann Arbor: Institute of Public Administration, University of Michigan, 1964.

Millett, John D. *Conflict in Higher Education: State Government Coordination versus Institutional Independence*. San Francisco: Jossey-Bass, 1984.

Mingle, James R., editor. *Management Flexibility and State Regulation in Higher Education*. Atlanta: Southern Regional Education Board, 1983. ED 234 705.

Mortimer, Kenneth P. and T. R. McConnell. *Sharing Authority Effectively*. San Francisco: Jossey-Bass, 1978.

Mosher, Edith K. and Jennings L. Wagoner, Jr. *The Changing Politics of Education: Prospects for the 1980's*. Berkeley, Calif.: McCutchan Publishing Company, 1978.

National Conference of State Legislatures. *State Issues 1992: A Survey of Priority Issues for State Legislatures*. Denver: National Conference of State Legislatures, 1991.

Ransome, Coleman B., Jr. *The American Governorship*. Westport, Conn.: Greenwood Press, 1982.

Ross, Michael J. *State and Local Politics and Policy: Change and Reform*. Englewood Cliffs, N.J.: Prentice-Hall, 1987.

Schmidtlein, Frank A. and Lyman A. Glenny. *State Budgeting for Higher Education: The Political Economy of the Process*. Berkeley: University of California, Center for Research and Development in Higher Education, 1977.

Skolnik, Michael L. "A Comparative Analysis of Arrangements for State Coordination of Higher Education in Canada and the United States. *Journal of Higher Education* 63 (March/April 1992): 121–42.

Slaughter, Sheila and Edward T. Silva. "Toward a Political Economy of Retrenchment: The American Public Research University." *The Review of Higher Education* 8 (Summer 1985): 295–318.

Snider, Clyde F. in collaboration with Samuel K. Gove. *American State and Local Government*. 2nd ed. New York: Appleton-Century-Crofts, 1965.

State Postsecondary Education Structures Handbook 1986. Denver: Education Commission of the States, 1986.

Thompson, Fred and William Zumeta. "A Regulatory Model of Governmental Coordinating Activities in the Higher Education Sector." *Economics of Education Review* 1, no. 1 (1981): 27–52.

Treadway, Jack M. *Public Policymaking in the American States*. New York: Praeger, 1985.

Wildavsky, Aaron. *The New Politics of the Budgetary Process*. Glenview, Ill.: Scott, Foresman, 1988.

LIBRARY FINANCE AND GOVERNANCE

Ackerman, Page. "Governance and Academic Libraries." *Library Research* 2 (Spring 1980): 3–28.
Allen, Kenneth S. *Current and Emerging Budgeting Techniques in Academic Libraries, Including a Critique of the Model Budget Analysis Program of the State of Washington.* Washington, D.C.: Council on Library Resources, 1972.
Association of Research Libraries. "Review of Budgeting Techniques in Academic and Research Libraries." *ARL Management Supplement* 1 (April 1973): 1–4.
Clapp, Vernon W. and Robert T. Jordan. "Quantitative Criteria for Adequacy of Academic Library Collections." *College & Research Libraries* 26 (Sept. 1965): 371–80. Reprinted in *College & Research Libraries* 50 (March 1989): 154–63.
Colorado. Formula Budgeting Committee. *Report of the Association of the College and University Presidents' Library Formula Budgeting Subcommittee.* 1977.
Curran, Charles. "Developing Patterns of Governance in Public Organizations." *Library Trends* 26 (Fall 1977): 161–80.
Govan, James F. "The Better Mousetrap: External Accountability and Staff Participation." *Library Trends* 26 (Fall 1977): 255–67.
Gregory, Vicki L. "Development of Academic Library Budgets in Selected States with Emphasis on the Utilization of Formulas." *Journal of Library Administration* 12, no. 1 (1990): 23–45.
Gregory, Vicki L. "Formula Funding in Academic Libraries." in *Encyclopedia of Library and Information Science* v. 49, Supplement 12 (1992): 259–67.
Jaramillo, George R. and Jan Squire. "UnCover—Instant Article Access." *Serials Review* 16 (Fall 1990): 29–37.
Josey, E. J. and Kenneth D. Shearer, eds. *Politics and the Support of Libraries.* New York: Neal-Schuman, 1990.
Kroeger, Marie. "Using UnCover (Article Access) in a University Library." *Reference Services Review* 18 (Winter 1990): 69–76.
Lohela, Shari and F. William Summers. "The Impact of Planning on Budgeting." *Journal of Library Administration* 2 (Sum./Fall/Win. 1981): 173–85.
McAnally, Arthur M. "Budgets by Formula." *Library Quarterly* 33 (April 1963): 159–71.
Mitchell, Betty Jo. *ALMS: A Budget Based Library Management System.* Greenwich, Conn.: JAI Press, 1983.
Munn, Robert F. "The Bottomless Pit, or the Academic Library as Viewed from the Administration Building." *College & Research Libraries* 29 (Jan. 1968): 52–54. Reprinted in *College & Research Libraries* 50 (Nov. 1989): 635–37.
Prentice, Ann E. *Financial Planning for Libraries.* Metuchen, N.J.: Scarecrow Press, 1983.
Voigt, Melvin J. "Acquisition Rates in University Libraries." *College & Research Libraries* 33 (July 1975): 262–82.

LIBRARY NETWORKS AND RESOURCE SHARING

Arms, Caroline, ed. *Campus Strategies for Libraries and Electronic Information.* Bedford, Mass.: Digital Press, 1990.

Brong, Gerald R. "The State of Washington's Search for Intrastate Cooperation." *Library Trends* 24 (Oct. 1975): 257-75.

Cooperative Library Resource Sharing among Universities Supporting Graduate Study in Alabama. Montgomery: Alabama Commission on Higher Education, 1983. ED 224 497

Cravey, G. Randall. "Networking in the Southeast." *Technical Services Quarterly* 4 (Fall 1986): 55-67.

Crowe, William J. and Nancy P. Sanders. "Collection Development in the Cooperative Environment." *Journal of Library Administration* 15, nos. 3/4 (1991): 37-48.

Culkin, Patricia and Ward Shaw. "The CARL System." *Library Journal* 110 (February 1985): 68.

Dalehite, Michele I. "Florida Center for Library Automation: The Organization." *Advances in Library Administration and Networking* vol. 3 (Greenwich, Conn.: JAI Press, 1989): 205-24.

Dougherty, Richard M. "A Conceptual Framework for Organizing Resource Sharing and Shared Collection Development Programs." *Journal of Academic Librarianship* 14 (Nov. 1988): 287-91.

Fayad, Susan. "Update on the Access Colorado Information Network." *Colorado Libraries* 17 (December 1991): 26-28.

Florida. Department of Education. Postsecondary Education Planning Commission. *Automation and Networking for Florida Libraries.* Tallahassee: PEPC, 1988.

Florida. Senate. Committee on Governmental Operations. *A Review of the Benefits, Costs, and Feasibility of a Statewide Network Linking the Libraries in Florida.* Tallahassee, 1989.

Gorman, Michael. "The Online Catalogue at the University of Illinois at Urbana-Champaign: A History and Overview." *Information Technology and Libraries* 4 (Dec. 1985): 306-11.

Griffiths, Jose-Marie and Donald W. King. *Massachusetts Libraries: An Alliance for the Future.* Knoxville, Tenn.: King Research, 1991.

Hawks, Carol Pitts. "The Integrated Library System of the 1990s: The OhioLINK Experience." *Library Resources & Technical Services* 36 (Jan. 1992): 61-77.

Henigman, Barbara. "Networking and Authority Control: Online Catalog Authority Control in Illinois." *Information Technology and Libraries* 10 (March 1991): 47-54.

Huseman, Dwight. "Access to Materials in Pennsylvania: Interlibrary Delivery." *Wilson Library Bulletin* 59 (Dec. 1984): 262-63.

LaCroix, Michael J. "Minitex and ILLINET: Two Library Networks." *Occasional Papers of the University of Illinois, Graduate School of Library and Information Science* no. 178 (May 1987): 3-15.

LaRue, James. "A Superhighway to the World." *Wilson Library Bulletin* 67 (May 1993): 35–37.

Lawhorne, Anne. "Missouri Research and Education Network: Catalyst for Change in Missouri Libraries." *Show-Me Libraries* 43 (Winter 1992): 18–21.

Markuson, Barbara Evans and Blanche Woolls, editors. *Networks for Networkers: Critical Issues in Cooperative Library Development.* New York: Neal Schuman, 1980.

McGinn, Howard F. "Electronic Services for Rural Libraries: Meeting the Challenge in North Carolina." *RQ* 29 (Sum. 1990): 492–96.

McGinn, Howard F. "Information and the Development of Rural North Carolina." *Southeastern Librarian* 40 (Sum. 1990): 75–79.

McGinn, Howard F. "Information Networking and Economic Development." *Wilson Library Bulletin* 62 (Nov. 1987): 28–32.

McGinn, Howard F. "The Role of Serials Location and Distribution in Economic Development." *Serials Review* 15 (Sum. 1989): 15–18.

Medina, Sue O. "The Evolution of Cooperative Collection Development in Alabama Academic Libraries." *College & Research Libraries* 53 (Jan. 1992): 7–19.

Medina, Sue O. "Network of Alabama Academic Libraries: An Emerging State Network." *Southeastern Librarian* 37 (Sum. 1987): 41–45.

National Commission on Libraries and Information Science, 1975. *Toward a National Program for Library and Information Services: Goals for Action.* Washington, D.C.: Government Printing Office, 1975.

Neumann, Joan. "The New York State Experience with Coordinated Collection Development: Funding the Stimulus." *Resource Sharing and Information Networks* 2 (Spr./Sum. 1985):115–28.

Oberlander, Susan. "The New Mexico Consortium of Academic Libraries, 1988–1990." *College & Research Libraries News* 52 (June 1991): 359–62.

Ohio Board of Regents, Library Study Committee. *Academic Libraries in Ohio: Progress through Collaboration, Storage, and Technology.* Columbus: Ohio Board of Regents, 1987.

Pitkin, Gary. "Access to Articles Through the Online Catalog." *American Libraries* 19 (October 1988): 770.

Rogers, Michael. "Automation News." *Library Journal* 117 (July 1992): 26, 28.

Sessions, Judith, Hwa-Wei Lee, and Stacey Kimmel. "OhioLINK: Technology and Teamwork Transforming Ohio Libraries." *Wilson Library Bulletin* 66 (June 1992): 43–45.

Wilcox, Alice E. "Library Networks Circa 1984 or One Blind Person Touching the Elephant." *Resource Sharing and Information Networks* 2 (Fall/Winter 1984): 27–40.

Wilson, Mark. "How to Set Up a Telefacsimile Network—The Pennsylvania Libraries Experience." *Online* 12 (May 1988): 15–25.

PROGRAM REVIEW

Barak, Robert J. and Robert O. Berdahl. *State Level Program Review in Higher Education.* Denver: Education Commission of the States, 1978.

Barak, Robert J. and Barbara E. Brier. *Successful Program Review: A Practical*

Guide to Evaluating Programs in Academic Settings. San Francisco: Jossey-Bass, 1990.
Gregory, Vicki L. "The Academic Library in the Program Review Process." *Collection Management* 12, nos. 3/4 (1990): 125–34.
Medina, Sue O. et al. *Collection Assessment Manual.* Montgomery: Network of Alabama Academic Libraries, 1987.

STATE LIBRARIES AND MULTITYPE LIBRARY SYSTEMS

Adams, Douglas M. *An Organizational Analysis of Multi-Type Library Cooperation in Utah: A Consideration of Basic Issues for Laypersons and Librarians.* Salt Lake City: State Library Division, Department of Community and Economic Development, 1987.
Casey, Genevieve M. "Administration of State and Federal Funds for Library Development." *Library Trends* 27 (Fall 1978): 145–63.
Epler, Doris M. and Richard E. Cassel. "ACCESS PENNSYLVANIA: A CD-ROM Database Project." *Library Hi-Tech* 5 (Fall 1987): 81–92.
Fiels, Keith Michael, Joan Newmann, and Eva R. Brown, comp. *Multitype Library Cooperation, State Laws, Regulations and Pending Legislation.* Chicago: Association of Specialized and Cooperative Library Agencies, 1991.
Ford, Sylverna. "Models of Access: The Oakland Library Consortium." *Resource Sharing and Information Networks* 7, no. 1 (1991): 67–80.
Givens, Beth. *Pilot Moncat: Making Way for Montana's Union Catalog.* Helena: Montana State Library, 1985.
Illinois Libraries 57 (June 1975). [Entire issue is devoted to ILLINET.]
Jackson, Mary, ed. *Research Access Through New Technology.* New York: AMS, 1989.
Markuson, Barbara Evans. "Analysis of Requirements of On-Line Network Cataloging for Small Academic, Public, School, and Other Libraries." Bethesda, Md.: ERIC Documentation Reproduction Service, 1977. ED 140 861
Mitchell, Thornton W. *The State Library and Library Development in North Carolina.* Raleigh: North Carolina Department of Cultural Resources, 1983.
New Jersey State Library. *A Developing State Plan for Library Services.* Trenton: Department of Education, 1980.
"North Carolina Information Network." *Tar Heel Libraries* 14 (May/June 1991): 5.
RMG Consultants, Inc. *Executive Summary of Plans and Recommendations for an Alabama Library Network.* Montgomery, Ala.: Alabama Public Library Service, 1985.
RMG Consultants, Inc. *Plans and Recommendations for an Alabama Library Network.* Montgomery, Ala.: Alabama Public Library Service, 1985.
State Library of Pennsylvania, Advisory Council on Library Development. *Improved Access to Pennsylvania's Library Resources: A Review of the Comprehensive Plan and Governor's Conference Resolutions.* Harrisburg: State Library of Pennsylvania, 1991.
Summers, William F. and Daniel D. Barron. *An Evaluation of the Two Multi-type*

Inter-library Cooperation Projects in Alabama. Columbia, S.C.: College of Library and Information Science, University of South Carolina, 1984.

Townley, Charles T. "College Libraries and Resource Sharing: Testing a Compact Disc Union Catalog." *College & Research Libraries* 53 (Sept. 1992): 405–13.

Townley, Charles T., Charles R. Peguese and Kenneth G. Rohm, Jr. "Academic Library-State Library Agency Relationships: The Pennsylvania Needs Assessment." *College & Research Libraries* 49 (May 1988): 239–50.

Turock, Betty J. "Organizational Factors in Multitype Library Networking: A National Test of the Model." *Library & Information Science Research* 8 (April/June 1986): 117–54.

Turock, Betty J. "Performance Factors in Multitype Library Networking." *Resource Sharing and Information Networks* 3 (Fall 1985): 15–38.

Index

Academic and state libraries: cooperation, 33–34, 36–39; relationship, 36–39
Academic and Student Affairs Task Force [Massachusetts], 134–35
Academic Committee on Libraries (ACL) [Georgia]: creation of, 144; GOLD, 149; library automation, 144–48; networking, 145, 147–48; Peachnet, 148–150, 152; resource sharing, 151–52
Access Colorado Library and Information Network, 78, 159–60
ACCESS PENNSYLVANIA, 78
ACHE. *See* Alabama Commission on Higher Education
ACL. *See* Academic Committee on Libraries (Georgia)
ACLCP. *See* Associated College Libraries of Central Pennsylvania
ACRL (Association of College and Research Libraries) Standards for College Libraries, 50–52
Administrative Committee on Academic Affairs [Georgia], 144, 148
Alabama Commission on Higher Education (ACHE), 63, 96
Alabama Public Library Service (APLS), 77–78
Alabama Union List of Serials (AULS), 77
Alaska Division of Libraries, Archives and Museums, 78
ALICAT [Alabama], 78
Allen, Kenneth, 49
ALMS (A Library Management System), 80
APCUP. *See* Colorado Association of Public College and University Presidents
APLS. *See* Alabama Public Library Service
Arkansas, 94
ARL. *See* Association of Research Libraries
ASERL. *See* Association of Southeastern Research Libraries
Associated College Libraries of

Central Pennsylvania (ACLCP), 69, 75
Association of Research Libraries (ARL), 31, 47
Association of Southeastern Research Libraries (ASERL), 146
Atkinson, Hugh, 81
AULS. *See* Alabama Union List of Serials

BCL. *See* Books for College Libraries Project [Massachusetts]
Berdahl, Robert, 4, 27
BITNET, 77
Board of Regents, Florida. *See* Florida, Higher Education
Blackwell North America, Inc., 147
Bolt, Nancy M., 37
Books for College Libraries Project (BCL) [Massachusetts], 124–25
Boston Library Consortium, 133, 137
Brong, Gerald, 62–63
Brownrigg, Edwin, 85
Budgets, Library: library standards in budgeting, 50–51; formulas, 47–54
Budgets, State: procedures in relation to higher education, 42–43; purpose, 41–42; types, formula, 46–47; types, line–item, 45–46; types, lump sum, 46; types, performance, 46; types, program, 46

Campus–wide information systems, 121
CARL. *See* Colorado Alliance of Research Libraries
CARL Systems, Inc. (CSI), 154, 158–59. *See also* Colorado Alliance of Research Libraries
California State University, Northridge, A Library Management System (ALMS), 80
Carlile, Huntington, 61–62
Carnegie Library of Pittsburgh, 76
Carnegie–Mellon University, 76
CCHE. *See* Colorado Commission of Higher Education

CCLA. *See* College Center for Library Automation
C.D. Cat, Union Catalog of the Associated College Libraries of Central Pennsylvania, 69
Central Florida Library Consortium, 77
Clapp–Jordan Formula, 51–52
CLSI, 79, 112–13
College Center for Library Automation (CCLA), 109, 117
Colorado Alliance of Research Libraries (CARL): funding, 154–56, 160–61; history, 153–59; membership, 153; organizational structure, 157–58; resource sharing, 156–57
Colorado Association of Public College and University Presidents (APCUP), 157, 159–60
Colorado Commission of Higher Education (CCHE), 155–56
Colorado Library Law, 34–35
Colorado Organization for Library Acquisitions Committee (CARL COLA), 159–60
Colorado State Library, 35, 80
Colorado State University, 156
COMCAT [Florida], 112
Committee on Library Resources of the Faculty Senate, State University of New York, 50
Connecticut State Library, 79
Consolidated governing boards, 29–30
Cooperative collection development, 60, 64, 157
Coordinating agencies of higher education: creation of, 3; membership, 27; program review, 90–94; role of, 4, 16, 20–21, 23, 25–26; types, 23–29
Council of Librarians [Alabama], 63
CSI. *See* CARL Systems, Inc. [Colorado]
Culkin, Patricia, 154

Data Research Associates (DRA), 69, 84, 117, 121

Index 189

DeGennaro, Robert, 62
Delaware, 77
Denver Public Library, 156
DePalma, Frank, 102
DLIS. *See* Florida Division of Library and Information Services
Document delivery: general, 64–65, 69, 137–38; telefacsimile, 65, 68
DRA. *See* Data Research Associates
Drexel University, 76
Duszak, Thomas, 76–78

Edinboro University of Pennsylvania, 76
Education Commissions of the States, 19–20,
Educational Amendments of 1972, 3
Educational Reference Materials (ERM)[Massachusetts], 125–56, 128, 140–41
ERM. See Education Reference materials (Massachusetts)

Fayad, Susan, 99, 159–60
Faxon, Inc., 148
FCLA. *See* Florida Center for Library Automation
Fife, Jonathan, 43
Fincher, Cameron, 144
FIRN. *See* Florida Information Resources Network
Florida, Higher Education: Board of Education, 101–4, 106; Board of Regents, 103, 106, 109, 113, 120–21; lottery, 119; organization, 103–4; public community colleges, 104, 115–17; Senate Governmental Operations Committee (GOVOP), 115–16; State Board of Community Colleges, 104, 115–16. *See also* State University System of Florida.
Florida Center for Library Automation (FCLA): establishment of, 106; funding, 111–12, 118–19; governance, 109–11; centralized planning, 69, 112–13; Public Services Committee (PSC), 110–11, 120; retrospective conversion, 108;
staffing, 109, 119; Technical Services Committee (TSC), 110–11, 120
Florida Division/Department of Library and Information Services (DLIS), 36, 113–14, 117
Florida Information Resources Network (FIRN), 113–17
Florida Northeast Regional Data Center (NERDC), 108–9, 118–19
Formula budgeting, *See* Budgets, Library; Budgets, State; and Funding formulas
Funding formulas: general, 48–54; fixed and variable costs, 46–47; specific states: Colorado, 155; New Mexico, 66–67.

Georgia Board of Regents, 143–45
Georgia academic libraries: Administrative Committee on Academic Affairs, 148; joint borrower's card, 150–52; library automation, 144–48; library funding, 143, 145, 149; retrospective conversion, 147; statewide telecommunications network, 148; union list of monographs and serials, 148. *See also* Academic Committee on Libraries; Georgia Online Database; Peachnet.
Georgia, Higher Education: funding, 143; structure, 143–44
Georgia Institute of Technology, 144–47
Georgia OnLine Database (GOLD), 149
Georgia State University, 148–49
Glenny, Lyman, 29, 42
Goglia, Mario J., 144
GOLD. See Georgia OnLine Database
Governing boards. *See* Consolidated governing boards

HECC. *See* Higher Education Coordinating Committee [Massachusetts]
Higher Education Act of 1965, 3

Higher Education Coordinating
  Committee (HECC)
  [Massachusetts], 124, 131, 135
Higher Education Facilities Act of
  1963, 3
Higher education: accountability, 4;
  centralization, 1–4; enrollments, 1–
  2; funding, 9, 11–12, 16, 43–45;
  gubernatorial oversight, 17–19;
  legislative oversight, 12–17;
  personnel issues, 14–15; trustees,
  11–13
  *See also names of states with
  subheading higher education; and
  names of specific institutions of
  higher education*
Hines, Edward R., 91

ILCSO. *See* Illinois Library
  Computer Systems Organization
Illinois Board of Higher Education, 80
ILLINET ONLINE (Illinois), 81–82
Illinois Library Computer Systems
  Organization (ILCSO), 81–82
Illinois Library System Act, 35
Illinois State Library, 82
Internet, 60, 76, 85–86

Joint borrower's card. *See* Statewide
  borrower's card

Kerr, Clark, 10
King Research, Inc.: Reports,
  Florida, 116; Massashusetts, 138–39
Krois, Jerry, 79

LCS (Library Computer System):
  Illinois, 81–82
"Learning at Risk: Long Range Plan
  for the Improvement of
  Massachusetts Public Higher
  Education Libraries," 129–135, 141
Library budget techniques, 47–54
Library Information Network
  Community Colleges [Florida]
  (LINCC), 117
Library networks: general, 60–63. *See
  also* names of individual networks.

Library Services and Construction
  Act (LSCA): administration of
  funds, 33–34; funding of multitype
  networks, 36–38, 75–82, 137–38
LINCC. *See* Library Information
  Network Community Colleges
  [Florida]
Line–item budgeting, 45–47
Littleton, Isaac, 49–50
LSCA. *See* Library Services and
  Construction Act
Lump sum budgeting, 46–47

Maine, 77
Massachusetts, Academic Libraries:
  formula budgeting, 136; funding,
  125, 128, 133–34; King Report, 138–
  39; resource sharing, 132–33, 135–
  38; Statewide Academic Library
  Planning Committee, 128–136;
  statewide library planning, 136–141;
  Union List of Serials, 137
Massachusetts Board of Library
  Commissioners, 137–39
Massachusetts, Higher Education:
  Academic and Student Affairs Task
  Force, 132; Board of Regents, 124,
  128–31; Higher Education
  Coordinating Committee (HECC),
  124, 131, 135; reorganization, 123–
  24, 131–33
Massachusetts Conference of Chief
  Librarians in Public Higher
  Education Institutions
  (MCCLPHEI), 124–25, 128–36, 139–
  41
McAnally, Arthur, 48
MCCLPHEI. *See* Massachusetts
  Conference of Chief Librarians in
  Public Higher Education
  Institutions
McKeown, Mary P., 50
Middlebury State College [Vermont],
  84
Millard, Richard M., 68
Miller, James L., 48–49
MINITEX (Minnesota Interlibrary

Telecommunications Exchange), 65–66
Minnesota Higher Education Coordinating Board (HECB), 65–66
Minnesota Interlibrary Telecommunications Exchange. *See* MINITEX
Minnesota Union List of Serials (MULS), 65–66
Missouri Coordinating Board for Higher Education, 60
Missouri Research and Educational Network (MOREnet), 60
MOREnet. *See* Missouri Research and Educational Network
MULS. *See* Minnesota Union List of Serials
Multitype Library Authority Committee [North Dakota], 35
Multitype library programs: legal basis, 34–35; funding, 73–74; membership, 74; relationship to state libraries, 73
Munn, Robert F., 55

NAAL. *See* Network of Alabama Academic Libraries
National Commission on Libraries and Information Science (NCLIS), 60–61
National Research and Education Network (NREN), 211
NCIN. *See* North Carolina Information Network
NCLIS. *See* National Commission on Libraries and Information Science
Nebraska Library Commission, 78, 80
NEON (Nebraska Online Catalog), 78
NERDC. *See* Florida Northeast Regional Data Center
Network of Alabama Academic Libraries (NAAL), 63–65, 78, 95–96
New Mexico Commission on Higher Education, 66
New Mexico Consortium of Academic Libraries (NMCAL), 66–67
NMCAL. *See* New Mexico Consortium of Academic Libraries

North Carolina Department of Cultural Resources, 82–83
North Carolina Information Network (NCIN), 82–84
North Carolina, State Library, 82–83
North Carolina Union Catalog, 83
North Carolina Union List of Serials, 83
North Dakota, 35, 66
NOTIS, 69, 108, 111, 113–14, 117–18, 120
NREN. *See* National Research and Education Network

Oakland Consortium [Pennsylvania], 76
OARNet. *See* Ohio Academic Resource Network
OCLC (Online Computer Library Center), Inc., 66, 75, 77–78, 84, 138
Ohio Board of Regents, 67
Ohio State Library, 67
Ohio Academic Resource Network (OARNet), 67–68
Ohio Library and Information Network (OhioLINK), 67–68
Oklahoma Network of Continuing Higher Education (ONCHE), 68–69
Olver, John, 139
ONCHE. *See* Oklahoma Network of Continuing Higher Education
Oregon, 37, 78–79

Packet Radio Internet Extension (PRIE)[San Diego], 84–85
Packet radio technology, 85
Panhandle Library Access Network [Florida], 77
Peachnet [Georgia], 148–50
PENN*LINK, 77
Pennsylvania, State Library of, 69, 75–76, 79–80
PEPC. *See* Postsecondary Education Planning Commission (Florida)
Performance budgeting, 46, 49
Pitkin, Gary, 160
Planning-Programming-Budgeting System (PPBS), 46, 49

Post–secondary Education Planning Commission (PEPC)[Florida], 103, 114–15
PPBS. *See* Planning–Programming–Budgeting System
Preservation, 79–80
PRIE. *See* Packet Radio Internet Extension [San Diego]
Program budgeting, 46, 49
Program review: general, 89–92; existing programs, 93–4; gubernatorial and legislative involvement, 15, 90–92; library-related procedures, 94–96; new programs, 92–93
Program review (specific state procedures): Alabama, 95–96; Arkansas, 94; North Carolina, 94; Oklahoma, 94; South Carolina, 90; Washington, 90–91
PSC. *See* Florida Center for Library Automation, Public Services Committee
Pullen, William R., 144

Reference and Research Library Resources System (3R's)[New York], 80–81
Reference Network (RefNet)[(Connecticut], 79
RefNet. *See* Reference Network (Connecticut)
Restricted library funding, 48
Riverbend Library System [Illinois], 82
RLG (Research Libraries Group), 112–14
RLG Conspectus, 64, 95
Rosenberg, Stanley, 139–40

San Diego State University, 84–5
Scheppke, Jim, 37
Scott, Robert W., 20–21
SEFLIN. *See* Southeast Florida Library Information Network
Self assessment, 160–173
Senate Governmental Operations Committee (Florida) (GOVOP), 201, 203
Shaw, Ward, 154
SOLINET (Southeastern Library Network), 63, 146–48
South Carolina Commission on Higher Education, 92
South Dakota, 66
Southeast Florida Library Information Network (SEFLIN), 77
Southeastern Library Network. *See* SOLINET
State Board of Community Colleges [Florida], 104, 115–16
State budget *See* Budgets, State
State libraries: administration of LSCA funds, 33; legal basic, 35–36; relationship to academic libraries, 36–38. *See also names* of *individual state libraries.*
State Library of Pennsylvania, 69, 75–76, 79–80
State University of New York, Committee on Library Resources of the Faculty Senate, 50
State University System (SUS) of Florida, 69, 101, 106, 109, 111–18
Statewide Academic Library Planning Committee (Massachusetts), 220–228
Statewide Borrower's Card, 80, 150
SUS. *See* State University System of Florida

Talbot, Richard, 135
Tampa Bay Library Consortium, 77, 79
Tennessee State Library and Archives, 77
3R's. *See* Reference and Research Library Resources System [New York]
Townley, Charles T., 76
Triangle Research Libraries Network (TRLN)[North Carolina], 69–70
TRLN. *See* Triangle Research Libraries Network [North Carolina]
TSC. *See* Florida Center for Library

Automation, Technical Services Committee
Tyson, John, 85–86

UnCover [CARL database], 76, 159
Union Catalog of the Associated College Libraries of Central Pennsylvania (C.D. Cat), 69
University of Colorado, 156
University of Denver, 156
University of Florida, 108–9, 111–13
University of Georgia, 146
University of Illinois at Urbana–Champaign, 80–81
University of Massachusetts, Amherst, 131, 140
University of Massachusetts, Dartmouth, 140
University of Northern Colorado, 156–57
University of Pittsburgh, 76
University of Vermont, 84
University System Advisory Council [Georgia], 143
University System of Georgia (USG), 143–45
USG. *See* University System of Georgia
Utah, 74, 77

VALS. *See* Vermont Automated Libraries System
Vermont Department of Libraries, 84
Vermont Automated Libraries System (VALS), 77, 84
Vermont State College, 84
Vickery, James, 63
Virginia Library and Information Network (VLIN), 85–86
Virginia State Library and Archives, 85
VLIN. *See* Virginia Library and Information Network
Voight Formula, 49, 53
Voluntary coordinating agencies, 26–27

Washington (State), 91–92
Washington State Formula, 49, 51–52
Western Library Network (WLN): network, 78; software, 82
Whitaker, Martha, 159
WLN. See Western Library Network
Wyoming State Library, 79

Z39.50 Protocol, 121

About the Editor and Contributors

VICKI L. GREGORY is Assistant Professor in the Division of Library and Information Science at the University of South Florida. Her previous publications have appeared in journals such as *Southeastern Librarian, College & Research Libraries*, and the *Journal of Library Administration*. An active member in the American, Florida, and Alabama Library Associations, serving on a variety of committees, roundtables, and divisions thereof, she is also a contributor to the *Encyclopedia of Library and Information Science* and served as the principal editor for *A Dynamic Tradition—A History of Alabama Academic Libraries*, published in 1991.

MICHELE I. DALEHITE is the Assistant Director for Library Services at the Florida Center for Library Automation where her responsibilities include management of the User Services Department. In addition to publishing in the field, her professional activities include membership in and Director-at-Large, 1991–1992, of the OCLC Users Council. She has also served on the executive boards of the Library and Information Technology Association (LITA), the Southeastern Library Association, and the Florida Library Association.

JANET FREEDMAN is the Dean of Library Services and Professor of Education at the University of Massachusetts Dartmouth. She is the author, with Harold A. Bantly, of *Information Searching: A Handbook for Designing and Creating Instructional Programs*. She is an active member of many organizations and has written numerous reviews and articles on both library and women's issues.

MARGARET A. HOGUE is the User Services Librarian at the Florida Center for Library Automation, where her responsibilities include user support for librarians at the Florida State University System Libraries. She is the co-author of an article entitled "The Academic Librarian as Entrepreneur" which appeared in *Infomediary*. Her professional activities have included serving as chair of the Library Administration and Management Association (LAMA) Circulation Services Committee.

GEORGE R. JARAMILLO is the Director of Public Services and Personnel, University of Northern Colorado Libraries, where his responsibilities include the formulation, establishment, and administration of policies, rules, and regulations for the provision of public services, and the development of the libraries collection and expenditure of the learning materials budget. He is the author of numerous journal articles. His professional activities include membership on the ACRL Academic Status Committee, the ALA Bibliographic Instruction for Educators Committee, and the LAMA Publications Committee.

HELEN I. REED is the Director of Library Access Services and Budgets, University of Northern Colorado Libraries. She is active in several divisions of the American and Colorado Library Associations and frequently conducts seminars and presentations at meetings of technical services and user groups, and has from time to time served as a consultant to university libraries and others around the country.

RALPH E. RUSSELL is University Librarian at the William Russell Pullen Library of Georgia State University. He is the author of numerous publications. He has served as a consultant on many occasions, including working with the South Carolina Commission on Higher Education. He was President of the OCLC User's Council in 1987–1988 and has been a member of the OCLC Board of Trustees since 1988. He has received, and acted as project director for, numerous grants including currently a $400,000 challenge grant from the National Endowment for the Humanities. He served as the program chair for the 1990 Georgia Governor's Conference on Libraries and Information Services and as a professional delegate to the 1991 White House Conference on Libraries and Information Services.